ST. MARY'S ... Y
ST. M...
T5-BZZ-691
4.57 Barnes & Noble 4-61 (Swearingen)

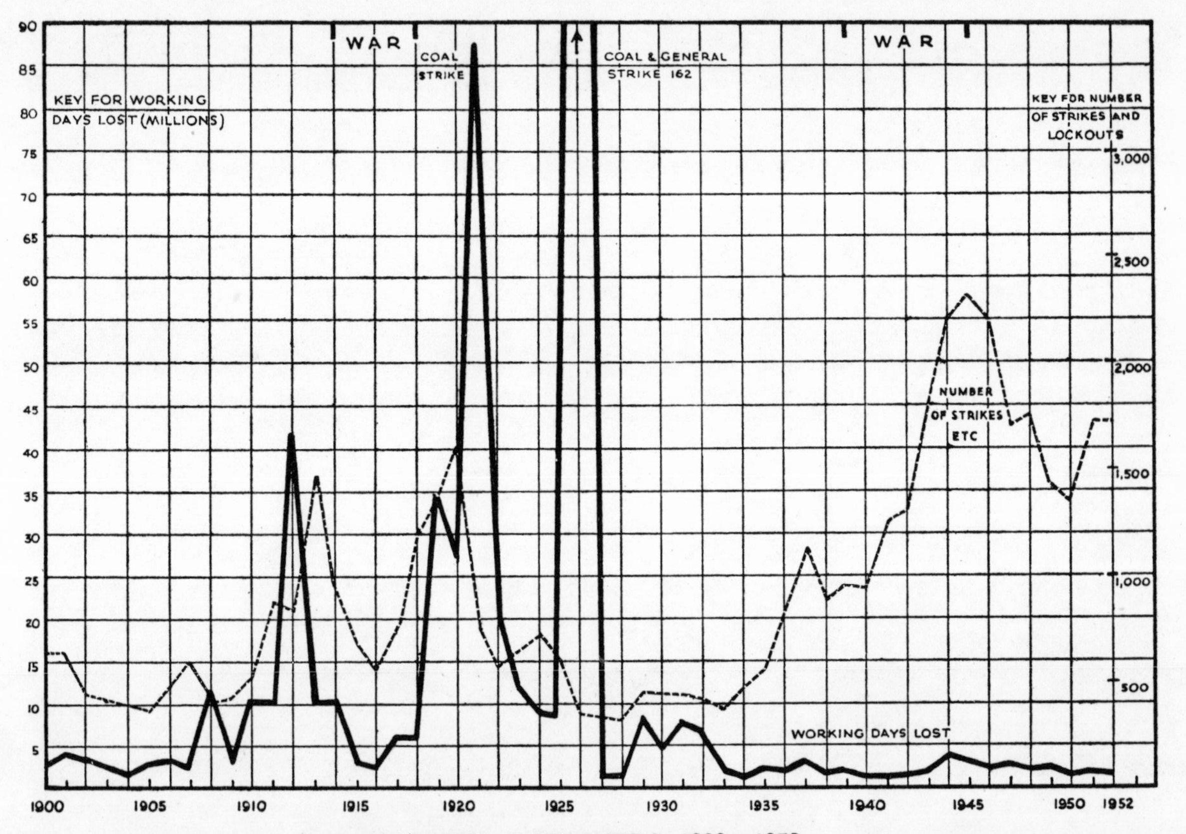

TRADE DISPUTES 1900—1952

G. D. H. COLE

AN INTRODUCTION TO

TRADE UNIONISM

GEORGE ALLEN & UNWIN LTD

RUSKIN HOUSE · MUSEUM STREET · LONDON

First published in 1953
Second impression 1955
Third impression 1962

This book is copyright under the Berne Convention. Apart from any fair dealing for the purposes of private study, research, criticism or review as permitted under the Copyright Act 1956, no portion may be reproduced by any process without written permission. Enquiry should be made to the publisher.

© *George Allen & Unwin Ltd* 1955

Printed in Great Britain
By Photolitho
in 11 point Imprint type
by Unwin Brothers Limited
Woking and London

21507

PREFACE

As long ago as 1918 I published a book with the title *An Introduction to Trade Unionism*, and with much the same intention as lies behind the present volume. This earlier book, in a revised form, was re-issued in 1924 with the title *Organised Labour*. It has been long out of print. In 1939 I edited, and wrote a considerable part of, a volume entitled *British Trade Unionism To-day*, in which I had the collaboration of a number of Trade Union leaders and other experts in the sections dealing with particular industries and problems. This work was re-issued in 1945, but has now been out of print for a considerable time. On account of its collaborative character, it would be exceedingly difficult to revise; and the situation has changed to such an extent as to exclude the mere revision of my earlier volume. I have accordingly now written an entirely new book, in which nothing survives from that of 1918 except a single chart illustrating some of the complexities of Trade Union organisation. This was re-drawn from my original by Miss M. Pulsford, then associated with the Labour Research Department, for which my original draft was prepared. With this one exception the present volume is entirely new. I have to thank Mr. Arthur Deakin, of the Transport and General Workers' Union, and Mr. T. Williamson, of the National Union of General and Municipal Workers, for help in compiling the table dealing with the ramifications of the membership of these two vast organisations; and I have also to thank a large number of Trade Union secretaries who have kindly supplied me with documents and information.

G. D. H. COLE

All Souls College, Oxford
April 1953

NOTE TO SECOND IMPRESSION . . . I have taken the opportunity afforded by a new edition to correct a number of errors.

CONTENTS

APPENDICES:

TABLES IN THE TEXT

CHARTS AND DIAGRAMS

CHAPTER I

TRADE UNIONISM IN GENERAL AND ITS VARIETIES

WHAT are Trade Unions? In Great Britain the legal definition of them, in the Trade Union Acts, includes employers' as well as workers' associations; and a few unimportant employers' bodies are actually registered as Trade Unions under the law. But in common parlance a Trade Union means an association of workers in one or more occupations—an association carried on mainly for the purpose of protecting and advancing the members' economic interests in connection with their daily work. This need not be its sole purpose; and in fact many Trade Unions do many things which either fall outside this range of objects, or are only connected with them indirectly. Trade Unions enter into educational activities over a wide field; they take part in politics; and they act as friendly societies for the provision of benefits in sickness or old age, as well as in cases of unemployment or trade dispute. Increasingly, where they are strong and have won a large measure of recognition from Governments as well as from employers, they appoint representatives to all manner of Councils and committees dealing with questions of social and economic policy; and in some cases they participate in the control or management of industrial enterprises or are given a special status in schemes for joint consultation concerning such matters as productivity or the prevention of accidents. Trade Union functions have developed rapidly in recent years in the countries where they are strongly organised; and these developments have raised a number of problems about Trade Union policy and method—problems to be considered later in this book.

But, whatever else a Trade Union may do, no body is commonly thought of as a Trade Union (or regarded as one by the law) unless one of its main purposes is the defence of its members' economic interests. A Trade Union is essentially a body of workers designed to do for its members by combination things which these persons, acting in isolation, could not do for themselves. It is meant especially to help them to get collectively better terms of employment or service than they could expect to get if each individual had to make a private bargain. Nowadays, this usually means that a Trade Union is a body which bargains collectively on behalf of its members either with single employers or business firms or with an association or federation of employers, or with a number of such 'opposite numbers'. Such bargaining commonly results in collective agreements laying down conditions of employment to remain in force either for a definite period or until they are revised by further negotiation, and these agreements often include provision for discussing and settling disputes that arise out of them, or while they are in force. Major agreements are nowadays usually written down and formally signed by representatives of the parties; but less important agreements are often made merely by an exchange of letters, and general agreements covering a whole trade, nationally or locally, and even agreements with single large firms, often give rise to numbers of supplementary agreements applying them in detail. Some of these last are written down; but many of them rest on unwritten understandings about workshop practices, or similar matters, or on a simple exchange of letters, or on minutes of a joint meeting. The number of collective agreements of these various kinds is very large, and big Trade Unions often issue booklets embodying the more important of them for the guidance of their officials and active members.

Thus, nowadays, in the countries where Trade Unions have firmly established their position, their main activity is collective bargaining on their members' behalf. It is, however, always possible that Trade Unions and employers, or employers' associations, may fail to reach agreement about the conditions of employment. In that event, save where strikes and lock-outs are forbidden by law—and sometimes even where they are forbidden —a Trade Union may call a strike of some or all of its members, or an employer, or employers' association, may decide on a lock-out. If either occurs, it will in most cases be ended by an agreement, drawn up in the light of the parties' trial of strength. But in many cases, where direct negotiations fail, either the parties agree to call in an arbitrator, or an arbitration board, to settle the dispute, or the Government steps in and either attempts to arrive at a settlement by conciliation (that is, by invoking the aid of a third party to bring the two sides together) or refers the matter to arbitration where it has taken legal power to intervene in this way. Many disputes are in fact settled by arbitration after direct negotiations have failed; and many agreements contain provisions for referring to arbitration any difference that may arise over their interpretation or their detailed application to particular cases. The strike or lock-out remains in reserve as a weapon of last resort; but more and more disputes tend to get settled without it as the scale of collective bargaining increases, so that a stoppage of work becomes a major event, costing huge sums of money and, especially in certain industries and services, seriously dislocating the affairs of the whole society.

Collective bargaining leading to agreements accepted by both parties did not always occupy this position of predominance in Trade Union activity : nor does it everywhere even to-day. Collective bargaining involves a preparedness on both sides to discuss the terms of employment; and this, in the past, many employers refused to do, as some attempt to behave now even in the countries where Trade Unions are well established. Nowadays, however, such refusals are not common in the economically developed countries, though they were very common until the 1930s in the United States, and are quite frequent in countries where Trade Unionism is still at an early stage of growth. In the past, employers in highly industrialised countries, usually with the approval of governments, often refused to bargain collectively with their employees, on the plea that terms of employment ought to be entirely a matter for individual contract between employer and worker, and that Trade Union bargaining was a denial of the individual worker's 'freedom' to accept employment on such conditions as he pleased. This view was put forward as a part of the economic doctrine of *laissez-faire* (sometimes called 'economic liberalism') by those who argued that the economic world was, or should be, ruled by a system of 'natural economic laws', with which neither the State nor any other collective agency could interfere rightly, or without disaster. The 'laws of supply and demand', it was argued, would, in a 'free' labour market, bring about levels of wages, hours, and other conditions of employment which would hold a right balance between employers seeking to buy labour as cheaply as they could and workers seeking to get as much as they could for their services; and under such conditions everyone would tend to receive the real value of his contribution to the work of production.

Such arguments were never popular with the working classes, whose spokesmen rightly maintained that the employer was himself in effect a 'combination' in relation to the isolated workman.

But they tended to be reinforced by the action of governments and of governing classes, because these were afraid, on political even more than on economic grounds, of workers' combinations, which they regarded as potentially dangerous threats to their own power at a time when government was regarded as the prerogative of the upper classes and the 'lower classes' were not looked upon as having any claim to political rights. During the period which followed the French Revolution of 1789, while in Great Britain the government was passing laws against workers' combinations as part of a wider policy of repressing movements of popular discontent, in France trade combinations were being suppressed no less rigorously in the name of the sovereign people, on the ground that all forms of sectional organisation were inconsistent with the right of the whole people to govern its collective affairs without being subject to any kind of 'monopoly' pressure. Thus, autocratic and aristocratic governments on the one hand and revolutionary advocates of popular freedom on the other were at one in supporting employers in their hostility to Trade Unionism; and Trade Unions were able to exist at all only because the instinctive drive towards combination was too powerful to give way even in face of severe legal repression.

In Great Britain, there were already, in the eighteenth century, a number of statutes forbidding workers' combinations in particular trades. Moreover, the courts of law had shown a growing tendency to outlaw all such combinations on the ground that their effect was to 'restrain trade' by interfering with the 'natural' liberty of all men to dispose of their labour as they wished. But, on account of the cumbrousness of the legal procedure, these repressive measures were not very effective. The principal purpose of the Combination Acts of 1799 and 1800 was to make them more so, both by declaring unequivocally that combinations were unlawful—indeed, criminal conspiracies against the public interest—and by providing simpler ways of proceeding against offenders. The campaign for the Acts was begun by certain employers in the machine-making industries, who demanded that the combinations among their own skilled employees, the millwrights, should be suppressed. The cry was taken up by anti-revolutionary politicians, who substituted for the particular measure directed against the millwrights a general prohibition of all workers' industrial combinations; and this prohibition remained in force until 1824, when, Napoleon having been defeated and the fear of revolution having died down, it was repealed by the efforts of certain Radicals who argued that, far from being effective in preventing Trade Unions, it positively encouraged them by leading the workers to believe that their wages were being kept down by legal repression rather than by the inexorable working of economic law.

When employers refuse to bargain collectively, there can be no collective agreements. In such cases Trade Unions, if they are able to exist at all, have to attempt to serve their members' interests by deciding on what terms they are prepared to advise their members to work, and thus seeking to compel employers to accept these terms, without formal agreements, by a concerted refusal to work under less favourable conditions. In fact, Trade Unions in the earlier stages of their development did largely act in this way: indeed, workers in a particular workshop or even in a whole trade often so acted even without having a formal Trade Union to support them. In many cases employers who refused to bargain with Trade Unions could be induced to accept conditions thus imposed, either because they could not get the skilled workers they needed on other terms or because they preferred a quiet life to constant bickering and discontent. Even when collective bargaining had developed to an advanced stage, this way of enforcing minimum conditions of employment without formal agreement remained of great importance, especially among skilled workers. It is still important in many occupations to-day. This informal kind of pressure has become embodied in a complex customary structure of trade practices, sometimes extending over a whole trade, nationally or locally, and sometimes peculiar to a single workshop or establishment, regulating such matters as the determination of the kind of worker who is to operate a particular machine, or the proportion of apprentices or learners to journeymen, or the special payments to be made for particular jobs within the framework of the general wage-rate applicable to a trade.

Indeed, this kind of common action goes back far beyond the establishment of formally organised Trade Unions. There never was a time when employers in fact habitually entered into a separate contract, written or unwritten, with each individual worker, without any reference to the general 'custom of the trade'; and this 'custom of the trade' was always in part an outcome of the natural disposition of groups of workers following a common employment to act together for mutual protection and advancement of their common interests. Trade Unions, as formally organised bodies, arose out of this natural tendency. Often they began mainly as friendly clubs of journeymen in a particular place, meeting partly for social intercourse but also to establish funds for mutual help in sickness or unemployment, or to aid members travelling in search of work. It was natural for such clubs to turn to the discussion of their members' conditions of employment, including not only such matters as wage-rates and hours of labour, but also the regulation of apprenticeship and the quantity of output constituting a fair day's work (known as the 'stint'). The name 'Trade *Union*', in Great Britain, seems to have been first used to describe joint activity by several of these little Trade *Clubs* in defence of the common interests of the workers in a whole town or area. The Clubs themselves were usually small: they usually met at a public house near the members' homes or places of work, and often they employed the landlord as the treasurer of the common funds. Such small bodies could not do much to regulate wages and general conditions of work unless several of them acted together: so they formed from time to time joint committees, or 'unions', to conduct a particular movement —for example, to resist a wage-reduction, or ask for an advance, or to prevent the employment of unapprenticed workers or an increase in the proportion of apprentices to journeymen, or to oppose night work or overtime. These 'unions' commonly dissolved, leaving only the constituent Clubs, when the particular purpose for which they had been formed had been fulfilled, or when they had failed in achieving it. But presently, in one case after another, the union became lasting ; and Trade Unions, with the little local Clubs as branches, came into being.

In the parlance of the early nineteenth century, a Trade *Union* was something more than a Trade *Club*, and a *Trades'* Union was more than either. *Trades'* Union meant a grouping of workers in more than one trade—for example, a Union including bricklayers', carpenters', and other types of building workers' Trade Clubs or Unions. The name Trades' Union was also used to designate the various attempts made at a quite early stage to bring together for common action not merely all the workers in a particular industry, but *all* workers. In Great Britain the first known attempts of this kind were made as early as 1818, during the disturbed years after the close of the Napoleonic Wars; and they reached a climax in the early 1830s, during and immediately after the struggle over the Reform Act of 1832. Their main purpose was usually that of organising mutual aid between the societies in different trades or districts in resisting wage-reductions. This, for example, was the main declared object of the National Association for the Protection of Labour, formed under John Doherty's influence in 1831. But the most ambitious of all these attempts, the Grand National Consolidated Trades' Union of 1833-4, in which Robert Owen's influence predominated, had much wider purposes—nothing less than the entire replacement of capitalism by a system of Co-operative Socialism. In this it stood alone as the exponent of a gospel of social regeneration to be brought about by mass industrial action; and the combined action of the Government and the employers speedily laid it low. With this exception the Trades' Union, or 'General Union', movements of the first three-quarters of the nineteenth century were primarily defensive. They were formed usually in bad times in the hope of offering concerted resistance to wage-reductions and to attempts to alter conditions of employment to the workers' disadvantage.

Trades' Unions came in for a great deal of attack even from those who were prepared to accept, or at least to tolerate, the existence of limited Trade Clubs of journeymen. The Trade Club was regarded as primarily a friendly society for mutual aid through the provision of friendly benefits in sickness or accident; whereas the Trade Union, and still more the Trades' Union, were accused of the cardinal sin of endeavouring to regulate wages and conditions which ought to be left to be settled by the unimpeded working of 'economic laws'. It was then generally held by orthodox economists that the share of wages in the product of industry was determined by inexorable laws, which many economists held to be based on the laws regulating the growth of population. Wages, it was said, could never rise more than temporarily above 'subsistence level', because if they did more children would be born, or more survive, so as to produce a surplus of labour. The competition for jobs would then force wages down to, or below, their 'natural' level. Economists who did not rely on this line of argument propounded another no less fatal to the claims of the Trade Unions. Wages, they said, were determined by the size of the 'wages fund', which was built up out of the profits saved by employers for use in further production. If the workers forced up wages at the expense of profits, the 'wages-fund' would not be replenished, and wages would inevitably fall until it had been restored. Thus, it was argued, Trades' Unions, in seeking to evade the operation of economic laws, were kicking vainly against the pricks, and ought to be put down in the interest of the workers themselves, as well as in that of general economic progress, which depended on rapid accumulation of capital out of profits.

Some who were on the workers' side accepted the force of these arguments. Francis Place, for instance, the 'Radical tailor of Charing Cross', was fully convinced that Trade Unions were powerless to influence wages and believed that the only way of raising them was for the workers to restrict the growth of population by artificial means. Nevertheless, he worked hard for the repeal of the laws against combinations, believing that the existence of these statutory laws blinded the workers to the real 'laws of economics', and that, if they were allowed to combine freely, they would soon realise the futility of trying to raise wage-rates by industrial action, and would confine themselves to Trade Clubs pursuing less misguided objectives.

Most of the leaders of the workers' movements did not accept these views. They believed that wages were low and conditions bad because employers and governments made common cause to repress the workers, and that the situation would get better if they could make their combinations strong enough to force the employers to concede better terms. Some of them, accepting the view that under capitalism wages were held down inexorably to subsistence level, insisted that it would be necessary to abolish the profit system in order to bring about a real improvement, and either preached a doctrine of revolutionary Trade Unionism designed to bring this about or urged the need for a political struggle to enfranchise the workers and thus make them masters of the State, which they could then use as an instrument for the furtherance of their own ends. But most of the men who played an active part in establishing and conducting Trade Unions in face of the hostility of both governments and employers simply believed that stronger Trade Unions would be able to win better terms, despite anything the orthodox economists told them to the contrary. In this, of course, they were entirely correct ; for even if there were 'economic laws' which governed the distribution of the total product of industry (and on the whole there were not), it did not at all follow that particular groups of workers could not better their conditions by combined action, but only that, when they did, there would be less left for others. As most Trade Unions grew up among relatively small groups of skilled workmen, and took the form of monopolies of particular kinds of skilled labour, there was nothing to prevent these workers from improving their lot by collective action, even on the assumption that the laws proclaimed by the economists were true. For nobody denied that 'monopolists' could gain an advantage for themselves by holding up the price of whatever they had to sell—in this instance, particular kinds of skill.

If, however, the economists were correct in what they said, it did follow that the benefits to be derived from sectional monopolies of skilled labour could not be generalised to cover the whole working class, and that attempts at 'general union', aiming at improving wages and conditions all round, were doomed to failure. This was what Francis Place believed ; but it was valid only on the assumption that the global division of the product of industry between capital and labour was fixed by inescapable economic laws, so that it was impossible for wages to be increased all round at the expense of profits. The opinion that this was so, held by those who followed the orthodox economists' teaching, was never accepted among the main body of the workers—or rather, most of those who were active in workers' movements never faced the question in this theoretical way, but simply continued, in commonsense fashion, to press for all they could get, and to form Trade Unions for this purpose despite all the obstacles which employers and governments put in their way.

These early Trade Unions had a hard struggle. The men who took the lead in organising them were very apt to find themselves discharged from their employment and to have much difficulty in getting fresh jobs ; and, over and above this, many of them were imprisoned when they organised strikes, or even simply for the offence of forming Trade Unions and presenting collective demands. In Great Britain, although workers' combinations were no longer absolutely forbidden by law after 1824, there remained many legal pitfalls for those who were active in them ; and it was not until 1871, after many of the skilled workers had won the parliamentary franchise under the Reform Act of 1867, that Trade Unions were given any secure legal position. Even after 1871 many employers still refused to recognise the right of collective bargaining, which was established only by stages, in one trade or industry after another. The railway companies and the ship-owners both stood out against it right up to the first World War, though the former were compelled to make some concessions a few years before 1914. In France, though Trade Unions in fact existed without any legal basis throughout the nineteenth century, no legal recognition was given to them until 1884, and they again and again underwent heavy persecution—especially after the defeat of the Revolution in 1848 and after the overthrow of the Paris Commune of 1871. In Germany, where industrial development came later than in either Great Britain or France, small Trade Clubs of skilled workers were tolerated throughout the nineteenth century, and no serious attempts were made to advance beyond them until the 1860s. Then, under Lassalle's leadership, a General German Workmen's Association was established, but as a political rather than an industrial body. Trade Unionism proper hardly began to develop until the 1870s, and thereafter it suffered from Bismarck's attempt, in the 1880s, to stamp out working-class movements with the aid of the Anti-Socialist laws, which were not repealed until 1890. Only then did the growth of large-scale Trade Unionism in Germany really begin. In the United States, on the other hand, Trade Unions found relatively few legal obstacles in their way till the latter part of the nineteenth century, when American big business set out to organise a formidable resistance to them. If they did not extend rapidly before this period, the reason was not so much that they were repressed as that the conditions were still unripe. The United States was still through most of the century predominantly an agricultural country, and as long as free land was available and the continent was still being opened up by the development of the West, wages and conditions were largely maintained by the competition for labour, and 'agitators' who might have been active in forming Trade Unions were diverted to other activities. Despite these conditions, Trade Unions did exist in considerable numbers from the 1840s onwards ; but they did not play, until well after the end of the nineteenth century, anything like so important a part in the national life as they did in the industrial countries of Western Europe. Indeed, the development of American Trade Unionism outside the skilled crafts and a few industries such as coal-mining, in which the lines between craftsmen and labourers are not clearly drawn, is mainly an affair of the past twenty years.

Thus Trade Unions, even in the advanced countries, have won their way to recognition of their right to bargain collectively on their members' behalf only after long struggles and in face of very obstinate resistance. Their growth and the recognition accorded to them have been part of a much wider process of democratic development which has brought with it the extension of the franchise, step by step, to include the whole adult population—women as well as men—and has profoundly altered the status of the working classes in society. This process has, of course, been closely bound up with the growth of industrialisation, which has gathered the workers together in great mining, metalworking and factory enterprises and has involved an immense movement of population from the agricultural countryside into towns and industrial areas. Scattered workers are always difficult to organise ; and as long as industry was mainly carried on under the 'domestic' system in small workshops or in the workers' homes, often in country areas, it proved impossible to build up stable Trade Unions, except for small groups of urban craftsmen who could easily meet together and had close bonds of neighbourhood as well as of craft. The textile workers, who were widely scattered until the advent of the factory system gathered them together, made many attempts at combined action in Great Britain during the eighteenth century ; but these movements were never lasting. One great reason for this was that such movements were powerless unless they were organised over quite large areas ; for it was easy for the merchants, who were in effect the employers and used workers drawn from a number of districts, to withdraw work from any one place where the workers tried to stand out for better terms, and combinations extending over a large area were difficult to maintain because of bad communications and were also more liable to be broken up by the strong hand of the law. Consequently, the earliest stable Trade Unions grew up among groups of skilled craftsmen in the towns ; and only with the establishment of factories using power-driven machinery were the main bodies of the textile workers able to follow suit. The miners were also, in general, late comers to Trade Unionism, partly because of their isolation in remote areas and partly because they were subject to the most severe repression of all. The great landowners who owned the mines and either worked them with paid overseers or leased them out to sub-contractors were in most cases the local magistrates as well, and often owned the houses in which the miners lived. They regarded attempts at combination as acts of rebellion against their feudal rights, and stamped them out by every means at their command, evicting strikers from their homes and making it impossible for 'agitators' to find work.

Of course, as industry developed at different times in different countries and areas, no definite dates can be given for the advent of the conditions which made it practicable for Trade Unionism to develop as a sustained movement outside the few skilled crafts in which it first established its position. In Great Britain, the cotton operatives began to organise on a substantial scale towards the end of the Napoleonic Wars and thereafter carried on a continuous agitation, though their Unions were often broken up and did not become really stable until the 1850s. The woollen and worsted workers were very active in the 1820s and 1830s ; but the power of their Unions was broken in the struggles of the early 'thirties, and they were long in re-building them on secure foundations. The mineworkers on the North-East Coast engaged in many struggles in the first three decades of the nineteenth century, and a powerful National Union extending to other coal-fields was established in the 1840s ; but it went down to defeat, and a new movement was built up only in the 1860s—to be almost destroyed again during the depression of the later 'seventies, and yet again re-built—this time on lasting foundations—after the formation of the Miners' Federation in 1888. The builders created a powerful Union in the early 'thirties ; but it was speedily crushed, and never fully re-made, though local federations of craft Unions became important in the 1860s, and the stonemasons and later the carpenters and joiners succeeded in maintaining powerful Unions on a sectional basis. The skilled engineers began to organise in the 1820s, chiefly on the basis of the new capitalistic industry of steam-engine and locomotive building ; but they did not consolidate their organisation till the Amalgamated Society of Engineers was founded in 1851.

Throughout the first half of the nineteenth century, in Great Britain, the Unions came and went. Some local societies of skilled craftsmen—for example, the London Compositors—were able to maintain a continuous existence ; but most even of such Unions were re-formed again and again, and there is no national Union of to-day, except the Boilermakers, and perhaps the Plumbers, that can truly trace its continuous existence far back beyond 1850, though a few older Unions, such as the Stonemasons, the General Union of Carpenters and Joiners, the Journeymen Steam-engine Makers, and the Ironfounders, have survived as constituents of existing amalgamations. Here is a list of a few of the more important of the older Unions which either survive to-day (1953) or have become co-founders of existing Unions in which they have been merged :

Date of Foundation	*Name*	*Existing Union*
1809	Friendly Society of Ironfounders	Amalgamated Union of Foundry Workers
1825	Journeymen Steam-engine Makers	Amalgamated Engineering Union
1827	General Union of Carpenters and Joiners	Amalgamated Society of Wood-workers
1832	United Society of Boilermakers	Still exists
1832	Operative Stonemasons' Society	Amalgamated Union of Building Trade Workers
1834	United Kingdom Society of Coachmakers	National Union of Vehicle Builders
1835	Bookbinders' Consolidated Union	National Union of Printing, Bookbinding and Paper Workers

From about 1850, however, the number of Trade Unions which have survived into modern times begins to increase rapidly. The Typographical Association dates from 1848, the Amalgamated Society of Engineers (now merged in the Amalgamated Engineering Union) from 1851, the Operative Cotton Spinners' Amalgamation from 1853. The Weavers' Amalgamation, though not fully consolidated until 1884, really began with the formation of the North-East Lancashire Weavers' Association in 1858. The Amalgamated Society of Carpenters and Joiners, the main nucleus of the present Amalgamated Society of Woodworkers, dates from 1860, and the National Plasterers' Association from 1861. The Amalgamated Society of Tailors, now merged in the National Union of Tailors and Garment Workers, was formed in 1866. The Brassworkers and the Patternmakers both date from 1872, and the Amalgamated Society of Railway Servants, the nucleus of the present National Union of Railwaymen, from the same year. This last was the forerunner of a new type of Trade Union, based on industry rather than craft and the first durable organisation to be formed among transport workers ; but its growth was slow, and it had a long struggle ahead of it before it achieved recognition from the railway companies.

In Great Britain the period between 1850 and the middle 'seventies was that during which craft Unionism among skilled workers became firmly established on a national scale. The late 'sixties and early 'seventies were also a time of rapid growth among the miners ; and in the early 'seventies Trade Unionism spread at a great speed to less skilled workers, such as gasworkers and railway servants, and also among agricultural labourers. But the depression of the later 'seventies, extending into the 1880s, brought most of the new Unions founded in the early 'seventies to grief ; and there was no large-scale revival until nearly the end of the 1880s, when the establishment of the Miners' Federation (now the National Union of Mineworkers) in 1888, and of the Dock, Wharf, Riverside and General Workers' Union (now the Transport and General Workers) and the Gasworkers' Union (now the National Union of General and Municipal Workers), both in 1889, ushered in the 'New Unionism' and made the organisation of the less-skilled workers a permanent feature of Trade Union activity. After the immense developments of these years there were serious setbacks in the 1890s ; but most of the new Unions managed to survive, and it is reasonable to say that in or about 1889 Trade Unionism became, for the first time since the collapse of 1834, a movement open to every kind of manual worker, with a tendency to spread beyond the manual trades into the fields of blackcoat and professional employment. The National Union of Teachers, first established in 1870 among elementary teachers, broadened its scope and reorganised its methods in 1888. The National Union of Shop Assistants, now merged in the Union of Shop, Distributive and Allied Workers, began in 1891, and the National Union of Clerks (now the Clerical and Administrative Workers' Union) in 1892. The Postmen's Federation (now merged in the Union of Post Office Workers) dates from 1891. The Railway Clerks' Association (now the Transport Salaried Staffs Association) came rather later, in 1897.

Thus, by the 1890s, Trade Unionism in Great Britain had taken on a shape recognisably like that of to-day, though the balance of forces within it was still very different. In the 1890s craft Unionism was still predominant : the Miners were rapidly building up their new organisation, but the new Unions of transport and general workers were struggling for their very existence, and the new Unions of non-manual workers still very weak. There was nothing analogous to the huge 'general' Unions of today. Coal, cotton and engineering were the three strongest groups at the annual Trades Union Congresses ; but the engineering group was still confined to skilled, or at the lowest, semi-skilled workers.

The Trades Union Congress had taken shape as a regularly constituted annual gathering in 1868, in the course of the struggle for legal recognition which lasted from 1867 to 1875. It was, industrially, a much less ambitious body than the earlier attempts to federate the Trade Unions for common action that had been made in the 1830s and again in the 1840s and in the middle 'sixties. Its purpose was, indeed, mainly political—to represent the movement in the legal struggle, to press for industrial legislation, and to provide a common platform for the expression of Trade Union views. It had no power over its constituent Unions, no common fund for use in trade disputes, no negotiating functions. Moreover, it retained this limited scope until after the first World War. The very name of its executive—the Parliamentary Committee—indicated how its main functions were conceived. When, in 1922, it was decided to replace the Parliamentary Committee by a General Council, chosen to represent each main industrial or occupational group, the new body was given somewhat wider functions, but was still left—as was the Congress itself—without power to bind any constituent Union against its will. The British Trades Union Congress has far less authority than the central Trade Union bodies in other countries where the individual Trade Unions have been largely built up under the auspices and influence of the common centre. In Great Britain, the older Unions were too strongly entrenched before the Congress became important to be induced to give up their independence. When the General Strike was declared in 1926 the body which was used to call it was not the Trades Union Congress General Council but a specially convened Conference of Trade Union Executives.

The main business of Trade Unions, we have seen, is the making of collective agreements on behalf of their members. These agreements, however, are of a peculiar kind. A Trade Union is not in a position to enter into a binding legal contract on behalf of its membership; for if it did this contract would be enforceable at law, and the Union would be legally liable for damages in respect of any breach of it by any member. This would create an impossible situation; for a Trade Union, though it can fine a member or in the last resort expel him for breach of Union discipline, cannot in practice make him pay if he prefers to resign. Union funds would be continually in jeopardy if they were liable for damages caused by the action of any members who chose to break an agreement or to go on strike. Accordingly, Trade Union agreements are not binding legal contracts: they do not bind either the Union or its members, save in certain indirect ways. Each employed worker is under a personal contract with his employer, even if the terms of the contract are the outcome of a collective bargain. In dealing with alleged breaches of contract, the law courts go, in the absence of written personal contract, by what is called the 'custom of the trade', which depends partly on unwritten custom and partly on the content of such collective agreements as are in fact being customarily observed. There has, indeed, grown up a custom by which employers usually accept collective notice from a Trade Union that its members wish to terminate their contracts when a strike is to be declared; but they are under no legal compulsion to do this, and have sometimes refused—in which case, legally, each individual has to tender his personal notice to end his engagement before he is free to strike. In practice, however, this cannot be insisted on.

As for the Trade Union itself, it is now clear that it cannot be sued on account of any breach by its members either of a collective agreement or of a legal contract. But this immunity was not secured without a great struggle. Up to 1901 it was generally believed that it had been secured by the Trade Union Act of 1871; but in 1901, in the celebrated case of the Taff Vale Railway Company *v.* the Amalgamated Society of Railway Servants, the House of Lords, sitting as a court of law, awarded heavy damages to the company on the ground that the Trade Union in question had been guilty of incitement to breach of contract in trying to prevent blacklegs engaged by the company from taking the place of men on strike. The effect of this legal judgment, which threatened all Trade Union funds and made it a perilous matter for a Union to call a strike under any circumstances, was undone in 1906, when the Liberal Government, under strong pressure from the newly constituted Labour Party, agreed to the enactment of the Trade Disputes Act, which gave the Trade Unions the immunity they now enjoy. We shall come back to this question when we deal with the legal position of Trade Unions in general : it comes in here as a necessary part of the explanation of the special status of Trade Union collective agreements.

Although such agreements are not legally binding, they have of course a strong moral force ; and modern Trade Unions attach the highest importance to the strict keeping of agreements into which they have entered. That is why so many small strikes, called in immediate reaction to a particular local grievance, are 'unofficial'—that is, unrecognised and unsupported by the Trade Union to which the strikers belong. Collective agreements nowadays usually embody a provision that no strike or lock-out shall be called until a prescribed procedure of negotiation has been gone through. This often takes a considerable time, which can be spun out to an unconscionable length by delaying tactics ; and sometimes the workers on the spot are not prepared to wait, especially when the grievance seems to need dealing with at once. Strikes, then, do occur in spite of collective agreements, and sometimes in violation of their terms ; and a good deal of internal trouble may arise when a Trade Union Executive not only refuses to support a strike, but takes disciplinary measures against its recalcitrant members. To this too we shall come back later, when we are discussing the internal working of Trade Unions and the conditions of strike action in the world of to-day.

What has been written in the foregoing paragraphs relates specifically to Great Britain ; but it holds good for all countries that Trade Union agreements do not constitute binding legal contracts, though in some the Trade Unions enjoy much less full legal immunity for *incitement* to breach of contract than in Great Britain. The collective agreement is an entirely different thing from the type of 'collective contract' that is sometimes made, especially in France, between an employer and a group or squad of workers engaged in a particular piece of work, such as erecting a big machine or building a bridge. In such contracts the workers concerned form in effect, and often under an actual constitution, a sort of producers' Co-operative Society which agrees with the employer to carry out the work for a collective payment, to be divided among them at their own discretion. This type of collective contract is rare in Great Britain—there have been one or two recent examples of it at the docks—but it is less uncommon in

France and Italy, which have both a stronger tradition of Producers' Co-operation.

Trade Unions are organised on a national basis ; and each national Trade Union movement has its peculiar characteristics. In a few cases, Trade Unions extend beyond national frontiers. Thus many of the American Trade Unions extend to Canada, and some to Mexico, as well as to the United States ; and, for historical reasons, a number of British Trade Unions have branches in the Irish Free State—and some also in the British Dominions. The French Trade Unions in some cases have branches in the overseas territories of the French Empire. But there are exceptions. Usually, Trade Unions are confined to a single country, and organised under its national law. They are, however, linked up internationally, in two distinct ways. National Trade Union centres are in most cases affiliated to an international federation, of which there are now three of importance—the International Confederation of Free Trade Unions, to which the British Trades Union Congress belongs ; the International Federation of Christian Trade Unions, which draws its membership chiefly from the Catholic Trade Unions of Western Europe ; and the Communist-dominated World Federation of Trade Unions, from which the British, American, and a number of other Trade Union centres broke away in 1947 to form the I.C.F.T.U. Secondly, there are a number of International Federations, or Secretariats, representing the workers in particular industries or occupational groups—transport workers, miners, textile workers, commercial employees, and so on—and in this field there are in many cases two rival bodies, sponsored respectively by the I.C.F.T.U. and the W.F.T.U. These international bodies have usually no real authority over their constituent organisations : they are chiefly debating assemblies, though many of them also work closely with the International Labour Organisation in pressing for and drafting International Conventions for the regulation of labour conditions. The I.C.F.T.U. and the World Federation of Trade Unions in addition pay, from their rival standpoints, much attention to the encouragement of Trade Unionism in the less developed countries ; and keen rivalry exists in this field.

In the countries in which Communism is the dominant system, and all large-scale industry is publicly owned and carried on under a national economic plan, Trade Unions necessarily occupy a position very different from that which they have in countries where parliamentary government exists and the greater part of industry is still privately owned and controlled. In the Soviet Union, for example, the Trade Unions are virtually part of the machinery of government. Their leaders are subject to the discipline of the Communist Party ; and their principal functions are to administer social service benefits which in the West are administered by government departments or agencies, and to do all they can to stimulate the workers to increase production in compliance with the national economic plan. The 'monolithic' theory and practice of Communism are entirely inconsistent with the existence of Trade Unions as independent bodies free to oppose the government. The government is regarded as the supreme representative of the entire working class, and the Communist Party as its supreme directing authority ; and there is accordingly no room left for any independent Trade Union power.

This view of Trade Unionism runs directly counter to the view which holds sway in the United States, where Trade Unions are regarded as essentially power groups independent of the government, and making their own policy in their members' interests. the United States, where there is no planned economy pre-ibing the distribution of the product of industry, the Trade ions in effect take it for granted that their function is to press or the highest wages and the best conditions they can exact from employers, leaving the economy as a whole to adjust itself to the results of their bargaining. No doubt, American Trade Unions often make it their business to encourage high production, in order to be able to exact better terms ; and of course under war conditions they acted within limits set by national needs. But, wars apart, they behave essentially as pressure groups, acting upon government and employers to the full extent of their independent power.

The American Trade Unions are able the more easily to behave in this way because there has never been a Labour Government and is not even a Labour Party to demand their loyalty. In Great Britain, on the other hand, the Labour Party is based largely on the Trade Unions ; and the Trade Unions have experienced a situation in which a Labour Government, including a number of their own leaders, has been in power. In such a situation, it becomes impossible for the Unions to act as they would if they had no political connections. They are compelled, when the Labour Party is in power, to take account of the repercussions of their industrial policy on the political situation. Moreover, in an economy so precariously balanced as Great Britain's has been since 1945, the Trade Unions cannot exert their full economic strength regardless of wider consequences even when a Conservative Government is in office. The British Trade Unions have not renounced their independence of the Government, even when their own party is in power ; but they have recognised that they must, in practice, put limits on the use they make of their industrial strength and take cognisance of the needs of the economy as a whole. They stand therefore in a position somewhere between the Soviet and American positions, but nearer the Americans because they are still working in a predominantly capitalist environment.

In France and in Italy yet another situation exists. The Trade Unions which command the widest following are under Communist leadership and in sharp opposition to the prevailing political régimes. They are, in the last resort, subject to the Communist Parties and to the policy directives which issue from Moscow ; but their power to follow the orders of these bodie[illegible] limited by their need not to lose the support of their memb[illegible] In rivalry with them there exist, in both countries, non-C[illegible] munist Trade Unions, connected with either the Internatic[illegible] Confederation of Free Trade Unions or the Internationa[illegible] Federation of Christian Trade Unions ; but these rivals are relatively small and ineffective, nor are they nearly so much involved in politics as the British Unions. In France and Italy, the main body of the Trade Union movement is not merely independent of the Government, as in the United States, but hostile to it ; and the non-Communist minority movements occupy an uncomfortable position between the Communists and the governments dominated by the capitalist parties.

In Germany, conditions are again different. Eastern Germany, dominated by the Soviet Union, reproduces in its Trade Union movement the pattern of Communist control. In Western Germany, on the other hand, the reconstituted Trade Union movement belongs to the I.C.F.T.U. and is largely under Social Democratic influence, though it includes the groups which were formerly organised in separate Christian Trade Unions under Catholic control. The West German Unions have been fighting since 1945 a battle with capitalism for a recognised share in the control of industrial policy, through the right to be represented on the Supervisory Councils of big business, and also on the managing boards. In this campaign they have achieved a limited success—how much in effect, it is still too soon to say.

In Yugoslavia there is yet another situation. The Yugoslav Trade Unions were built up under Communist tutelage while Yugoslavia was still part of the Moscow-dominated world. Since the break with the Soviet Union, the Yugoslavs have been making great efforts at decentralisation and towards handing over the control of the factories and workshops to the workers' own representatives. The Trade Unions still work in close association with the Government; but the Government has evidently been trying to give them a real measure of independence—with what success, it is again too soon to tell.

In the Scandinavian countries the position of the Trade Unions is most like that of the British Unions, except that in Sweden and Denmark the Social Democratic Parties are not based directly on the Trade Unions, as they are in Great Britain. In Holland, there are five rival Trade Union movements, working for the most part together on wage questions, but divided sharply by political and religious differences. In Belgium the main Trade Union body is integrally connected with the Belgian Labour Party, but there is keen rivalry between it and the Catholic Trade Unions, which are more loosely related to the Catholic Party. In Switzerland the movement is well-organised and on good terms with the Socialist Party, but independent of it.

In other continents, except Australasia, Trade Unionism is still for the most part at an early stage of development. The South African movement is mainly among the white workers, and attempts to organise the Africans have been bitterly opposed. In Australia the Trade Unions dominate the Labour Party; but there have been in recent years fierce struggles within them between Communists and anti-Communists, with governments intervening to prevent Communist control. The same struggle has taken place in New Zealand, where the Communist-controlled Unions at the ports were broken up in 1951 and replaced by new Unions under anti-Communist leadership. In India there are rival movements headed by Communists and by Socialists and adherents of the Congress Party. In China a vast new Trade Union movement is being established under Communist control.

In Japan the Unions have been set up on a non-political basis under the American occupation, but are now a battleground of rival political tendencies. In Malaya there is a struggle between Communist-dominated groups and new Unions set up with official encouragement on West European lines. In the West Indies, Trade Unions established mainly among plantation workers under nationalist leadership have passed from tumultuous beginnings to serving as the main support of nationalist politicians in office. In West Africa, again, nationalism has played a large part in the growth of Trade Unions, which tend to be fully as much political as industrial organisations. In French Northern Africa there is a struggle between Communists and anti-Communists for the control of Unions still for the most part at a rudimentary stage of growth.

Thus, in each country, Trade Unionism is shaped not only by the form and stage of economic development, but also by the political conditions and by the general structure of the society in which it has to act. This book is mainly about Trade Unionism in Great Britain, where the movement has the longest continuous history. But it seemed best to begin by saying a little about Trade Unionism in general, and about its varieties. The last general point it seems necessary to make is that in most countries Trade Unionism remains predominantly an urban movement. There are quite strong Unions of agricultural workers in Great Britain, among the vine-growers in France, and in a few other countries. But there is little room for agricultural Trade Unionism in peasant countries—peasants organise mainly in Co-operative Societies of various types—and even in industrialised countries firms are often fairly small, so that the hired workers are widely scattered and difficult to organise. In countries dominated by 'plantation economy', there is more scope for Trade Unions ; but they are often bitterly opposed by the planters, and in a good many cases the plantations are manned largely by imported workers, who cannot easily combine with others in a country from which they expect to return home later on.

CHAPTER II

TRADE UNION GOVERNMENT

I. THE BRANCH

THE simplest type of Trade Union, which was also at one time the most usual, consists of a small group of workers following a common trade and meeting from time to time for the discussion of their common affairs. Such Trade Unions, or Trade Clubs—to give them their older name—hardly exist to-day in Great Britain. They have been absorbed into larger bodies, either turning into mere local branches of Unions covering a larger area, or simply disappearing, to give place to Trade Unions catering for a more diverse membership. Even the local branches of modern Trade Unions restricted to workers following a single craft are usually much larger than these little societies used to be. They resemble rather the local federal committees, or 'Unions', that used to be formed when a number of the little Clubs came together to organise a joint movement, either for the purpose of claiming improved conditions or, quite as often, for resistance to an attempt by employers to reduce wages or to abrogate some cherished protective 'custom of the trade'. Even the purely local Trade Union of to-day, even the local branch of a national or regional Union, is seldom a 'face-to-face group' to anything like the same extent as these primitive Trade Unions used to be. The nearest thing to them that exists nowadays, save quite exceptionally, is the single branch of a craft Union in a not very numerous craft in a small town, meeting in a public house within easy reach of the members' houses, and still serving a social and convivial as well as an industrial purpose. But the meetings of such branches in these days very seldom bring together more than a small fraction of the total number of persons on the books of the branch, or, even if a higher proportion put in an appearance now and then, most of them attend only to pay their contributions, and perhaps to take a drink in the bar, without playing any part or taking any interest, save on quite exceptional occasions, in the business that is being done. Branches of this kind may retain their social character ; but the social element nowadays appeals only to a few, who are largely the persons who run the branch's affairs and form a small *élite* with only loose contacts with the main body of members.

In rather larger towns, some of the craft unions may have several branches, each with its own meeting place and group of cronies who attend with fair regularity. Many craft Unions—or Unions which were once confined to skilled workers in a particular trade, even if they have now widened their range of membership—still prefer to keep their branches fairly small, and to open new branches as their membership increases. But this type of small branch is now regarded as old-fashioned and is seldom found in the newer Unions catering for mass-memberships or for less skilled workers. It is, indeed, chiefly a survival of a type of organisation which has largely lost its original character. The single-branch Trade Club was, as we have seen, in most cases a friendly society fully as much as a Trade Union. Its funds, raised by weekly contributions, were spent largely on mutual benefits—on sickness pay, unemployment pay, funeral benefit, and so on—and it had often a 'benevolent fund' out of which grants could be voted to members to meet special misfortunes. But to-day most friendly benefits, where they exist, are administered nationally according to strict rules which leave the local branches little to do in debating claims ; and a very large part of what Union members formerly had to do for themselves by voluntary mutual aid has been taken over by the State under compulsory schemes of National Insurance, supplemented by National Assistance paid for out of public funds. 'Benevolent funds' still exist, but they are now of much less importance ; and it is no longer a regular task of the branch to go through a series of claims to benefit or requests for aid, and to adjudicate upon them in the light of close personal knowledge of each member's personal affairs. This has removed one large element of interest from the business of most Trade Union branches.

Moreover, the centralisation of a great deal of collective bargaining has meant that the local Trade Union branch has little or nothing to do with the fixing of wages or general conditions of labour. Where there is only one branch of a particular Union in a town, the branch is still to some extent concerned with such matters as the local application and implementation of national agreements ; but where more than one branch exists, these questions are usually dealt with by a District Committee made up mainly of branch representatives but also nowadays often including shop stewards chosen to represent the members in the principal establishments in the area ; and the District Committees, in carrying out their functions, will in many cases deal rather with the bodies of shop stewards or works representatives in the particular establishments than with the Union branches as such. Very commonly such questions affect the members of more than one Union, and the District Committees of the Unions concerned need to take action in concert. Even where this complication does not exist, a trouble arising in a particular establishment may involve members who belong to a number of different branches of the same Union ; and the District Committee will then find it more convenient to deal with them all on a works basis, through their shop stewards, than to refer to a number of branches most of whose members are not directly concerned. This complication does not arise in those Unions which organise their branches so as to group together the members employed in the same establishment rather than those who live in the same neighbourhood. But the more this is done, the less can the branch serve as a social club ; for it means that neighbours will be enrolled in different branches, and also usually that branch meetings will be held in a hurry by members eager to leave for home.

The modern tendency is for wage rates and general working conditions to be settled by negotiations covering large areas, and for the detailed working out of the application of such agreements to be done more and more in particular establishments, mainly by shop stewards and works committees rather than by discussion in trade union branches—except, of course, where the works and the branch units coincide. They tend to coincide chiefly in such industries as coal-mining or steel, where a single colliery or steel works may dominate a district and provide the only field for employment of a particular kind of worker. Where there are many establishments in an area belonging to the same industry, if the branch is based on the place of employment rather than on where the worker lives, a shift from one job to another involves moving to a different branch, and there are in few cases effective arrangements for automatic transfer of membership. That is one reason why many Trade Unions prefer branches based on place of residence to works branches ; another is that such branches constitute the traditional type and still preserve in many cases relics of their social character. The effect, however, is that the branch counts for less and less in the actual running of the Union. In some cases, it is still the body which is entitled to send a representative to the National Conference of the Union, as well as to the District Committee ; but in some of the big Unions there are too many branches for this to be possible and they have to be grouped for the purpose of choosing delegates. This, again, weakens the branch ; for a delegate representing several branches has no longer the same direct contact with those who have chosen him and cannot be instructed in the same way as the nominee of a single branch.

Trade Union branches used to meet largely in public houses, many of which had special rooms set aside for meetings of Clubs, Friendly Societies, and Trade Unions, where the property of the branch could be kept in a locked chest and the walls were often hung with the emblems of societies meeting on the premises. But at an early stage objections were raised to meeting on licensed premises ; and some branches preferred to meet in coffee-houses or in halls belonging to chapels, or indeed wherever they could find a place ready to receive them. In the early days there was often great difficulty in finding meeting places. While Trade Unions were still forbidden by law, publicans were often threatened with the loss of their licences if they harboured 'seditious' meetings ; and Trade Unions had to pose as friendly societies in the hope of escaping the ban. Only a few chapels, where the ministers held radical opinions, would receive them ; and only radical coffee-house keepers, who often set up shop for the purpose, wished for their presence. Sometimes they were able to meet on the premises of Owenite Socialist groups or in Secularist 'Halls of Science' ; but these were to be found only in a few places. Gradually these difficulties became less ; but through most of the nineteenth century public houses offered the easiest way out, as landlords hoped to attract regular custom and to make some profit on the drink consumed. Only when the Trade Unions, or some of them, became strong enough to build or lease halls of their own, or when some benefactor—usually anxious to get them away from the public houses—presented the local Trades Council with a building of its own, did the practice of meeting on licensed premises go out of fashion ; and even to-day it continues, especially in some of the branches of the older craft Unions.

Trade Union branches used to meet oftener than most of them

do nowadays. Weekly meetings used to be common, when they were also social events. In these days, some branches meet fortnightly, but more only once a month, unless a special meeting is called to deal with an urgent problem. There is usually a good deal of rather formal business—reading of correspondence from the Union's head office, or from its regional officers, and from outside bodies, reports from shop stewards or representatives on the state of membership in the various establishments covered (but in Unions with several branches in a town this is usually dealt with at the District Committee level), passing of applications for membership, and so on. In some Unions, contributions are still collected at the branch meetings and members file in and out making payments while the business is being done. But more often, in these days, contributions are collected by stewards, or special collectors, at the workplaces, or even in some Unions by collectors who go round the members' homes. Very occasionally, there is an outside speaker or lecturer who addresses the branch ; and there are sometimes visits from Union officials, especially when there is trouble afoot.

Save at exceptional times, branch meetings are not exciting, and it is not surprising that attendance is often small. A good many Unions nowadays have very large branches, with a considerably diverse membership, and the meetings are held in rooms that would not hold more than a small fraction of those entitled to attend. Especially in such cases, but also to a considerable extent even where branches are smaller, the membership is in practice divided into an active minority and an inactive majority. The former consists mainly of those who hold or hope to hold some office in the Union, or to be elected as delegates to represent it on other bodies, such as the Trades Council or the local Labour Party, and take their membership seriously because of their interest in the wider working-class movement. From this active nucleus are drawn those who serve as shop stewards or collectors ; and most men and women who rise to positions of wider influence in the Trade Union movement begin with activity in the branch. The majority of the members can be divided into the occasional attenders and those who are never seen at all at a branch meeting. The contact of the latter with the Union is entirely with the collector or delegate to whom they pay their contributions or with the shop steward in their department (who may or may not be the same person), or, sometimes, is kept up through meetings held at the factory when a particular grievance or problem is being discussed. In the less skilled Unions with their large branches and rapid turnover of members the contact between the Union and its less active contributors is often very tenuous indeed. It has to be admitted that many join a Union not out of any interest in its doings but simply because it is the 'done thing' in their place of employment, or even because membership is in effect a condition of getting or holding the job.

There is nothing to be surprised at in this widespread apathy. When membership was much smaller, working conditions much worse, and bargaining mostly local, those who joined a Trade Union mostly did so because they hoped to help make it a means of improving their lot and the lot of their fellow-workers and knew it could not be effective unless they worked hard for it, and that a good local branch might be able to make a real difference to local wages and conditions. But nowadays wage-rates and general conditions are for the most part settled either nationally or over large areas, and the branch as such can do nothing about them, while the local implementation of agreements takes place in each separate establishment, through the action of shop stewards and works committees, rather than as a result of action by the branch. No doubt, the power of the Unions as a whole to make good agreements depends in the last resort on the quality, as well as on the number, of its members; but this quality finds scope for exercise more and more elsewhere than in the branch meetings. Moreover, it has to be recognised that most workers are much more interested in other leisure-time activities than in Trade Union business; and as Trade Union membership spreads from the few to the majority, it is bound to include a high proportion whose interest in Trade Union affairs is very slight.

Trade Union branches, then, and indeed Trade Unions in general, are carried on by active minorities, with very little participation by most of the paying members. This is sometimes said to be 'undemocratic'; but of what type of group or society is it not true? It is certainly true of politics, in which the majority of voters play very little part beyond casting their votes—when they do even that; and it is true of practically every kind of voluntary society. In Trade Unions, as in other types of association, democracy consists in giving every member a chance to participate actively if he wishes: it cannot extend to securing the active participation of the majority save at highly exceptional moments of crisis—if even then.

Trade Union branches elect their own officers, and usually branch committees as well. The only exception is when a large branch has a full-time secretary, who may in some Unions be assigned to it by the head office : even if locally elected, such full-time officers are usually paid by and responsible to the Union as a whole. The vast majority of Trade Union branches have no paid officers : the work is done by volunteers, who usually receive small sums in part compensation for their spare-time labour, or for loss of time when they have to be absent from work on Union business. The number and the titles of the branch officers vary from case to case. There is always a Secretary, nearly always a regular Chairman and a Treasurer or Financial Secretary ; and there may be others—collectors, doorkeepers (a survival from the days of secret meetings, when precautions had to be taken to keep out spies), trustees, and so on. There are also, when the branch is based on a particular place of employment, shop stewards and other works representatives, sometimes chosen in the branch meeting, sometimes elected by the workers in the several shops or departments. It is often difficult to find enough suitable members for all these positions, which mostly involve a good deal of unpaid, or very ill-paid, work. That is why it is often fairly easy for minority groups to get control of a branch by volunteering for offices which no one else wants. It helps to account for the fact that in some Unions Communists are able to exert an influence in the branches far beyond their numerical strength. But even when they have secured election they have to be cautious in using their powers if they are not to lose the confidence of the rest of the members, or to bring down on the branch disciplinary action by the higher authorities of the Union. In most Unions, the Executive Committee has power to suspend, or in the last resort to dissolve, a branch which it considers to be acting against the Union's interests ; and a few Unions have recently imposed a ban on known supporters of the Communist Party holding any Union office.

In the Mineworkers' Union, the local branches are called 'lodges', and usually consist of the workers employed in a particular colliery or pit, though sometimes several small pits are grouped together, or a big colliery has several lodges for different pits or 'districts'—i.e. sections of the colliery. The miners' lodges have thus a much closer contact with workplace problems than Trade Union branches in most other industries, and are apt to be much more lively and better attended and to play a much more important part in the discussion of matters of policy. This tendency is reinforced by the fact that the lodges now appoint the worker members of the Consultative Committees which have to be constituted at all pits as part of the machinery of Joint Consultation set up under the Act nationalising the coal industry.*

It will be seen that, in most industries, the Trade Union branch no longer plays so important a part in the life of the Union as it formerly did. It has been superseded in some of its former activities by the District Committee which links together all the branches of a Union in a particular town or area, in others by the development of national bargaining, and in yet others by the central control of benefits and by the growth of state insurance and assistance. It has also largely lost its social function as a meeting-place where members could get to know one another; and the development of joint consultation at the workplace and of other forms of works organisation has further narrowed its functions. It remains, however, the basic unit on which the Trade Union is built up. Every member of a Trade Union belongs to a branch, and is entitled, subject to his contributions being paid up (with some latitude for a few weeks' arrears) to vote at the branch meeting. Some Unions, especially in the building trades, do a large amount of voting at branch meetings, not only on local issues, but also on national questions referred to them by the Executive Council of the Union; but this type of branch referendum is much less practised in the newer Unions. In the Mineworkers' Union, and in some others, it is a regular practice for the lodges to vote instructions to the delegates they send to district or area Conferences; and most branches have the right to initiate resolutions on almost anything they please and forward them for consideration to the Union Executive or to the District to which they belong. In many Unions, too, the delegates to the Union Conference are elected by the branches, though in some the smaller branches have to be grouped for this purpose in order to keep the Conference down to a manageable size. In some cases, full-time officials are elected by voting in the branches, whereas in others the Conference or the Executive Council is the appointing body. Again, in some Unions the members of the Executive are

*For a discussion of Joint Consultation, see page 118.

elected by a vote taken in the branches ; but for this purpose the branches are grouped into Districts or Regions, usually much larger than the Districts previously referred to as entrusted with local collective bargaining.

Thus, the branch remains an essential part of Trade Union structure, though it is no longer so significant as it was in relation to collective bargaining. Its importance lies rather in its place in the internal structure of the Union, as the basic unit on which the higher levels of Trade Union government are built up. If the branch fails to attract a sufficient number of members to activity in Union affairs, Trade Union democracy is threatened with erosion at its roots, and bureaucracy is bound to take its place. But equally, if the branches are captured by minority groups which are perpetually at loggerheads with the Union leadership, the Union cannot work well whether the minorities in question are right or wrong. The problem of Trade Union democracy is to sustain a co-operative relation between the local units—branches and workplace organisations—and the directing agencies of the Union as a whole. This does not require that all the members, or even a majority of them, shall be active in Union affairs—that would be asking too much ; but it does require a sufficient number of active members, drawn from a fairly wide range of opinion, to create at any rate some healthy competition for minor offices and membership of committees, and so to protect the Union from becoming either a battle-ground for the conflicts of the head Office and the so-called 'rank-and-file' or a tool of outside groups manipulating it for their own purposes. It cannot be denied that in many Unions to-day the active nucleus is too small to satisfy these conditions, or that too little is done to arouse the members' interest and ensure their participation. In particular, it needs to be considered whether the branch based on place of residence rather than on place of work may be in process of becoming obsolete, and whether a larger recognised place should be given to Union groups based directly on the place of employment. This, as we saw, would have disadvantages where members shift often, or in large numbers, from one employer to another. It might involve, in large Unions, making the District, rather than the branch, the basic unit of enrolment, and sorting the district membership out according to place of employment, with improved provision for ensuring continuity of membership from job to job. But these questions can be better discussed when we have considered more closely both the district organisation and the methods of Trade Union activity at the level of the workshop and establishment.

II. WORKS AND WORKSHOP ORGANISATION

In most industries, a factory or work-place will have in it members of more than one Trade Union. Even where Trade Unionism is organised on an industrial basis this is likely to be the case. Not only are supervisory workers usually organised, if at all, in separate Unions : there are also, in most establishments, members of specialist grades, manual or non-manual, which have Unions of their own. In a good many industries, the main body of workers is spread out among a number of Trade Unions, each organising its own craft or department ; and there is often in addition a 'general labour' Union which caters for some or all of the less skilled workers. Often, in this last case, there is overlapping between the 'general' Union and one or more of the other Unions ; and there may be overlapping even among the Unions catering for the more skilled grades.

Thus, action at the workplace level, in order to be comprehensive, usually calls for the collaboration of a number of Trade Unions, which may, or may not, be actually rivals in the enrolment of members. This situation can give rise to many complications. These are least serious as a rule where either a single, 'industrial' Union holds a preponderant position, or each of a number of Unions has a clearly defined sphere. In the building industry, for example, there are separate Unions of Woodworkers, Woodcutting Machinists, Plasterers, Plumbers, Heating Engineers, Painters, Slaters and Tilers, Constructional Engineers, Electricians, Street Masons, Asphalt Workers, and Bricklayers and Stonemasons—the two last belonging to a single Union, the Amalgamated Union of Building Trade Workers. There was also a National Builders' Labourers' and Constructional Workers' Society, now merged in the A.U.B.T.W. Of the labourers, others belong to 'general' Unions, but the majority are still unorganised. As between the Unions catering for the various skilled crafts there is very little overlapping, though demarcation disputes sometimes arise, especially between the Plumbers and the Heating Engineers. In some of these crafts there are separate Scottish Unions (Painters, Plasterers, Slaters), whereas in others the same Unions cover the whole of the United

Kingdom. There is also a separate Association of Building Technicians. All these Unions, except the Heating Engineers, belong to a common federation, the National Federation of Building Trades Operatives, which also includes the two big 'general' Unions—the Transport and General and the General and Municipal.

The building industry is of course peculiar in that most of its members work not in factories but on building sites which shift as one job is finished and another begun. Most building firms have some nucleus of permanent employees and many have substantial workshops ; but a large proportion of the workers are employed discontinuously and shift from one employer to another as the work fluctuates. A good many of them shift from place to place as well as from firm to firm ; and all this makes Trade Union organisation a good deal more difficult than in factory industries or in other more stable occupations. These conditions largely account for the relatively poor state of Trade Union organisation in the industry—though the Woodworkers, Plumbers and Plasterers stand out as highly-organised sections.

In the building industry, Trade Union organisation at the work-place level has for the most part to be improvised on each site, though in some cases—e.g. the building of a New Town, or of a suburb—the organisation may last for years. On a well-organised job, each craft will have its delegate—the equivalent of the shop steward in a factory—and, because of the conditions of work, it is relatively easy for the men of a craft, or for representatives of them all, to come together for common discussion. In building operations, the working group has a considerable power to settle its own pace and conditions of work on the job, and a good deal is done in this way without any formal use of Trade Union machinery. The working groups can, when they wish, call in a Trade Union official to help them, and can resort through him to the formal machinery of collective negotiation with the employers. But much is done on the spot, without such formal reference. By the test of active participation at the workplace, the building Trade Unions are highly democratic : their weakness lies in the instability of these working groups and in the difficulty of maintaining continuous membership.

Another example of an industry in which a number of sectional Unions share the field is printing. There are separate Unions of compositors, correctors of the press, printing machine managers, printers and assistants, lithographic artists, lithographic printers, electrotypers and stereotypers, and typefounders, and a combined Union of Printing, Bookbinding and Paper Workers which organises not only the paper-makers and bookbinders, but also such unskilled workers as are not enrolled in specialist Unions. Here again there is a separate Scottish Union of compositors and some related groups—the Scottish Typographical Association; and in England the London Compositors have their own society—a very old one—separate from the Typographical Association, which organises compositors in the provinces. As in the building industry, the printers' Unions have a federation—the Printing and Kindred Trades Federation—to which all these Unions and also the National Union of Journalists belong. There is little overlapping, and in general the Unions work harmoniously together, each insisting on a good deal of independence in its own field.

The compositors take rank as the pioneers of formal workshop organisation. The institution known as the 'Chapel', which began with the compositors but has now spread to most of the other printing trades, long antedates any wider form of Trade Union organisation: it was well established throughout the eighteenth century, and probably much earlier. The 'Chapel' is a grouping of all the compositors in a particular workshop, under the presidency of a senior compositor, known as the 'Father of the Chapel'. Through him, it watches over the interests of the craft—for example, in regulating the distribution of work and taking up questions of special payment for tabular or other exceptional kinds of type-setting. The compositors are jealous of their freedom from detailed supervision by foremen, and very insistent on their traditional customs; and other trades in the printing industry largely follow their example. The industry is one which employs a high proportion of skilled workers and in which special problems of work-arrangement constantly arise. Its workers are for the most part highly literate, and strongly individual in outlook; and the proportion of members playing an active part in Union affairs is large. But this activity is much centred on the place of work, which is the real basis on which the whole Union structure is built.

A third example of an industry organised mainly in sectional Unions is cotton. In this case there are four main branches, which are usually not all carried on in the same establishment. These are preparing the cotton for spinning, spinning of the yarn, weaving of textile fabrics, and bleaching and dyeing. A fifth, knitting, is usually reckoned as belonging to the distinct hosiery industry, which covers woollen and other textiles as well as cotton. So, indeed, does dyeing ; but its cotton-dyeing section is often reckoned as part of the cotton industry. Trade Union organisation in the main, though not entirely, follows these divisions. The preparing sections are covered mainly by the Card and Blowing Room Operatives' Amalgamation ; but this Union also covers ring-spinning, which has been gradually ousting the older process of mule-spinning for the coarser kinds of yarn, and can be done by relatively unskilled labour. The mule-spinners have their own old-established Union, the Amalgamated Association of Cotton Spinners, which is confined to men and has exceptionally high rates of contribution. It also enrols the 'piecers', who assist the spinners and provide the material from which the spinners are recruited. The manufacturing section is organised mainly in the Amalgamated Weavers' Association, which includes a number of subsidiary grades ; and there are also a separate Amalgamation of Beamers, Twisters and Drawers and of Power-Loom Overlookers, and also a Union of Textile Warehousemen and a few lesser bodies. Finally, the Bleachers and Dyers, who used to have a separate Union of their own, are now amalgamated with the main body of workers in the woollen industry in a National Union of Dyers, Bleachers and Textile Workers.

For the most part, these Unions negotiate separately with the employers. Preparing and spinning are commonly carried on in the same establishments, and sometimes weaving as well ; but most weaving is done in separate works and by different firms. Bleaching and dyeing are usually in the hands of entirely separate firms. The Cardroom Amalgamation organises the least skilled section—mainly women : the Spinners' Amalgamation the most skilled—entirely men. The Weavers' Amalgamation includes both men and women of varying degrees of skill. The Overlookers, and also the Beamers, Twisters and Drawers, are skilled workers : the Dyers and Bleachers include both skilled and unskilled. Here, as in the printing industry, the 'general' Unions play no part, except in a few mills in areas remote from the main centre of the industry in Lancashire and Cheshire.

The cotton industry is one in which there has not been, in the past, a great deal of scope for workshop organisation. The processes are highly mechanised, and, until recent years, they were not subject to rapid change. There were many complicated problems of measurement, especially in the weaving sections, involved in the determination of piecework prices—the cotton industry works almost wholly on a system of piecework payments—but these consisted mainly in the arithmetical calculation of prices in accordance with standard lists drawn up by agreement between the Union and the employers' association. These calculations were mainly a matter for full-time officials, who were required to be experts in this field. In the spinning section of the industry, the chief troubles arose out of faults in the materials supplied, as faulty or unsuitable material caused frequent breakages, which affected piecework earnings. There was, however, usually little either in preparing or spinning rooms or in weaving sheds to give rise to the need for frequent negotiations at the workshop level ; and no shop steward system made its appearance in the cotton industry until quite recently. Apart from this, the practice of employing collectors to collect Union subscriptions from door to door at the workers' homes removed the need for collections in the workshops. Only of late, in connection with changes in machine-operation, especially in the weaving section, have workshop problems become important. This has occurred particularly where automatic looms have been introduced, or old looms fitted with semi-automatic devices, so that the weaver has been given a larger number of looms to work, and new systems of payment have been introduced. But even today, the shop steward system has very little hold, and there is relatively little development of workshop organisation or of negotiation or joint consultation at the factory level. The Trade Unions in the cotton industry are organised on a basis of considerable autonomy to the localities : indeed, the Weavers' Amalgamation is still made up of a number of local bodies registered as separate Unions, carrying on their friendly benefit activities on a local basis, and united only for industrial action. The Spinners and the Cardroom Amalgamation, though rather more centralised, are also made up of local bodies which enjoy a considerable autonomy. Each local Union or district has its own full-time officers, who do most of the detailed negotiation under the auspices of the elected local or district committees, the central Amalgamations dealing only with general questions. The Amalgamations are, indeed, joined together federally in the United Textile Factory Workers' Association ; but this is in the main not a negotiating body but an agency for representing the common interests of the industry in relation to trade policy and industrial legislation and for political action through the Labour Party. The manufacturing section has a rather closer federation, the Northern Counties Textile Trades Federation, which links together the Weavers and the other trades connected with weaving and kindred processes ; and this body has local federations in the various manufacturing centres, and acts to some extent as a negotiating agency. The Dyers and Bleachers negotiate quite separately, with different employing groups.

The engineering industry has a Trade Union structure differing widely from the three so far described. Engineering is not so much a single industry as a group of industries connected at one end with the industries engaged in metal manufacture and at the other with such industries as shipbuilding and the making of motor-cars and aircraft. No one can say where precisely engineering begins or ends, and its Trade Union organisation reflects this uncertainty. The iron and steel manufacturing industry stands clearly apart from it, but employs a good many skilled engineers : the ironfounding industry is pretty separate, but many ironfounders are employed in the moulding shops of engineering firms : marine engineering is closely connected with shipbuilding : electricians are employed partly in engineering factories and partly in other industries, including building : the motor and aircraft constructional industries are engaged partly in engineering and partly in body-building and in the making of electrical and other specialised equipment ; and there is hardly any industry in which skilled engineers are not employed to some extent. The biggest overlap of all is in the locomotive constructional and maintenance establishments carried on by the railways, which can be regarded as belonging either to the railway or to the engineering industry, or in a sense to both. Engineering was formerly organised mainly on a basis of craft, with a number of separate craft Unions each catering for a particular kind of skilled worker, and the Amalgamated Society of Engineers, founded in 1851, was designed to bring together in one society a number of related crafts. Among the trades which had separate Unions competing with the A.S.E. were the patternmakers, the blacksmiths, the coppersmiths, the brassfounders and brass finishers, and a number of lesser crafts. The central core of the A.S.E's membership consisted of fitters and turners, millwrights, and the operators of machines needing a fairly high degree of specialised skill—milling machines, screw-cutting machines, and a number of adaptations of the centre lathe. In direct competition with the A.S.E. were the highly-skilled Steam Engine Makers, and also the Toolmakers and the United Machine Workers' Unions, which included many workers who were hardly more than semi-skilled. The A.S.E. was also open in theory to ironfounders, electricians, and a number of other skilled grades whose members in practice belonged to other Unions. As all these Unions consisted mainly of skilled workers, or at least of workers who had some pretension to rank as skilled, the rapidly growing numbers of less skilled workers and labourers would have been left almost unorganised had not the 'general labour' Unions set out to enrol them. As they did, there appeared an overlapping area, in which some of the workers were in the craft Unions, others in the 'general' Unions, and yet others in certain areas in small Unions restricted to engineering labourers. Confusion became greater as some of the craft Unions, including the A.S.E., opened their ranks to the unskilled and attempted to enrol them as members entitled only to an inferior position in the Union, without eligibility to office. During the first World War women entered the industry in large numbers—they had previously been employed in it to some extent in the Midlands—and were enrolled, some in the general labour Unions catering for both sexes, and some in the separate National Federation of Women Workers, which subsequently merged with the General and Municipal Workers' Union. At the end of the first World War the A.S.E amalgamated with the Steam Engine Makers, the Toolmakers, and the United Machine Workers to form the Amalgamated Engineering Union, which thereafter tended to become more and more an industrial Union, opening its ranks first to less skilled males and later to women workers. But the 'general' Unions were too firmly entrenched to be driven out; and to-day the less skilled workers are divided between them, the A.E.U., and a number of more specialised Unions, such as the Foundry Workers and the Electrical Trades Union.

The engineering Unions cover marine engineering and the engineering branches of the motor-car and aircraft manufacturing industries. But the shipbuilders proper have their separate Unions—the Boilermakers' and Iron and Steel Shipbuilders' Society, and the Shipwrights' Association; and the Woodworkers, Plumbers, Upholsterers, Painters, Electricians, and a number of other Unions have also a considerable shipyard membership. The coachbuilding and body-making sections of the motor-car and aircraft industries are largely organised by the National Unions of Sheet Metal Workers and Vehicle Builders. In addition, there are a host of minor metal-manufacturing trades whose skilled workers belong largely to the various engineering Unions, while their less skilled operatives are catered for mainly by the 'general' Unions. Finally, in the railway constructional and maintenance shops, both the engineering and the 'general' Unions are in competition with the National Union of Railwaymen, which enrols many of the less-skilled workers and some even in the skilled grades.

This is a very confusing picture. At the workplace level, it involves that there are usually a considerable number of Trade Unions represented in any factory of substantial size, and even in many that are quite small. Moreover, these Unions have not, in many instances, clearly defined spheres of operation, but are in competition for the adherence of the same workers—though this condition of affairs is made less intolerable by many local inter-union agreements, written or unwritten, to assign particular groups to one Union rather than to another. In some big establishments there may be as many as fifty different Unions, though some of these will have only a very few members.

Most of these Unions are joined together in the Confederation of Shipbuilding and Engineering Trade Unions, which includes the 'general' Unions as well as those which have their main strength among the various skilled grades. This federal body nowadays takes charge of general wage movements and of some other general questions ; but each Union is autonomous in its own affairs and negotiates separately on matters special to its own membership. As against this, the employers have two main Federations—of Engineers and of Shipbuilders—and a number of more specialised associations for particular branches of production.

At this stage, our concern with this most complicated Trade Union structure is with its reactions on organisation and bargaining at the workplace level. The engineering group of industries is that in which the shop steward holds the most outstanding position. The shop steward began as a very minor functionary of the craft Union, with the duty of trying to ensure that the skilled workers employed belonged to the Union and paid their contributions regularly. He had at the outset no authority to negotiate, or even to deal with workshop grievances beyond reporting them to the Trade Union branch or District Committee. But even before 1914 in some establishments—notably Woolwich Arsenal—the shop stewards had in fact assumed considerable importance as workshop negotiators, and in some cases had come together in workshop or works committees, either confined to stewards belonging to a particular Trade Union or, occasionally, including the stewards of a number of distinct Unions.

The first World War led to a very rapid development of the shop stewards' movement. Under war conditions, changes in workshop practice were continually being made, and trade customs were formally suspended for the war period in order to allow what was known as 'dilution of labour'—that is, upgrading of less skilled workers to skilled jobs, breaking up of jobs previously done by skilled workers into their skilled and less skilled components, extended employment of female labour, and so on. These changes had to be introduced by negotiation at the workshop level ; for they were far too many and diverse to be handled by full-time Trade Union officials or by district negotiation. They came to be handled mainly by shop stewards and shop stewards' committees ; and, whereas the pre-war shop steward had been definitely an agent of the Union, and under its authority, under war conditions many groups of workers elected in the workshops stewards who owed no allegiance to a Trade Union (though they were nearly always members of one) and often represented members belonging to a number of different Unions. Thus, there were in many factories, official Trade Union stewards side by side with unofficial stewards ; and sometimes both kinds served on the same Shop Stewards' Committee covering a whole factory or a department.

It was not long before the Shop Stewards' movement, in one place after another, fell foul of the official Trade Union machine. The Trade Unions in the munitions industries had agreed not to resort to strikes during the war, and a little later (in 1915) compulsory arbitration had been imposed by the Munitions Act, and dilution of labour had thereafter been widely extended under government auspices. Thus, workers who were discontented with the conditions laid down under the machinery set up by the government had either to accept them or to take action against them without official Trade Union support, and usually in violation of the law. In these circumstances the leadership of the movements of protest tended to pass into the hands of the Shop Stewards' Committee, which included unofficial as well as official Trade Union stewards. As the war continued and more and more workers were called up, from the munitions factories as well as from other occupations, anti-war feeling increased, and there was a growing sentiment in favour of 'peace by negotiation'. The shop stewards' movement became closely identified with this attitude ; and after the Russian Revolution of 1917 it moved rapidly leftwards. Quite a number of its leaders, indeed, took part later in the formation of the Communist Party of Great Britain in 1920. By that time, however, the movement had largely collapsed. As soon as the war was over and the engineering industry began to contract, many employers hastened to get rid of the most militant among their employees and refused to bargain any more with unofficial workshop representatives. The shop stewards did not die out ; but their numbers were greatly reduced, and the unofficial stewards disappeared, leaving only stewards appointed by the Trade Unions to represent them and enjoying much less wide powers than the movement had been able to assume under the stress of war. At the same time, something was done by a number of Trade Unions, including the newly established Amalgamated Engineering Union, to give their stewards a rather improved status. The A.E.U. for example included a small representation of its shop stewards on its District Committees and developed a practice of meetings between the shop stewards and the District Committees for consultation about the conduct of the Union's local affairs.

Nevertheless, in many establishments the shop steward system almost died out during the years of depression that followed the first World War, and everywhere it ceased to provide a militant leadership. It then gradually began to grow again, particularly in the developing aircraft industry ; but it did not regain much driving force in most branches of engineering until after the end of the great depression of the early 1930s. As rearmament developed gradually in the later 'thirties, there was some further growth ; but large-scale expansion came only with the second World War, and especially after 1940, when the war entered on its decisive phase.

This new shop stewards' movement was in certain respects

widely different from that of the years after 1914. It was mainly an official movement, supported by the Trade Unions and led by men who were supporters of the war effort and ready to help in the drive for higher production. Up to 1941 the Communists were in opposition ; but from the moment of the Nazi attack on the Soviet Union they were among the most enthusiastic supporters of the war effort, and, despite their relatively small numbers, their keenness enabled them to play a considerable part. Between 1941 and 1945 Communists and non-Communists in the workshops were acting mainly together in pursuance of the same immediate objectives.

The growth of the shop steward system during the second World War was also accompanied, and helped, by the development of Joint Production Committees in most of the larger factories. These Committees were not intended to be negotiating bodies, or to take over any Trade Union functions : they were meant specifically to help in increasing output by promoting more co-operative relations between workers and managements. It could not, however, be easy in practice to draw a clear line between measures designed to encourage higher production and matters of Trade Union concern ; and even if the J.P.C.s did not negotiate, their discussions often affected the conditions of wage-payment and other terms of employment in the war factories. In some factories, J.P.C.s and Shop Stewards' Committees existed side by side, usually with overlapping membership. In others there was no Shop Stewards' Committee representing all the workers, but there were groups of shop stewards representing the several Unions and in practice often taking common action either directly or through the J.P.C.s. By the end of the war, workshop organisation in both forms was very widespread in the engineering and kindred industries and had also spread quite largely in a number of others.

After 1945 many of the J.P.C.s were wound up, though some remained ; but the shop stewards' movement suffered no such major setback as after 1918. There were several reasons for this—the much greater strength of the Trade Unions, the fuller recognition of the shop stewards in the Trade Unions, the absence of serious unemployment, and the presence in power of a Labour Government favourable to joint consultation and to full recognition of Trade Union rights. The Labour Government, indeed, refused to make joint consultation compulsory on private employers ; but it did establish the system throughout the industries that were taken over by the State—including mines, railways, docks, road transport, civil aviation, gas and electricity supply. At the same time a good many of the bigger firms, faced with strong Trade Unions and conditions of labour shortage, felt it to be to their advantage to bring the workers into consultation in the hope of securing their help in the readjustment of industry to the post-war situation and of disarming their hostility to the adoption of new methods based on war-time experience. In the big mass-production firms especially, the actual conditions of work came more and more to depend not only on the terms of general collective agreements between Trade Unions and associations of employers, but also on special arrangements related to the particular methods in use in each separate establishment ; and in making these adjustments within the general conditions laid down for the whole industry, bargaining at the factory and workshop level came to assume a high importance. This was especially true of the bonus arrangements which became common, of special arrangements for the grading of labour on a factory basis, and of the conditions to be adopted for various kinds of team or squad work, or where one shift of workers alternated with another on a continuous process.

The effect of this development has been that in practice shop stewards and works negotiating bodies have become of much more significance in determining the actual conditions of work than they used to be, or than they are even now recognised as being by the formal constitutions of many of the Trade Unions. Nor is it likely that this trend will be reversed. The more new processes and machines develop, and the larger the scale of factory organisation becomes, the more each establishment tends to be a law unto itself, needing to make its own working arrangements in regular consultation and detailed bargaining with its own employees. This does not do away with the need for wider forms of bargaining to settle general wage-rates and conditions ; but it does mean that district officials and committees of Trade Unions cannot tackle the tasks arising in each establishment without the aid of strong organised agencies representing the employees and organically connected with the Trade Union as a whole.

III. DISTRICT AND REGIONAL ORGANISATION

We have seen that a Trade Union, when it has more than one branch in a town or district, usually provides for the election of a District Committee, chosen mainly by the branches, to take charge of its local affairs. But this is not always the case. Some Unions have only wider Area or Divisional Councils linking up their branches over quite extensive regions ; and some have both. There are also great differences in the powers given to district or regional bodies. In the Amalgamated Engineering Union, for example, the District Committees are the responsible bodies in charge of local negotiations and for the maintenance of the local organisation. A few of the largest have full-time officers of their own ; and they occupy a position of key importance. The much larger Divisions of the A.E.U. are mainly electoral districts for the choosing of members for the Executive Council and also organising areas, in each of which the Union maintains a full-time organiser (Organising District Delegate) whose function is to keep a general eye on the districts and branches within his division and to go where he is needed to help when troubles arise. The Division is not a negotiating body, and has no regular administrative functions in the conduct of the Union's affairs.

The National Union of Mineworkers presents a pattern different from either of these. It began as a Federation of a number of independent Unions in the various coalfields, each with its own separate finance and its ultimate independence, though as a rule in matters of common concern all the affiliated Unions followed a concerted policy. Only at the time when the industry was facing nationalisation did these Unions combine to form a single national Union ; and even thereafter the former Unions, while becoming Districts of the national body, kept a large part of their old powers, continuing to negotiate separately on matters affecting a particular coalfield, and largely maintaining their separate financial arrangements. The Districts of the N.U.M. still possess many of the characteristics of distinct Trade Unions, though general policy has become a good deal more closely co-ordinated since their amalgamation. This, however, would have been bound to happen in any case when the whole industry was taken over by a single employing body—the National Coal Board.

The 'Amalgamations' in the cotton trade, described in a previous section, resemble the Mineworkers in this respect. They too arose out of a linking up of previously existing local or district Unions, which kept after the fusion a good deal of independence. The main purpose of amalgamation in both cases was to secure unity of action in matters of general industrial policy, rather than to take local matters out of local hands or to establish any uniform system of friendly benefits over the whole area of the combined body.

The Mineworkers' Districts, like the coalfields on which they are partly based, are of very different sizes. For example, the very small Kent coalfield forms one District, and the whole of Scotland another. All South Wales is one District, but the small North Wales coalfield is separate. In Scotland there were formerly separate county Unions in Ayrshire, Lanarkshire, Fife, and other counties; but these joined up in a Scottish Miners' Federation which joined the Miners' Federation of Great Britain as a body and then became rather more closely united in a National Union of Scottish Mineworkers before it turned into a District of the N.U.M. These and other Districts—Yorkshire, Durham, Northumberland, Nottinghamshire, and others—have a long tradition of independent organisation behind them, going back in most instances a long way further than the M.F.G.B. itself—which was formed only in 1888. This long record of independence causes them to behave as autonomous units in a central body rather than as mere sections of it. Moreover, some of the larger are broken up in turn into district or area groups which have their own representative machinery and a good deal of power of local action within the general activities of the N.U.M. District.

It is much easier for this considerable autonomy to exist within a national Union where the latter has come into being on a basis of separate regional Unions than where it has developed from the first on a national basis or has been formed by the fusion of related or rival separate national Unions. Other cases in which federations of regional Unions have turned into national Unions by amalgamation include the Blastfurnacemen, the Sheet Metal Workers, and, much longer ago; the Typographical Association, as well as the principal Unions in the cotton industry. Even where federation of this type leads to amalgamation, a good many powers which it does not seem necessary to centralise are apt to be left in regional hands. On the other hand, national Unions which have not passed through this stage usually concede only specific delegated powers, and not residuary powers, to the regional or district bodies set up under their rules, and in a great number of cases of this latter type finance is almost completely centralised.

Naturally, the extent of regional decentralisation or autonomy has also something to do with the structure of the industry in which its members are employed. Even before the railways were nationalised, it would have been impossible for the railway Trade Unions to give wide powers to local or regional agencies, because each railway company operated on a national scale and there was usually more in common among railwaymen employed by the same company in different areas than among those employed by different companies in the same area. The Post Office, being throughout under central government management, requires a large amount of centralised bargaining, though regional agencies have had rather more scope since an attempt at decentralisation of management was made as an outcome of the Bridgeman Report of 1932. Building, on the other hand, is a highly localised industry, in the hands largely of purely local firms—though there are some big contractors operating on a much larger scale. Accordingly, the building Trade Unions have a large measure of local autonomy, and also a good deal of regional co-ordination and negotiation over and above their internal arrangements for collective bargaining on general issues.

Local and regional autonomies of these types remain in being ; but the tendency has been for more of the collective bargaining to be conducted on a national scale. Sometimes this means the fixing of uniform national wage-rates and general conditions : more often, even if general conditions are settled on a uniform basis, even national agreements make provision for local variations in wage-rates. Sometimes the variations are between London, other big towns, and small towns and rural areas over the country as a whole : sometimes they are regional—the reasons for such differences being mainly historical. The variations have tended to become less in recent years, largely because cost-of-living differences have grown smaller, but also as part of a general tendency to reduce real wage differentials as money wages have increased.

It is impossible to go further into these differences of regional and district structure between one Trade Union and another without discussing each Union separately ; and that would take much too long. Some further light on the differences will however be thrown when we come to deal with particular aspects of Trade Union activity in later chapters.

IV. EXECUTIVES AND CONFERENCES

Over the work of each Trade Union presides, between its periodical Conferences, an Executive Council. In all cases save a very few the members of these Councils are actual workers employed in the trades or industries served, not full-time officials of the Union—though in troublous times some of them may need to spend a good deal of their time on the Union's business. They receive no salaries, but are paid delegation fees for attending meetings and compensation for lost time, and also of course expenses for travelling and hotel bills when these have to be met. These Executive Council members are usually elected for several years, and are re-eligible ; but some Unions insist on an interval before a retiring member is allowed to stand for re-election. In most cases each Executive member is elected by the members in a geographical region ; but in some Unions some or all of the members represent different trade groups, where the Union enrols a wide range of workers of different types. Some Unions elect their Executive members at their delegate Conferences, and a few by postal ballot ; but it is more usual for the voting to take place in the branches, by individual ballot. In most cases a member is eligible only if he has been in the Union continuously for a certain number of years, and is in good financial standing.

Trade Union Executives usually meet at fixed, often quarterly, intervals, for several days at a time ; and special meetings can be called when they are needed to deal with urgent matters. National negotiations are usually entrusted to special committees, chosen from the Executive and officials, sometimes with other members added when the affairs of a particular section are at issue. The Executive normally has a long agenda to handle at its regular meetings, including a full report by the General Secretary on the work done since the previous meeting. In addition to the full Executive there are usually a number of Committees, or Sub-Committees, sometimes including a General Purposes Committee which meets more often than the full Executive. In addition, Executive members, or groups of them, are often sent on 'delegations' to represent the Executive in particular areas, or to sit on joint committees with representatives of other Unions or on related bodies.

A very few Trade Unions—the Amalgamated Engineering Union and the Boilermakers' Society—have Executive Councils consisting of full-time members elected to represent large geographical regions. In such cases, the Executive members undertake many administrative duties which in most Unions are undertaken by elected officers. The system has not found favour, because it leaves the Union to be administered entirely by men who are no longer working at their trades—and may find great difficulty in returning to them if they are not re-elected. It tends to give the Executive a high degree of permanency, because in most cases the sitting member does continue to be re-elected until he retires. But this does not always happen. The system also means that a good many questions which in most Unions would be disposed of at Executive meetings are brought up at the Union Conference, which affords the only opportunity for the members working at their trades to make their opinions felt. A further consequence is that, when the Executive is in permanent session, the General Secretary and the other leading officials have a good deal less power.

Trade Union Executives have very large powers. In nearly all cases, nowadays, funds are highly centralised, and branches and districts have only quite small sums at their disposal without Executive sanction—sometimes none at all. Expenditure on strike or lockout benefits practically always requires Executive approval. The Executive is the body which controls the industrial and negotiating policy of the Union—subject to such directions as it may receive from the Conference, though in practice, officials, or at any rate General Secretaries, enjoy a large discretion between Executive meetings.

In earlier times, it was not practicable for Trade Unions covering large areas to be governed by Executive Councils representing the entire membership. The device most commonly used when representatives from different areas could meet but seldom was that of the 'governing branch'. A delegate Conference, meeting at rare intervals, would appoint one branch, or a group of neighbouring branches, to provide the Executive Council for a period, until the delegates could meet again ; and the Council thus chosen would take charge of the Union's affairs in conjunction with the General Secretary. At a later stage, use was sometimes made of two bodies—an Executive chosen from a particular area, and a larger General Council of delegates from the whole country, meeting much less often or even only when summoned to deal with a crisis. This General Council sometimes took the place of the still larger Delegate Conference ; and in such cases frequent use was made in some Unions of the referendum as a means of taking the members' opinions. The voting then took place in the branches, and was limited to those attending the branch meetings. This type of Trade Union government, though it survives in a few craft Unions, can now be regarded as obsolete. Both easier travel and the larger funds available have made it possible for all modern Unions of any substantial size to have periodically meeting Executive Councils chosen from a wide geographical area.

Although in most Unions the Executive Council consists of members actually employed at their several trades, it sometimes happens that this is not wholly so. In the Mineworkers' Union for example, the National Executive Committee consists partly of men who are full-time officials of the Districts of which the Union is made up. This practice began when the Miners' national organisation was a federation of independent district and county Unions, whose officers were eligible as members of the federal Executive ; and it continues in the amalgamated Union. This, however, does not mean that the Miners' Union is run by full-time officials without the active participation of working miners ; for the Union makes very frequent use of National Conferences for settling questions of policy, and the delegations consist largely of working miners. The National Union of Mineworkers has in fact a very democratic structure, with provision for frequent consultation at all levels.

Another instance of full-time officials sitting on the Executive is the National Union of General and Municipal Workers. This Union has two distinct executive bodies—a General Council and a smaller National Executive chosen from among the General Council. The Council is made up of two representatives from each District—one the District Secretary, who is a full-time official, and the other a 'lay member', that is, either a member actually working at his trade, or a local officer. Each of the four largest districts has an additional 'lay' representative. As the two leading national officials are also members of the General Council, this body comes near to having a majority of official members. The National Executive chosen by the Council consists of one representative from each District, with the proviso that half the persons chosen must be 'lay members'. Thus, the N.U.G.M.W. goes much further than most other Unions towards executive government by full-time officials. Its chief rival, the Transport and General Workers' Union, does not allow any full-time officials to sit as voting members on its Executive, which is made up of one 'lay' representative from each Region and one from each of the National Trade Groups into which the membership is divided functionally.

National Executives are in theory the 'Cabinets' of Trade Unions, whereas National Conferences are their Parliaments. But the analogy does not fully hold ; for the General Secretary by no means occupies the place of a top civil service official. He is very much more, being in most cases an elected leader, chosen by the entire membership, or sometimes by the Conference, with a mandate fully as ample as that of the Executive with which he works. The relations between Executives and full-time officials can, however, be better discussed later, when we have considered the 'legislative' aspect of Trade Union government.

As we saw, the highest organ of the Trade Union is usually a Conference of elected delegates, representing the branches. Save in a few cases, when there are very many branches of small size, each branch has one representative—larger branches often more if they wish. A good many Trade Unions hold an Annual Conference—a few, including the vast Transport and General Workers' Union, convene their Conferences only once in every two, or even three, years. The Trade Union Conference has three principal functions—to make and amend the Constitution, to pass policy resolutions, and to act as an appeal court from Executive decisions. Occasionally, the last of these functions is exercised by a separately elected Final Appeal Court, much smaller than the Conference ; but this is unusual. In some cases, rules revision is either carried out at special Conferences, or not allowed to come up each year, even when an Annual Conference is held. At Conference, except when a general revision of rules is being made, the main business is, first, the hearing and approval or criticism of the work of the Union and of its sections, where it covers a number of distinct groups or has separate machinery for the administration of different aspects of its work ; and secondly the consideration of resolutions submitted either by the branches or by the Executive. For example, the Conference may consider a new programme, or a new proposed system of grading labour, or a demand to be put forward in collective bargaining. It may also adopt, or reject, resolutions covering a wide range of subjects, political as well as strictly industrial. It may consider a project of amalgamation or federation with some other Union or Unions. It may pass in review an immense mass of detail relating to conditions of work in the trade or industry concerned. It may also conduct elections, as far as Conference is responsible for them. Special Conferences, unless they are called to deal with proposed amalgamations or revisions of rules, are most frequently concerned either with wage or other applications to employers, or with acceptance or rejection of terms proposed in the course of collective bargaining. In the big 'general' Unions, however, such matters are usually handled either by the Executive or by conferences representing only the particular sections of the membership concerned.

The Trade Union Conference is an outing and a friendly meeting place as well as a legislative convention. It is used by the Union leaders not only to tell their members what they are doing—through the delegates, who are expected to report back to their branches on their return, and often also through special numbers of the Union journal—but also as an occasion for making pronouncements and testing opinion. The coming together of a large number of delegates makes it possible for many unofficial contacts to be made, and for coming men to get known beyond their own branches or areas. The Conference also serves to advertise the Union, both in the district in which it is held and through newspaper reports.

Many Conferences are held largely in public, with provision for private sessions when confidential matters are discussed. But some sit in private, sending out such reports as are thought fit to the press, but often circulating fuller reports to their own officers and branches. There are often lively policy debates; but the Executive is usually in a strong position for carrying the resolutions it wants unless feelings are very strongly aroused. Some Unions discourage, or even prevent, branches or groups from seeking to canvass opinion in advance on the resolutions they submit to Conference, mainly in order to make it more difficult for outside bodies to organise campaigns for capturing the Union or for getting a particular resolution accepted.

Naturally, the Conference plays a bigger part in those Unions in which it meets at least once a year than in others ; and it plays the biggest part of all where the practice is to summon a special Conference whenever a vital decision affecting the whole Union has to be taken. This, as we have seen, is the practice particularly of the Mineworkers.

V. OFFICIALS

The chief officer of a British Trade Union is its General Secretary, who save in a few very small Unions is always a full-time servant of the Union. The President is usually much less important : indeed in most Unions he is not a full-time officer, but a leading member of the Executive Council, who serves as its chairman, and continues to work at his trade—though in fact he may spend a great deal of time away from it on Union business. A number of Unions have Presidents who are more than Executive chairmen and chairmen at Conferences : and some of these are salaried full-time officers. But even so the British tradition normally gives the highest standing to the General Secretary. In a few cases, this situation may be changing, where a strong full-time President is in office ; but the British tradition differs from the American, in which the President rather than the Secretary takes pride of place.

The General Secretary is usually elected by the whole membership—or rather by those who trouble to vote. Sometimes, however, he is chosen by the Delegate Conference ; and in at any rate one Union—the Iron and Steel Trades Confederation—the choice is in the hands of the Executive. Election by the members at large is felt to confer the highest democratic status. The choice may be for a term of years, with eligibility for re-election ; but it is usually for life—or rather up to a fixed retiring age. General Secretaries have a very great security of tenure : only on the rarest occasions do they vacate their offices before retiring age (which is often sixty) save by their own choice. There have been a number of voluntary retirements in recent years on account of the appointment of Trade Union Secretaries to the Boards of nationalised industries, or to similar posts. Ernest Bevin retired on becoming a Cabinet Minister.

In large Unions there are also a number of Assistant Secretaries, usually including an Assistant General Secretary and the Secretaries in charge of various departments of the Union work. Such officers, or some of them, may be elected in the same way as the General Secretary ; but some or all of them are often appointed by the Executive rather than elected. The larger Trade Unions have in addition Organisers, some attached to their head offices, but others working in particular localities or regions. These again may be either elected, or appointed by the Executive. Where they are elected to serve in particular areas, the election is often in the hands of the members in the area concerned ; but some Unions—notably the big 'general' Unions—prefer to appoint their local full-time officers centrally, in order to make sure that they work under the orders of the Executive and the head office rather than of the local membership. This is a most important aspect of Trade Union centralisation. Organisers may, however, be elected regionally—as in the Amalgamated Engineering Union—and at the same time be put under the orders of the centre rather than of the area in which they serve.

Most Trade Union officials are not highly paid. Even the General Secretaries of the biggest Unions do not draw salaries comparable with those paid by big Unions in the United States or with the salaries paid in capitalist business. Lesser officials mostly get quite modest salaries, in return for what is usually exacting work. The Trade Union official is very apt to spend a large proportion of his week-ends as well as his week-days on the job, and may easily have his holidays interrupted by an outbreak of trouble affecting his department. Nevertheless, if he belongs to the negotiating team of the Union, he will almost inevitably take to leading a life which is more like that of a middle-class person than like the traditional ways of working-class life. He will inevitably get used to staying in hotels and meeting with men much better off than he is from the employers' side, and will have to be enabled to do this by adequate expense allowances. There used to be some Trade Unionists who argued that the Trade Union official should not be paid more than the average wage or salary of the workers he represented ; but this became unworkable long ago, and little is heard of it now except in certain highly paid occupations, in which there is no difficulty. Indeed, the cry has died down as working-class standards have risen, and as there have come to be, even in manual trades, some workers who earn as much as most of the officials who represent them.

The General Secretary is in charge of the Union's head office and of its general administration. Some of the older Unions still try to recruit their office staffs largely from among their own members; but this practice is dying out. Specialists, such as accountants, have to be recruited from outside; and most Unions now draw their clerical workers, male as well as female, from the general labour market. These staffs are usually organised in the Clerical and Administrative Workers' Union, or sometimes in other Unions; and collective bargains are made regulating their wages and conditions. Trade Unions are usually good employers, giving good conditions as well as fair wages to their clerical staffs.

The General Secretary, as head office administrator, may be helped by a special assistant; but the authority is his. He is finally responsible to the Executive and to the members for every letter or circular that goes out of the office, and for the paying of proper attention to incoming correspondence. The other officers, even those who are separately elected, work under him, and must consult him when matters of importance come up for decision. It is his task not only to supervise the administration and the organising and negotiating work of the Union but also to act as the chief policy-maker, with the necessity of carrying the Executive, and in due course the Conference, along with him when controversial issues arise. Being at work all the time, he is necessarily in a better position than an Executive which meets only from time to time to keep a constant watch and hold on the Union; and he is also its powerful representative in dealing with other Unions and with outside bodies. The General Council of the Trades Union Congress is made up largely of General Secretaries of important Unions. In 1952-3, out of 35 members of the General Council, 24 were General Secretaries and 2 full-time Presidents of affiliated Unions, and 6 more were full-time officials of Unions whose General Secretary was also serving on the Council. The remaining three were other leading officials.

The General Secretaries of the leading Unions, with a very few others, thus form the central 'Cabinet' of the Trade Union movement. Their duties are heavy, and they mostly work very hard. Only two of the General Secretaries on the General Council, and no other General Secretaries of Unions affiliated to the Congress, are also Members of Parliament. They have not the time. The two who are are both Secretaries of fairly small Unions, who can manage the dual job—or think they can. It used to be much more common, in the Labour Party's early days, to find such 'twicers', as they used to be called. Nowadays, both Union work and work in Parliament are much more exacting than they used to be.

The Trade Union official, unless his work is entirely in the office—which is rare—needs to know his members, and to be able to tackle an unruly meeting at need. He has to be a competent speaker, though he need not be an orator ; and he has to be a competent negotiator as well. For these and for his many other tasks he usually receives no special training : he has learnt them, as a rule, in working for the Union as committee-man or unpaid officer before he became a salaried official ; and for the rest he picks them up as he goes along. This gives rise to some difficulties in occupations in which negotiations are coming to be more and more technical ; and a few Unions have recently taken to sending some of their younger officials to special courses in such subjects as time and motion study and rate-fixing or job evaluation, as well as to arranging short courses for shop stewards on methods of negotiation and related matters ; but this is still exceptional. Most Trade Union officials have picked up, and not been taught, their jobs ; and some are very scornful of the notion that there is any other way of learning them. In this they are doubtless right ; but it does not follow that some training might not be a useful supplement.

Some Unions now have research departments of their own, to help their officials in preparing briefs for negotiation and for collecting and arranging statistics ; but many still have not. Research officers are usually appointed, not elected, and are often taken from outside the Union. I believe I was the first Union research officer ever appointed—by the Amalgamated Society of Engineers—as long ago as 1915. Even now, Trade Union research departments are usually on a very small scale, and staffed by quite junior officers—who may be none the worse for that.

The balance of power between General Secretaries and their subordinate officials on the one hand and between General Secretaries and Executive Councils on the other depends much on personalities, as well as on formal arrangements and methods of election. The General Secretary of a British Trade Union is not usually expected to behave in so dominant a fashion as is common among Union Presidents in the United States ; but a strong personality can become very powerful, above all in a Union made up of a heterogeneous membership. Ernest Bevin was for many years almost omnipotent in the Transport and General Workers' Union, and so was John Hodge, in the Steel Smelters and later in the Iron and Steel Trades Confederation ; but for an equal dominance it is necessary to go a long way back—to such men as Richard Harnott, of the Stonemasons, or Robert Applegarth, of the Carpenters, in the middle of the nineteenth century ; and part of their power was due to the greater difficulty of consulting the membership in former days. Short, however, of quite so commanding a position, a capable and energetic Secretary can concentrate a great deal of power in his hands, and can use it either to reduce his fellow-officers to mere subordinates or to induce them to work as a responsible team under his leadership. By way of contrast, when the General Secretary is weak or indolent, the other leading officials are apt to go their several ways without much regard for him, and jealousies and 'empire-buildings' easily arise. J. H. Thomas, who was a very powerful leader of the railwaymen, actually pushed himself into the key position while he was still holding only subordinate office.

Naturally, a powerful Executive tends to deal directly with other leading officials as well as with the General Secretary ; and this tends to weaken his authority, though not necessarily with bad results, if the Executive does its work well. The best results, however, usually arise when the Executive, and especially its President or Chairman, and the General Secretary work harmoniously together, and when the General Secretary is content to give his principal subordinates a real share in Executive discussions. These conditions cannot be altogether easy to realise, especially in a big, complex Union ; but on the whole the task is usually tackled fairly well, each 'side' respecting the others' functions and trying to work out a reasonable practical adjustment. The laws of such accommodations have to be unwritten ; for no Union constitution or standing orders can effectively define the respective spheres.

General Secretaries are often fairly senior before they reach that high office. But some have risen young. Bevin was only forty when he became General Secretary of the newly formed Transport and General Workers' Union ; but his rise had been remarkably swift. J. H. Thomas was forty-four when he became General

Secretary of the National Union of Railwaymen. John Hodge was but thirty-one when he attained to the same office in the Steel Smelters' Union ; but he had just virtually created the Union, and at first the office carried no regular salary. Arthur Deakin succeeded Bevin as General Secretary of the Transport Workers at fifty : Tom Williamson became General Secretary of the General and Municipal Workers' at forty-nine : J. B. Figgins, of the National Union of Railwaymen at fifty-five : Arthur Horner, of the National Union of Mineworkers at fifty-two, and his predecessor, Ebby Edwards, at forty-eight. The Trade Union leadership is thus made up mainly of men who are getting on in life, but not, because of compulsory ages of retirement, really old. The lesser officials are of all ages ; but not many are very young, for, as we saw, a man usually graduates to office from voluntary Trade Union work.

The Trade Union hierarchy, despite the large numbers of women members, includes few women in its highest ranks. In 1953 there was one woman, Dame Anne Loughlin, as General Secretary of a big Union including both sexes—the National Union of Tailors and Garment Workers ; and there were of course both women Secretaries of women's Unions, and many women as organisers and lesser officials of mixed Unions. The General Council of the Trades Union Congress has two seats specially reserved for representatives of women workers. In 1952-3 the General Council actually included three women.

Most of the bigger Trade Unions now have their head offices in London. There used to be many more in Manchester and other northern towns. There are a few big ones still left outside London, notably the Shop, Distributive and Allied Workers, in Manchester, the Boilermakers, in Newcastle-on-Tyne, the Foundry Workers, the Woodworkers, the Cotton Spinners, the Typographical Association, and the Health Service Employees, all at Manchester, the Blastfurnacemen, at Middlesbrough, and the Painters, at Salford. The Dyers are at Bradford, the Weavers at Accrington, the Hosiery Workers at Leicester, the Boot and Shoe Operatives at Northampton, and the Pottery Workers at Stoke-on-Trent. A number of purely Scottish Unions have their headquarters in Glasgow, and others in other Scottish towns. But the main concentration is in London, with a second, much smaller group in Manchester and Salford. In London are the head offices of the two great 'general' Unions, the Mineworkers, the Engineers, the Iron and Steel Workers, the three Railwaymen's Unions, the Post Office and Civil Service Unions, and a great many more. The constant business with government departments, employers' national federations, and Parliament itself has made nearness to London a more and more important consideration. This is in some ways a pity, because it removes the leaders of many of the Unions from the districts in the north and midlands, and hands over the direct care of these areas to officers of the second rank. It is, however, unavoidable in the case of industries and services which have either been nationalised or are continually having to deal with Governments and Parliament.

VI. TRADE UNION GOVERNMENT AS A WHOLE

We have seen in the foregoing sections of this chapter that within a broad common pattern there are many varieties of Trade Union government and administration. Each Union has its own peculiar internal structure, based partly on its history, partly on the kinds of employer it has to deal with, partly on the range and character of the occupations it covers. The differences begin at the branch level, with branches of widely differing size and homogeneity, and with some based on the place of employment and some mainly on the place of home residence. Thus some Unions have a strong workplace organisation distinct from the branch, some none, or almost none. Some Unions have District Comittees, linking up neighbouring branches, with large functions and powers : others have none, and associate their branches only on a much wider divisional or regional basis, or in effect not at all. Some Unions are largely divided up in their working into separate sections, representing particular trades or departments of work : others have almost no such functional division. Some Unions make much use of the referendum for settling matters of policy : most make none, or almost none. Some have frequent, others infrequent Delegate Conferences. A very few have full-time, salaried Executive Councils. All have elected Executives, but these are elected in widely varying ways.

There are also great differences in the methods of choosing officials—from nomination by the Executive to election by vote of the members. The General Secretary, however, is usually, though not quite always, chosen by a popular vote. Most Unions nowadays embody a high centralisation of power in the hands of their Executives and General Secretaries, who share it in different ways ; but some, including the Mineworkers, are very tenacious of control from the bottom upwards. So, in certain respects, are the Engineers, and a number of the older craft Unions. The big 'general' Unions are in practice the least democratic, not so much because of anything in their rules as because their membership turns over so rapidly and attendance at Union meetings is usually so low—and also, of course, by reason of their sheer bulk and of the heterogeneous elements of which they are composed.

For the present, no attempt will be made to consider whether there are means open for improving the internal structure and working of the Trade Unions. This will come later, when their main activities have been passed in review. At this stage it need only be pointed out that systems of Trade Union government have for the most part not been deliberately constructed, but have grown over long periods. Even when a big new Union has been established, this has usually been done on the foundations laid by a predecessor whose tradition it has largely inherited. Thus, the National Union of Mineworkers grew out of the Miners' Federation and its constituent Unions ; the National Union of Railwaymen mainly out of the older Amalgamated Society of Railway Servants ; the Amalgamated Engineering Union out of the Amalgamated Society of Engineers, and that in turn out of the Journeymen Steam-engine Makers ; the General and Municipal Workers out of the old Gasworkers' Union ; and the Transport and General Workers' Union largely out of the Dockers'. The non-manual workers' Unions, for the most part, go back less far ; but they too have had time to gather, and to transmit, traditions. The Shop, Distributive and Allied Workers go back to the old Amalgamated Union of Co-operative Employees, more than to the Shop Assistants, with whom they have merged. The Union of Post Office Workers goes back to the Postmen's Federation and to the Postal and Telegraph Clerks ; and the Civil Service Clerical Association has grown out of earlier sectional societies.

The day-to-day working of the various types of Trade Unions whose forms of government have been outlined in this chapter absorbs a great deal of labour, voluntary as well as paid. The Transport and General Workers' Union alone has more than 4,000 branches, each needing its complement of officers and other

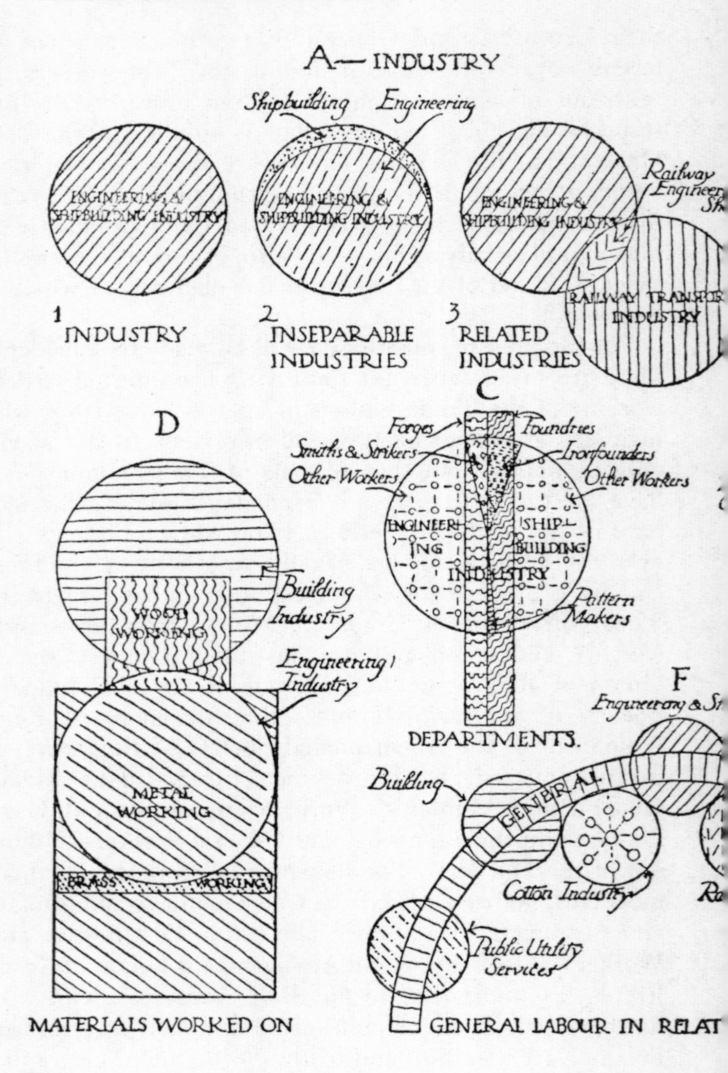
A— INDUSTRY
Shipbuilding
Engineering
ENGINEERING & SHIPBUILDING INDUSTRY
ENGINEERING & SHIPBUILDING INDUSTRY
ENGINEERING & SHIPBUILDING INDUSTRY
Railway Engineering
RAILWAY TRANSPORT INDUSTRY
1 INDUSTRY
2 INSEPARABLE INDUSTRIES
3 RELATED INDUSTRIES
C
D
Forges
Foundries
Smiths & Strikers
Ironfounders
Other Workers
Other Workers
ENGINEERING
SHIPBUILDING
INDUSTRY
Pattern Makers
Building Industry
WOOD WORKING
Engineering Industry
METAL WORKING
BRASS WORKING
DEPARTMENTS.
F
Building
GENERAL
Cotton Industry
Public Utility Services
MATERIALS WORKED ON
GENERAL LABOUR IN RELAT

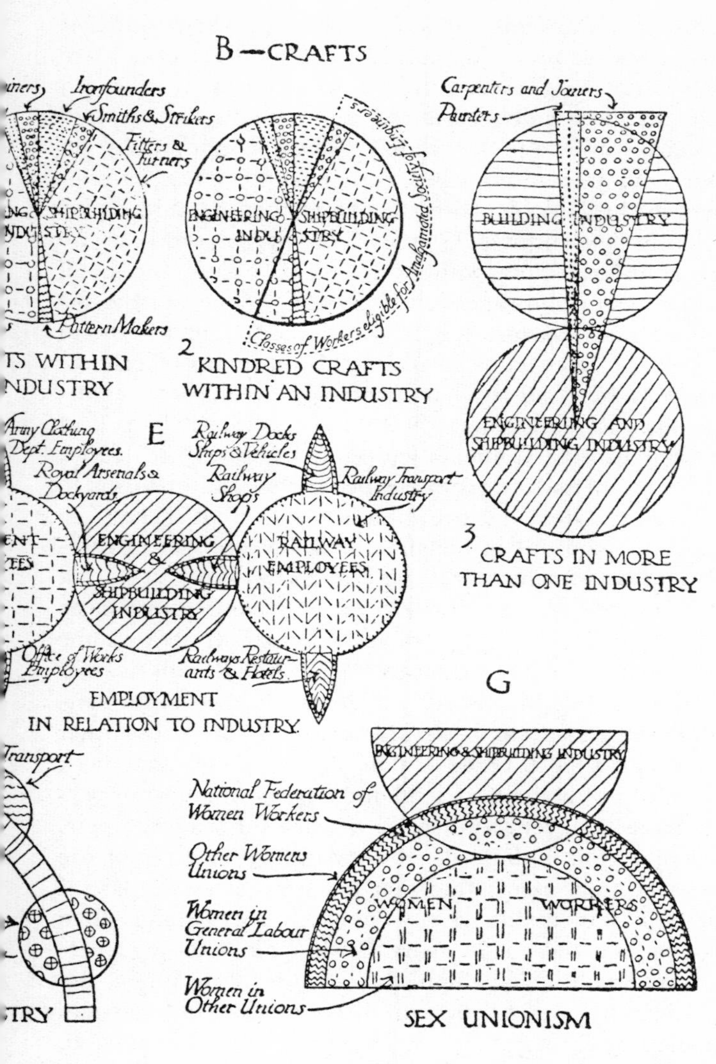

Drawn by Miss M. Pulsford from a design by G. D. H. Cole

active members ; and many other Unions count their branches by hundreds, and some by thousands. Post Office workers are found everywhere ; railwaymen in all towns and many villages ; builders too are very widely scattered, and printers, bakers, and road transport workers pretty widely. These conditions mean keeping open many small branches, and enlisting a great number of members in the Union's work—far more than need be active in more closely concentrated Unions. This branch work, as we have seen, is mostly done without payment, except for small sums in expenses or allowances : it is in effect done mostly 'for love', or sometimes because a man (or woman) wants to stand well with his (or her) fellows. Over and above this local unsalaried work there is all the labour of paid organisers, negotiators, and office administrators, and all the unsalaried work of members of Executive Councils and committees at the higher levels. There are masses of letters to be written and of forms to be filled up : a great deal of accounting for small sums received in contributions or paid out in benefits ; and any number of individual cases to be somehow dealt with and grievances to be put right. These individual cases include not only such questions as whether a worker is getting the wages due to him, or in some cases the promotion he has a right to expect, but also all manner of cases arising out of dismissals, accidents, illness due to conditions of employment, and, in practice, a great many other matters. The good local Trade Union officer, branch secretary, or shop steward needs to be a friend and adviser to a host of persons ; and there is never any dearth of work for willing takers.

The Trade Union is, indeed, an outstanding example of the kind of non-statutory association that forms an essential part of the democratic way of life. I say 'non-statutory' rather than 'voluntary' because there is in many Trade Unions to-day a certain element of conditional compulsion—that is, of making at any rate formal membership a condition of holding a particular job. But this conditional compulsion is a long way off being general, or there would be many more Trade Unionists than there are. It is limited to certain trades and establishments, and is directed much more against bad payers of contributions than against real objectors. The latter, indeed, are seldom numerous, except when a feud has arisen between one Union and another, or an internal quarrel has led to a split or breakaway. In such cases very awkward problems can arise ; but they are exceptional. In most cases, even when the Trade Unions are strong, their aim is rather '100 per cent membership' than the absolutely 'closed shop'—the essential difference being that in the latter case employment is barred to non-members, whereas in the former there is only pressure on them to join when they are employed.

No doubt, as we saw, a great many workers—especially among women and the less skilled men—join a Union less out of conviction than because it is the custom of the trade or of the establishment. But the Unions could not keep going on compulsory members : they require a large nucleus of willing volunteers to keep their organisation alive and in good condition. A Trade Union that loses this driving force is in danger of withering away; and employers know they need pay no great attention to it.

Who are these active participants, who keep the Unions alive and alert ? They are of all ages ; but they are not, in most Unions at most times, drawn mainly from the youngest adults. Especially among the more skilled workers, they include a high proportion of men in the thirties and forties, and a considerable number of older men. There are many fewer of them, in proportion to total numbers, among women than among men, largely because many women still leave work on marriage, or, even if they do not, are less interested in the affairs of work than in home and leisure-time pursuits. Nevertheless, many women do excellent work in the Trade Unions, and have done ever since they first got their big chance, outside a very few Unions, during the first World War, when for the first time many women became branch secretaries or organisers of mixed Unions.

The weakest spot of the Trade Union movement is its relatively scanty provision for the adolescent worker, who is usually given little chance of interesting himself in Union affairs. Some Unions, indeed, now negotiate on behalf of apprentices—concerning whom employers used often to refuse to bargain—and take part in drawing up plans of apprenticeship and training. Some Unions in the professional or semi-professional ranges—for example, the Engineering and Shipbuilding Draughtsmen and the Post Office Workers—interest themselves in the technical education of their young members ; but there is still very little attempt to educate them in Trade Union or Labour matters, or to provide opportunities for recreation or club life. Most Trade Unions are in spirit adult bodies, and do not accommodate themselves too easily to the ways of youth.

CHAPTER III

TYPES OF TRADE UNIONS*

I. CRAFT, INDUSTRIAL AND GENERAL UNIONS

THE simplest type of Trade Union, and the earliest to appear in the countries of Western Europe—and perhaps nearly everywhere—is the society consisting of members who follow a common craft. In the trades in which such societies developed the craft was usually learnt by means of apprenticeship to a master ; and by law or custom, especially in the older towns, only men who had been through an apprenticeship were allowed to work at the trade. This system of trades closed to unapprenticed men had come down from the Middle Ages, and in Great Britain was incorporated in the Elizabethan Statute of Artificers—which, however, was not held by the lawyers to apply to newer trades. Right up to the early years of the nineteenth century the craftsmen in London and other towns fought repeated battles to enforce the Apprenticeship Law, either by industrial action or in the law courts ; and the courts had sometimes to recognise their claims. But in practice industries escaped more and more from this form of regulation, especially where employers set up in business outside the old, corporate towns. Indeed, this movement out of the old towns was partly made for the purpose of escaping regulation ; but by the beginning of the nineteenth century both governing-class and employing-class opinion were turning sharply against such regulation, as savouring of monopoly ; and in 1814 Parliament repealed the clause of the Elizabethan statute from which it derived its force.

The repeal did not prevent bodies of craftsmen from continuing to attempt to enforce the old custom ; but it left them to depend entirely on their own strength. To a considerable extent they were successful, in those trades which continued to be carried on in small workshops with little or no use of power. Where industry moved into factories using power-driven machinery, the system of apprenticeship sometimes disappeared altogether, as it did for example in weaving, which had formerly been learnt in this way. But some of the new crafts which developed for the construction of the new power-driven machinery were

*See the diagrams on pp. 72-3.

able to introduce their own systems of apprenticeship—for example, engineers, ironfounders, and patternmakers ; and in the building industry, where the traditional crafts persisted almost unchanged, the apprenticeship system continued in force. On the other hand in coal-hewing, in which a sort of apprenticeship had existed in the North-East of England, the system died out ; and it was never introduced into the new craft of cotton-spinning, though the spinner's assistants, the piecers, learnt their craft under his supervision.

The foundation of early craft Unionism lay largely in the system of apprenticeship, which defined the persons eligible for membership. The craftsmen had an interest in preventing the taking on of too many apprentices, for fear of unemployment if too many men were trained ; and one of the most important functions of most craft Unions was the regulation of the number of apprentices and of their proportion to the adult craftsmen employed in a particular workshop. This still remains an important activity of certain craft Unions, notably in the printing trades, and also in the smaller engineering and metalworking crafts, such as patternmaking, coppersmithing and sheet metal working. In the greater crafts the growth of the large factory has made regulation much more difficult ; and in the main the concern of the Unions is more with regulating the conditions of apprentices than with limiting their number. The building Unions still attempt to limit the proportion of apprentices to adult craftsmen, but cannot do this very effectively in dealing with the big firms of contractors. Indeed, in the building industry the system of apprenticeship has been for a long time in danger of breaking down ; and, despite attempts to revive it after 1945, it still works only in part, and many skilled workers manage to pick up a training without ever passing through a real apprenticeship. In the past, apprentices were usually engaged—or at least supposed to be—under written contracts. Nowadays, in both building and engineering, the written contract is exceptional ; and in many trades the once clear line between apprenticed and unapprenticed men is by no means so clear as it was.

Craft Unions, uniting skilled workers in a single craft, now exist mainly in the printing and kindred trades—compositors, lithographic printers, etc—in the building trades—plasterers, plumbers, painters, slaters, and so on—and in certain engineering, metal-working, and kindred trades—patternmaking, coppersmithing, etc.,—and also in a miscellaneous group of skilled crafts in textiles and in a number of other manufacturing industries which need the services of groups of highly skilled craftsmen. In other cases, a number of related crafts have combined to form a single Union. The Amalgamated Society of Engineers, formed in 1851, was a combination of skilled fitters, turners, millwrights, brass-finishers, and a number of other kinds of craftsmen employed mainly in engineering factories. It attempted to enrol a number of crafts whose members for the most part refused to give up their separate societies—e.g. patternmakers and ironfounders—but even without these it included a wide range of skills. The Amalgamated Society of Woodworkers is an amalgamation of older Unions of carpenters and joiners with societies of cabinet-makers and other skilled workers in wood; but it has never been able to persuade the Woodcutting Machinists to merge their separate Union in a wider body. In the cotton industry, as we saw, there are a number of separate craft Unions for the various trades; but several of these include a number of related crafts—for example, the Weavers.

The kindred craft Union rests on the same principle as the craft Union in the narrower sense; but it can easily lead on, in appropriate conditions, to a further step—the admission of certain kinds of less skilled workers. The earlier craft Unions were very often operating under conditions in which the entire body of employed workers in a workshop consisted of craftsmen and apprentices, without any separate grades of unskilled or less skilled employees. This was never the case in the building industry, at any rate in modern times. There were always labourers who had no expectation of ever rising to be craftsmen. But it was only with the rise of the factory system that in most industries separate grades of labourers, and later of semi-skilled machine-minders, appeared. Thus, many of the early craft Unions were, in effect, setting out to organise *all* the workers in their workshops. But as mechanisation developed and as the factories grew there came to be in many cases bodies of skilled workers who were the fellow-employees of unskilled workers and could not combine the attempt to preserve their craft privileges with the acceptance of the open door for these workers to become members of their Unions.

Thus, there grew up in a great many trades a type of craft Union that was definitely exclusive, and fought for its own hand largely regardless of the grievances and claims of the less skilled workers, or even in hostility to them. This kind of Unionism developed not only in building and engineering and shipbuilding and in the steel industry, but also even in coal-mining in certain areas. It was at its height in Great Britain during the third quarter of the nineteenth century, and was not seriously challenged until the rise of the New Unionism at the end of the 1880s. There was, however, a wide difference between those industries in which there was no sharp division between skilled and less skilled—e.g. the cotton manufacturing industry, as distinct from cotton-spinning, and some, though not all, of the coalfields—and those, such as building and engineering, in which there was a great gulf fixed between the skilled, apprenticed workers and the less skilled.

The exclusive type of craft Union was largely responsible for the fact that when, after 1889, Trade Unionism began to spread to the less skilled workers, new Unions sprang up to meet their needs, and there was no fusion of skilled and less skilled workers into a single Union in each industry. At the docks, for example, there were craft Unions in London for the lightermen and for the stevedores (specialists in loading and stowing cargoes) ; but the main body of dock workers became organised in a separate Union catering for all grades—the Dock, Wharf, Riverside, and General Workers' Union. In the case of the gasworkers there was no organisation at all, except for a few skilled men who belonged to engineering craft Unions ; and the gasworkers became organised in a new Union which, like the Dockers, at once opened its ranks to labourers in other industries. In face of the unwillingness of the Engineers' and other craft Unions to open their ranks to the unskilled, the labourers and less skilled machine operatives in the various branches of engineering, where they became organised at all, joined one of the new 'general' Unions, which also began to enrol all kinds of workers for whom craft Unions did not exist. In the building industry there arose separate Unions of builders' labourers ; but many of the less skilled workers in building shifted to and fro between employment as builders' labourers, work on the roads or at the docks, or other forms of heavy unskilled labour, and a good many of these shifting workers enrolled in the 'general' Unions, which thus came to be competitors with the builders' labourers' Unions. The general outcome was that in the metal trades and in building the skilled and the less skilled came to be members of different Unions, and a great deal of friction arose as the craft Unions attempted to defend their monopolies of certain types of work against employers who wished to introduce less skilled workers at lower wages.

A leading part in organising the less skilled workers was indeed taken by certain skilled workers who were Socialists and wanted to espouse the claims of the whole working class. John Burns and Tom Mann, who played key parts in the London Dock Strike of 1889, were both skilled engineers: Ben Tillett, the other outstanding leader, was himself a dock worker. The attitude of the New Unionists gradually leavened the older Unions, and made it possible for skilled and less skilled to act to some extent together in pressing for better conditions. But a wide gap remained: the craftsmen were mostly determined to defend their exclusive privileges, and the less skilled workers' leaders were apt to resent the attitude of superiority and patronising support with which they met the attempts of those lower down in the social and economic scale to assert their rights.

Presently, a few of the craft Unions, realising the danger of division from the less skilled workers, decided to open their ranks to them. The Amalgamated Society of Engineers, for example, started a 'Class F' of membership open to engineering labourers. But the craftsmen were not prepared to give the unskilled equal rights. The A.S.E. admitted them with lower contributions and lower benefits, but refused them the right to hold office in the Union, with the consequence that most of the less skilled who joined a Union at all still preferred to become members of a 'general' Union. The real pressure on the craft Unions to change their attitude came in those industries in which, as an outcome of technical change, there was a great growth in the demand for semi-skilled workers to operate automatic or semi-automatic machines. These machine-workers became more and more the direct competitors of the skilled craftsmen, as more processes requiring skill were broken up and transferred piecemeal to single-purpose machines that could be operated with relatively little training. The skilled workers' Unions first tried to oppose these changes and to refuse to recognise their effects; but gradually the pressure became too strong to be resisted. This happened especially during the first World War, which had a great effect in breaking up processes into elements needing less skill and in admitting less skilled workers to types of work previously reserved for skilled craftsmen. It was at the end of the first World War that a number of engineering craft Unions, including the A.S.E. and several which had developed to cater for the higher groups of semi-skilled machine-operators, joined forces to form the Amalgamated Engineering Union, which opened its ranks to all male engineering workers, and later, during the second World War, to women as well.

The A.S.E., which had been essentially a Union of skilled craftsmen, thus turned into the A.E.U., which remained under the leadership of skilled workers, but set out to enrol skilled and less skilled alike. The change brought it into full direct competition with the 'general' Unions which had already enrolled a considerable proportion of the less skilled workers, both men and women ; but the latter were too strongly entrenched to be driven out, and to-day the less skilled workers in engineering continue to be divided between the two groups. Similarly, a number of craft Unions in other industries and occupations gradually opened their ranks to admit less skilled workers. This resulted in the development of a type of Union which was neither exactly a craft Union nor a Union based on the principle of 'organisation by industry'; and to this we must turn before we examine any further what happened to these 'diluted' craft Unions under the changed conditions.

'Union by industry' means an attempt to enrol in a single Union, regardless of skill or occupation, all the workers who are employed in the same industry. In some cases it is easy, in others very difficult, to define exactly what is meant by an 'industry'. For example, coal-mining, cotton-spinning and manufacturing, printing, building, boot and shoe making, and seafaring are fairly clear instances of industries which are distinctive, and can be marked off from others. But when we come to railways, the question at once arises whether we mean only railway *transport*, or include the engineering works in which the railway concerns make and repair their locomotives and railway carriages, or the hotels and restaurants which they conduct. Do these latter belong to the railway industry, or to the industries of engineering, vehicle-building and catering respectively ? Or, again, is distribution—i.e. retail and wholesale shopkeeping—an industry, or is the great Co-operative movement an industry apart, including not only distributive workers, but also productive workers employed in its numerous factories, transport workers, workers in restaurants, and a number of other groups? Each of these questions has given rise to acrimonious disputes between Unions based on rival principles of organisation; and some of these disputes have not been settled even to-day.

The case for 'union by industry' is, broadly speaking, that it unites the workers employed by a single employer, or group of employers, in a single combination transcending the differences between grades and degrees of skill. It has been favoured, historically, by those who have wished to unite the workers in a common struggle on a class basis, and have been shocked by the gulf between the craft Unions and the less skilled workers. It has also been advocated by those, such as the Syndicalists and Guild Socialists, who have looked forward to the day when the organised workers will take over the control of industry on a basis of economic self-government; for clearly the workers cannot do this without possessing an organisation inclusive of the whole industry.

There are, however, two forms of 'union by industry'; and these are sometimes confused. In the first form, all that is meant is that all the workers in the same industry should be enrolled in a single Union, in order to be able to present a common front to the employer, or group of employers, concerned—or, of course, to participate in management and ultimately take over control of the industry if these objectives are in view. In the second form of the idea, which is often called 'Industrial Unionism', the stress is laid on all workers in all occupations being enrolled in a single Union—the 'One Big Union'—which is then to be divided into industrial sections, one for each industry. The underlying notion in this case is that of all-inclusive Unionism on a basis of class, for the purpose of carrying on a revolutionary struggle against capitalism. This idea has its germ in the attempts at 'General Union' in Great Britain during the first half of the nineteenth century; but in its more recent manifestations it has been chiefly American. In the United States the Order of the Knights of Labor, founded in 1869 by Uriah Stephens, set out to enrol in a single Union the active workers in all types of employment, and succeeded in building up a powerful movement which, after a period of success, began to disintegrate in the 1880s, as more and more groups of skilled workers broke away to establish separate Unions of their own. The American Federation of Labor, based on independent Unions in the various trades, then took its place.

But the notion of a single Union was soon revived on a more definitely Marxist basis by Danial De Leon, the Socialist leader, who founded first the Trades and Labor Alliance and then the Industrial Workers of the World. De Leon's notion was that the I.W.W. should act in close alliance with the revolutionary Socialist Party—the Socialist Labor Party—of which he was the leader. But disputes soon arose between the followers of De Leon and the Anarchists and Syndicalists, largely immigrants from Europe but also including important groups of miners and oil-workers in the Far West, who joined the I.W.W.; and this body soon split into two rival I.W.W.s, one continuing to follow De Leon, while the other, much the larger, went over to Anarcho-Syndicalism under the leadership of W. D. Haywood. From the United States the I.W.W., in its Syndicalist form, spread to Canada and to Australia and on a small scale to Great Britain during the years just before 1914. In Great Britain the De Leon-ites also found a small following, especially on the Clyde, and there were for a time two rival movements at work. But neither secured, under British conditions, any large success ; and in the United States both I.W.W.s were almost entirely stamped out during the first World War, though traces of them remained for some time longer.

The essence of this second type of 'union by industry' lies in its revolutionary basis. Its exponents argue that separate Trade Unions divide the workers into contending groups, instead of uniting them for the struggle to overthrow the capitalist class. As a next best to the 'One Big Union', they usually support industrial Unions for particular industries as against craft Unions, because industrial Unions at least bring better and worse paid workers together and thus come nearer to a 'class' basis of combination. But of late very little has been heard of the 'One Big Union', except in a few undeveloped countries in which the workers are beginning to be organised under nationalistic revolutionary leadership, usually with Communist support.

Union by industry in the narrower sense, on the other hand, is a very live issue. It lay at the root of the dispute which, in the 1930s, divided Trade Unionism in the United States into two great contending groups. As we saw, after the decline of the Knights of Labor the American workers became organised largely in the American Federation of Labor. The A.F. of L. had—and has—no one clearly defined principle of organisation ;

but it includes a large number of craft Unions representing exclusively or mainly skilled workers and enrolling such workers according to the crafts they practise irrespective of the industries in which they are employed. Unions of this type entirely failed to enrol the main body of less skilled workers in the great mass-production industries, such as automobiles, steel, oil and rubber ; and many of these workers were organised in 'fake' Unions set up by the employers in order to keep real Trade Unionism at bay. Then, in the 1930s, such company Unions were made illegal under the New Deal, and the workers were given by law the right to set up or join free Unions if they pleased. The A.F. of L. failed to put itself effectively at the head of the drive to organise these workers ; and one of its own affiliated Unions, which was an industrial Union—the United Mine Workers, led by John L. Lewis—joined forces with a number of others in setting up a Committee for Industrial Organisation designed to establish new mass Unions where no existing Union was able or willing to undertake the task. This was followed by a bitter dispute with the A.F. of L. The offending Unions were driven out or seceded ; and the Committee became an independent central Trade Union federation—the Congress of Industrial Organisations. In 1953 the main body of American organised workers is still divided between the A.F. of L. and the C.I.O., though some of the original seceders, headed by the United Mine Workers, have broken away from the C.I.O. This body now has its greatest strength in the automobile industry, which it completely dominates, and is also the predominant element in the steel, rubber, oil, and men's clothing industries, and in some others. The longshoremen (dockers) are divided : the railway workers have their own independent craft 'Brotherhoods', which belong neither to the A.F. of L. nor to the C.I.O.*

We have seen that 'union by industry' is a less simple principle than it sounds, because of the difficulty of agreeing on the definition of an industry. Let us come back, by way of illustration, to the case of the engineers. A typical engineering factory employs a considerable number of skilled craftsmen belonging to

* Late in 1952 the leaders of both the A.F. of L. (William Green) and the C.I.O. (Philip Murray) died ; and their successors announced their willingness to give way if this would help to bring about fusion. There are, however, many difficulties besides personalities in the way of this—above all else, differences concerning the basis of organisation between the craft Unions in the A.F. of L. and the industrial Unions in the C.I.O.

various metal-working crafts—fitters, turners, millers, borers, slotters, electricians, coppersmiths, sheet-metal workers, iron-founders, brassmoulders, brassfinishers, smiths, boilermakers, die-sinkers, drop hammer forgers, and so on—the list of such crafts varying considerably from factory to factory according to the goods produced. It also employs a much smaller number of craftsmen who are not metal workers—for example, carpenters and joiners, bricklayers, painters, upholsterers. Then it has probably a large complement of less skilled machine-operators, men and in many cases women as well, and a corps of labourers for heavy work. It has in addition stationary enginemen, transport workers of various kinds, and probably canteen workers. Its non-manual staff will include draughtsmen and tracers, clerks and typists, and technicians and their assistants in laboratories and testing departments. Then there will be foremen, under-managers of various kinds, and finally the higher managerial staffs, including working directors, or personal employers where the principal owners take an active part. There may also be an office at a distance from the factory ; and of course the same firm may have more than one factory.

If organisation is to cover all these persons, except those who are regarded as definitely on the 'employers' side'—and even perhaps some of these—how are they to be enrolled ? A complete industrial Union would presumably include them all ; but in order to do so it would have to repel a number of rivals. These would include the following, and perhaps others too :

(*a*) Craft Unions catering for skilled craftsmen in particular engineering crafts—*e.g.* coppersmiths, sheet metal workers, smiths, boilermakers ;

(*b*) Similar Unions, based on a particular craft, but enrolling also less skilled workers attached to that particular craft or department. (This would apply to several of the examples given under (*a*) ; for many of the craft Unions have thus opened their ranks in recent years) ;

(*c*) Craft Unions, whether or not open to less skilled workers, whose members are occupied mainly outside the engineering industry—*e.g.* enginemen, electricians, carpenters and joiners ;

(*d*) General labour Unions, enrolling less skilled workers in any industry, or in a wide range of industries ;

(*e*) possibly, specialised Unions of engineering labourers or semi-skilled workers (but these are few and small) ;

(*f*) possibly transport workers' Unions (but most transport workers concerned will be catered for by the Transport and General Workers' Union);

(*g*) Specialised Unions of non-manual workers, such as draughtsmen, clerks and typists, technicians and laboratory assistants—*e.g.* the Association of Engineering and Shipbuilding Draughtsmen, the Clerical and Administrative Workers' Union, and the Association of Scientific Workers;

(*h*) Unions or associations of supervisory and managerial workers—*e.g.* the Association of Supervisory Staffs, Executives and Technicians.

In addition, if the factory in question belongs to British Railways, or to the Post Office, there will arise the question whether it forms part of the engineering industry or of the railway or the communications industry. Actually the Post Office engineering department has a separate Union of its own—the Post Office Engineering Union—while in the railway engineering shops most of the highly skilled workers belong to one or another of the engineering or woodworking Unions, and the less skilled are divided between these, the general labour Unions, and the National Union of Railwaymen.

There is, however, a further complication. An engineering Union—such as the Amalgamated Engineering Union—which opens its ranks to all workers in the engineering industry does not thereby agree to give up organising skilled engineering craftsmen who work in other industries—for example, as seagoing engineers, or mine-mechanics, or engineers in the B.B.C., or as maintenance or toolroom men in almost any kind of big factory or establishment that uses much machinery. The skilled engineer can transfer from one industry to another over a very wide range, and does not wish to change his Union every time he moves, or to lose the protection of a Union which looks after his interests as a skilled engineer. Sometimes, this difficulty is met by providing for dual membership. The Mineworkers, for example, insist on mine-mechanics belonging to their Union and on controlling their industrial bargaining affairs; but the mine-mechanic who has come from another industry and thinks he may go back, or wishes to keep his rights to friendly benefits in his old Union, can remain a member of the A.E.U. under a special agreement between the two Unions. Such formal agreements are not common. In most cases, the A.E.U. negotiates on behalf of skilled engineers (and other craft Unions on behalf of other craftsmen) employed outside the engineering industry. Often, firms in other industries agree to pay the standard engineering wages : sometimes separate bargains are made. Special bargains applying to a particular firm or establishment have been frequent in recent years.

Thus, such a Trade Union as the A.E.U., now that it has opened its ranks to the less skilled workers in the engineering industry, is in effect both a craft Union and an industrial Union. It is an industrial Union for engineering, but a craft Union for engineers, in whatever industry they are employed. In practice, it does not go quite so wide as this. It leaves alone certain kinds of craftsmen for whom powerful separate Unions exist (e.g. ironfounders, boilermakers, electricians) ; and it also refrains from organising certain kinds of engineers (e.g. Post Office engineers). But its range is even so very wide.

In effect, since many craft Unions have opened their ranks to less skilled workers—as a response to technical changes which they can no longer resist—the distinction between craft Unionism and industrial Unionism has become blurred at many points. A craft Union which opens its ranks does not indeed usually turn into an industrial Union : that occurs only where it organises a number of crafts together, covering most of an industry. More often, it turns into what can best be described as a 'departmental' Union.

This type is not new. It arose first where a particular craft was normally recruited from a particular grade below, through which everyone passed on his way to becoming a full craftsman, and there were no separate classes of apprentices learning a craft and labourers without prospect of promotion. On the railways, for example, the locomotive engine-drivers are recruited from among the firemen, who are usually promoted from among the engine cleaners. These three grades form a department, and are mainly organised in the Associated Society of Locomotive Engineers and Firemen. Similarly, the cotton spinners are recruited from among the piecers ; the blacksmiths from among the strikers ; and so on.

Finally, to complete the list of the main types of Trade Unions, there are Unions in which women are organised separately from men. These are now fairly uncommon. The great general labour Unions organise both sexes together—the pioneering National Federation of Women Workers having been absorbed into the

General Workers' Union soon after the first World War. Similarly, separate Unions of women boot and shoe operatives, hosiery workers, bookbinders, and a number of others, have been merged into Unions catering for both men and women. The only purely women's Unions now left in the Trades Union Congress are a small society of Felt Hat Trimmers, run by the same Secretary as the male Journeymen Felt Hatters' Society ; and the Women Public Health Officers' Association. There is also—outside the Congress—a small Union of Women Teachers, strongly feminist and standing for equal pay. But 'sex' Unionism, which played an important part in promoting the organisation of women workers in the early stages, is now practically extinct in Great Britain.

So is sectional Unionism based on religion, which has never taken any substantial hold in Great Britain. There used to be a few small Catholic Trade Unions among the Lancashire weavers; but they disappeared in the 1920s. British Catholic Trade Unionists have an association of their own which acts as a pressure group within a number of Trade Unions ; but there is nothing analogous to the separately organised Catholic Trade Unions of Belgium, Luxemburg, Holland and parts of France. The British Trade Union movement has never been either hostile to religion, or disposed to base its organisation upon religion. It has been an essentially secular movement.

II. AMALGAMATION AND FEDERATION

The development of the great Trade Unions of the present day is the outcome partly of sheer growth and partly of amalgamation of what were previously separate Trade Unions to form a single organisation. Every one of the largest Unions connected with the British Trades Union Congress is an amalgamation of a number of Unions into one. The Transport and General Workers' Union is the old Dockers' Union swollen by amalgamation with several other dockworkers' Unions, with the United Vehicle Workers (themselves a fusion of busmen, tramwaymen, and others), the Vehicle Workers (carters and lorrymen), and with the Workers' Union (a 'general' Union of most miscellaneous membership, including an agricultural section), the Scottish Farm Servants, and a large number of other societies. The National Union of General and Municipal Workers is the old Gasworkers' Union, *plus* the Municipal Employees' Association, the National Amalgamated Union of Labour, the National Federation of Women Workers, and a number more. The Amalgamated Engineering Union has risen out of the Amalgamated Society of Engineers (itself a fusion of 1851), together with the Toolmakers, United Machine Workers, Steam Engine Makers, Smiths and Strikers, and other craft Unions of metalworkers. The National Union of Mineworkers is a fusion of the numerous district Miners' Associations to form a national body, with the addition of the specialist Unions of colliery enginemen, mechanics and coke-oven workers. The National Union of Railwaymen was formed by the coming together of the Amalgamated Society of Railway Servants, the General Railway Workers' Union, and the Signalmen and Pointsmen. The Union of Shop, Distributive and Allied Workers is a fusion of the Shop Assistants with the Distributive and Allied Workers—the latter being the outcome of an earlier fusion between the Co-operative Employees and the Warehouse and General Workers.The Amalgamated Society of Woodworkers is based on three previous Unions of Carpenters and Joiners, *plus* the Cabinet-makers. The Union of Post Office Workers was formed by the joining of the Postmen, the Postal and Telegraph Clerks, and the Fawcett Association (sorters). The National Union of Tailors and Garment Workers brought together the Tailors and Tailoresses and the United Garment Workers, both the outcome of earlier amalgamations. Of the dozen biggest Unions in the Congress, only two—the Electrical Trades Union and the National Union of Public Employees—have grown mainly by straight recruiting of members without much absorption of other societies. Nor would the picture be much altered if the dozen next largest Unions were studied in the same way. In this group, the Civil Service Clerical Association, the Printing, Bookbinding and Paper Workers, the Iron and Steel Trades Confederation, the Building Trade Workers, the Dyers, Bleachers and Textile Workers, the Foundry Workers, and the Furniture Trades Operatives are all the outcome of amalgamations ; and the Weavers are a close federation of local associations that were formerly much more independent than they now are.

The process of amalgamation between independent Unions is regulated by statute. Up to 1917, when the Trade Union Amalgamation Act was passed on the initiative of the Labour members of Lloyd George's war coalition, it was very difficult to satisfy the legal requirements. Each Union wishing to amalgamate with another had to get a two-thirds majority, not merely of those voting, but of its entire membership. In 1912 the Unions which formed the National Union of Railwaymen managed to achieve this ; but it may have been fortunate that no one was concerned to scrutinise closely the methods by which it was done. Under the Act of 1917 the requirement was reduced to a majority of 20 per cent on a vote of not less than half the total membership.

Even this is a little difficult to meet ; for not nearly half the members are likely to attend branch meetings or to fill up a voting form sent to them through the post. The only way of getting so big a vote is to get the shop stewards, or special representatives, to take the ballot papers to the workers at the works—and probably spend weeks gradually gathering in the necessary number of votes. Because of the difficulty, many Trade Union amalgamations have been arranged in such a way as to evade the legal requirement. This can be done if the smaller Union agrees to dissolve—the rules of each Union contain provisions governing the method of dissolution—and if its members then individually join the larger body—or rather are deemed to have done so and are issued by it with fresh contribution cards in its name. The dissolving Union usually votes its assets to the Union to which its members are being transferred ; and there is a written agreement before the dissolution for the larger Union to take over the debts of the smaller, to find jobs for its officials, and to put its members at once into full rights to benefits. This method involves certain risks that members may be lost in the transfer ; but such risks exist even in cases of formal amalgamation—for there is nothing to prevent a member from dropping out when he likes, except where the Union is so strong as to be able to make continued membership virtually a condition of employment.

In one important case, that of the Iron and Steel Trades Confederation, a different method was used, not only in order to avoid legal difficulties, but also because something a little short of complete amalgamation was desired for the time being. The iron and steel workers' societies which desired to join forces formed two new bodies—a Confederation which they all joined, and a new Union—the British Iron Steel and Kindred Trades Association. This second body was to be the exclusive recruiting agency for new members, and it was to be open to the old Unions to transfer any or all of their members to it at any time. Thus the old Unions were gradually to disappear, as their members were transferred, retired or died ; and the biggest Union—the Steel Smelters—led the way by transferring its entire membership. The others followed as soon as complications about benefit rights could be straightened out. Only the National Union of Clerks (Steel Section) remained as a separate entity within the Confederation but outside the new Union.

This ingenious device was not widely imitated. After 1917 most amalgamations were achieved either by dissolving the smaller society or by somehow mustering enough ballot papers to give the amalgamation legal force. The general effect was that, despite the establishment of a good many new Trade Unions, mainly among non-manual workers, the total number of Trade Unions known to the Ministry of Labour fell steadily—from 1,302 in 1900 and 1,254 in 1918, rising to 1,425 in 1920, to 1,019 in 1939 and 704 in 1951. Of the 704, only 183 were affiliated to the Trades Union Congress, but they included all the largest except the National Union of Teachers and the National Association of Local Government Officers. As we shall see, a number more belonged to the Scottish Trades Union Congress or to the General Federation of Trade Unions.*

Trade Unions often wish to act together without complete amalgamation. If so, they can form federations, handing over greater or smaller powers to the joint agencies. These federations are broadly of two kinds—groupings of similar, or of dissimilar, societies. Federations of similar societies are usually formed by the coming together of a number of local Trade Unions in the same trade or branch of industry—e.g. mineworkers, blast-furnacemen, sheet metal workers, cotton spinners, compositors—and they sometimes lead later to complete, or more nearly complete, amalgamation, as has actually occurred in all the five instances just cited. Federations of dissimilar societies are usually made up of sectional or craft Unions concerned in a particular industry—building, printing, shipbuilding and engineering, for example. They may be, as we have seen earlier, either completely distinct in the types of workers they enrol, or overlapping to a greater or smaller extent ; and they may include sections of the big general labour Unions, where these are active among the less skilled workers in the industries concerned. Thus, both the Transport and General Workers' and the General and Municipal

*See pages 126 and 140.

Workers' Unions are members of the National Federation of Building Trades Operatives and of the Confederation of Shipbuilding and Engineering Trade Unions ; but neither belongs to the Printing and Kindred Trades Federation, as the printers have separate Unions which enrol the less skilled workers in the printing and paper-making industries.

Federations of *similar* local societies often have common funds for industrial purposes—seldom for friendly benefits, which are usually left to the local bodies. Common funds, beyond what is needed to cover purely administrative costs, are much less often found in federations of *dissimilar* societies, even where the federations act as negotiating bodies on matters of common concern. Usually, in such federations, the seat of final power remains with the individual Unions ; and it is not uncommon to find a Union withdrawing temporarily from federation when it cannot agree with the majority on an issue it regards as important. Secessions are most apt to occur when a federation gives an equal weight to each affiliated Union, or fails to give enough weight to the larger Unions. The Engineers were for a long time outside the Engineering and Shipbuilding Trades Federation (the predecessor of the existing Confederation) because they were again and again outvoted by a combination of much smaller societies. There have been several occasions on which one or another of the building Trade Unions has been temporarily outside the National Federation of Building Trades Operatives. But the seceders usually return when the quarrel blows over, or when the Federation changes its rules to meet a real grievance.

Some federations undertake the greater part of the work of negotiation in the industries concerned. But more usually they deal only with general movements affecting the industry as a whole, and each Union reserves its rights of negotiation and action in sectional matters affecting only its own members. If, however, a Union wishes to call on the other Unions for help, it is usually under an obligation to consult the federation and either to abide by its advice or not to expect assistance. The situation in this respect is however often left not very clearly defined.

A few federations have no negotiating functions at all, and exist purely for purposes of consultation. This was the position of the Federation of General Workers which existed before the two big general workers' Unions were formed.

In many trades there were formerly local federations, made up either of local Unions or of branches of national Unions, or of both—for example, in the building and engineering trades. These local federations have now mostly either disappeared or become district sections of the national federations. They still exist in the manufacturing section of the cotton industry, but are virtually agencies of the Northern Counties Textile Trades Federation, which is the national body linking together the Weavers' Amalgamation and the smaller craft Unions in this section of the industry.

CHAPTER IV

COLLECTIVE BARGAINING

I. GENERAL

We have seen that the most essential part of a Trade Union's business is the making of collective bargains about its members' wages and conditions of work. Such bargains may affect an entire trade or industry, or only a part of one—a particular district or region, or a single establishment, or sometimes a group of establishments belonging to a single business. The bargain, when made, is usually nowadays embodied in a written agreement if it applies to more than a single workplace, and sometimes even when it does not.

Broadly speaking, Trade Unions make two kinds of collective agreements with employers or employers' associations—agreements laying down terms of employment, and procedural agreements. Sometimes the two are included in the same document ; but more often they are distinct. Procedural agreements prescribe the methods to be used in negotiating and varying agreements which determine actual conditions of employment. Perhaps, nowadays, a third kind should be added—agreements for the setting up of machinery for joint consultation, as distinct from ordinary Trade Union negotiation.

Procedural agreements usually constitute some form of regular negotiating machinery, such as a joint board or conference representing the parties. In many cases more than one Trade Union is a party to them, and sometimes more than one body of employers. Some federations of Trade Unions are entitled to negotiate and sign such agreements on behalf of their affiliated societies. In national agreements the employers' body is often a federation of local associations.

It seems best to begin with national agreements on procedure covering an entire trade or industry—or rather, all the firms in it connected with the employers' federation and having members of the Trade Union or Trade Unions concerned. The simplest form of this kind of agreement merely makes provision for joint meetings of representatives of the parties to discuss any questions arising between them in connection with wages or working conditions. These meetings may be held either at regular stated intervals or as and when required. There is often a provision that a meeting must be held at least once a year. The agreement usually lays down in addition that no stoppage of work shall take place until the prescribed procedure has been gone through, and often adds that the meetings required at successive stages of negotiation shall be held within certain limits of time. Usually, no penalties are laid down for breach of these provisions ; but when they are broken the aggrieved party often refuses to negotiate until they have been complied with—for example, if a stoppage occurs before the procedure has been carried through, until the strikers have returned to work. This is sometimes a source of difficulty when a group of Trade Unionists has declared an unauthorised strike and refuses to go back until its grievance has been met. In such cases, the Trade Unions usually succeed in the end in persuading their members to go back in order to allow negotiations to proceed. But this does not always happen, and occasionally, despite agreed rules of procedure, negotiations go on during a strike or lock-out. Of course, they often do so after the negotiating procedure has been gone through without a settlement being reached.

Procedural agreements often provide for both national and local negotiation. Some questions arise nationally, and need to be dealt with at once by national bargaining—for example, proposed general changes in wage-rates, or hours of labour, or other general conditions of work. Others arise locally, and are dealt with first at local joint meetings, being subsequently referred to national meetings only if the local negotiations fail. In most occupations, wage-rates used to be settled locally ; but they are nowadays much more often determined by national bargaining. Hours of labour, and such matters as paid holidays, and standard rates of payment for overtime and night work are most often settled on a national scale.

Procedural agreements often run for an indefinite duration, until either side gives notice of termination or amendment. Some, however, run for a fixed period or for a minimum period and thereafter subject to prescribed notice. Agreements laying down actual wages and conditions, on the other hand, are usually made for definite periods, with or without provisions for varying them within fixed limits while they remain current.

One of the best known and longest-standing procedural agreements is the document known as the 'York Memorandum', or 'Provisions for Avoiding Disputes', in the engineering industry. A large number of Trade Unions are signatories, headed by the Amalgamated Engineering Union, which inherited the agreement from its predecessor, the Amalgamated Society of Engineers. It dates back to an agreement of 1907, which was amended in 1914. Under the agreement it is laid down that when trouble arises in a particular establishment, an attempt shall be made to deal with it on the spot, by what is called 'mutuality'. This means that the individual workers concerned are to take the matter up with the foreman in the workshop and, if he cannot deal with it, by deputation to the management. If it cannot be settled there, the local Trade Union body concerned can refer the matter to a Local Conference with the local employers' association ; and if there is still no agreement it can be further referred to a National Conference between the national Trade Union, or Unions, and the employers' national federation. This body in turn can refer it back for further consideration locally, or can settle it, or can record disagreement—in which case either party is free to take what action it thinks fit. That is to say, a strike or lock-out can be declared, but only when the procedure has been gone through right to the end.

This description refers to disputes which begin in a particular establishment. Of course, a question of wider bearing can be raised initially at a higher level—local or national. In any event, there is no provision for settlement except by agreement between the parties. There are no outside participants in the negotiations, and there is no mention of reference to outside arbitration—though of course during and for some time after the war such reference was legally compulsory quite apart from the terms of the agreement.

One form or another of direct negotiation on these lines is nowadays the most usual method of bargaining in trades and industries in which wages and conditions are not subject to any special government regulation. The form, however, differs considerably from case to case. Some industries have formal conciliation boards : some agreements contain provisions for referring to arbitration any points of interpretation, and sometimes other points, arising out of their terms. Some negotiating bodies have outside chairmen, with or without voting powers, or power to recommend a settlement. The type of conciliation board with an 'impartial chairman' used to be much more frequent than it is to-day. The Mineworkers, for example, used to do most of their negotiations through such boards, for particular areas. The system began a long way back, near the middle of the nineteenth century, with the board started in the hosiery trade under the influence of A. J. Mundella and with local boards in the building industry, of which Sir Rupert Kettle was the pioneer. This was at a period when most employers were still refusing to bargain collectively with Trade Unions. In 1867 the Conciliation Act was passed to authorise the Government to use its good offices to bring together the parties in industrial disputes ; but the Act conferred no compulsory powers and was not of much effect. It was, none the less, the first small step towards the much wider influence exercised later by the Board of Trade—and later still by its successor in this field, the Ministry of Labour.

To-day, almost every trade and industry has its own negotiating machinery, resting on some kind of formal agreement. The instruments used range from Joint Conferences like those of the engineering Unions to Joint Industrial Councils set up under the Whitley Council Report of 1917.* Moreover, in a good many trades there is statutory wage-fixing machinery in existence side by side with the provision for direct negotiation between the parties. This applies to trades and industries under the Wages Councils Act of 1945. which has replaced the earlier Trade Boards of 1909 and 1918 ; and there are a number of other occupations, including agriculture, road transport and cotton weaving, for which special schemes of regulation have been put into force by Acts of Parliament. We shall consider later the nature and effects of these statutory regulations : the immediate point is that they necessarily affect the processes of voluntary collective bargaining in the occupations concerned. The statutes indeed only set up machinery for determining *minimum* rates and conditions ; and there is nothing to compel any body of workers to accept the determinations made in this way. But it is not really practicable to have two entirely distinct processes for settling wages, the one statutory and the other voluntary ; and in practice, in the trades for which statutory wage-fixing bodies exist, most of the discussion at the national level is done through them, and the wages they fix become standard as well as minimum wages, leaving the Trade Unions, where they can, to negotiate better terms with

*See page 119.

particular employers, and to deal by means of ordinary collective bargaining at all levels with matters that the determinations of the statutory Wages Councils do not cover.

Quite apart from statutory Wages Councils or similar bodies, the system of compulsory arbitration which was established during the war and remained in operation, with some modifications, until 1951 deeply affected the working of collective bargaining. Both parties got used to referring their disputes to arbitration and to dispensing with the strike or lock-out as a means of settling their differences ; and this both made it less likely that they would come to an agreement in cases of serious difference and made them think of arbitration as a natural resort even when it had ceased to be compulsory. Under conditions of rising prices and full employment, arbitrators hardly ever gave less than employers had been prepared to offer : so that, if strikes were ruled out, the Unions had usually nothing to lose by arbitration, and might have something to gain. When compulsion was ended, the conditions continued to be those of rising prices and fairly full employment, and the Unions had accordingly still in most cases an interest in pressing for arbitration unless employers offered favourable terms. Employers, for their part, found it difficult to resist such demands, and in fact usually preferred arbitration to strikes extending over a whole trade with Trade Union support. Arbitration, therefore, continued to be widely used, even when the freedom to strike or lock-out had been restored.

Indeed, as we shall see when we come to consider strikes and lock-outs, the tendency to avoid large-scale disputes has been growing for at least a quarter of a century, partly because collective bargaining procedures have been improved and have come to cover the vast majority of industries and services, but also because, as negotiations have become more centralised, the stoppages resulting from their breakdown have threatened to be much bigger and to command larger resources than before. A strike or lock-out covering a whole industry is too expensive and too risky a venture to be embarked on lightly ; and Trade Unions are much more reluctant than they once were to become involved in one. Moreover, employers, both because of the much greater strength of Trade Unionism and because economic conditions have been favourable to profit-making—and to the passing on of wage-increases to the consumers—have usually been much more willing than in the past either to come to terms directly or to accept arbitration. In these circumstances Trade Unionism has shed much of its militancy.

The matters with which collective bargaining is most usually concerned are, first, wages, including both general wage-rates and conditions of payment for piecework, overtime, nightshift, and other special circumstances ; secondly, grading and classification of jobs, including manning of machines, conditions of apprenticeship or learnership, and promotion ; thirdly, hours of labour, including shifts, rosters, and similar matters ; fourthly, holidays, including holidays with pay ; fifthly, such matters as provision of uniforms, overalls and tools ; sixthly, safety provisions, and arrangements affecting health and amenity. This is not meant to be an exhaustive list ; but it covers most of the ground as far as working conditions are affected. Of course, collective bargaining often deals also with such matters as recognition of shop stewards and methods of workshop negotiation—which have been considered elsewhere ; and employers' associations and Trade Unions may also meet to discuss many other matters, such as government policies affecting an industry or the methods to be used in joint consultation.

At the national level, collective bargaining is normally conducted mainly by full-time Trade Union officials, usually accompanied by members of their Executives, who may or may not play an active part. At regional levels, much the same conditions may apply, with regional officials playing a large part, but with regional Executive members doing rather more, and with national full-time officials sometimes coming in on an important case. In district or local bargaining, the conditions vary much more. Some Unions do most of their local bargaining through spare-time officers or members of district Executives, whereas in others a full-time official, stationed in the district but employed by the Union headquarters, plays a greater part. This latter is the case especially with the general labour Unions, whereas craft Unions tend to make more use of local spare-time officers and committeemen. Bargaining at the workshop or establishment level is usually in the hands mainly of shop stewards or members of works or workshop committees ; but a full-time official is often called in when difficulties arise. Indeed, in the general labour Unions the local full-time officials may do a good deal of the bargaining, even at the establishment level.

II. WAGE BARGAINING

Trade Unions have struggled throughout their history to establish and maintain standard rates of wages for particular kinds of job. Standard rates, indeed, go back a long way further than Trade Unions : they were well-recognised in the medieval gilds, and were incorporated for each type of skilled craftsman in the 'custom of the trade'. Such 'customs' were mainly local, and applied most regularly in the corporate towns. There was much more variation in the wages paid in market towns and country districts, into which employers often moved in search of cheap labour, or where urban merchants gave out work to craftsmen working in their own homes. Some of the early attempts at combination extending beyond a single town were made with the purpose of enforcing the town rates in the surrounding areas, or of establishing uniform rates in scattered industrial districts.

These early wage-rates could be either daily or weekly timework rates of wages, or piecework prices fixed for particular jobs. Most country, and many town, workers either worked in their own homes at piecework prices or were employed in small workshops by employers who were often themselves sub-contractors employed by bigger employers or merchants. The employees of these small masters were sometimes pieceworkers, but were also sometimes employed at day wages, the master making his income by the difference between the day-wages and the piecework payment he got from the big employer or merchant. The worst wages and conditions were often found among such dayworkers ; and the early Trade Unions spent much effort in fighting against the system. Old Trade Union rule-books often contain rules against the 'piecemaster' (sometimes called the 'piecework') system—by which is meant not individual piecework in the modern sense, but the employment at day wages of workers whose direct employers were in receipt of piecework payments.

In the urban crafts, before the coming of the factory system, timework and piecework existed side by side, the latter especially in the textile trades. In some trades, for example tailoring, there was a system which combined the two. The worker was paid a daily wage, but this was limited to a certain quantity of work, known as the 'stint'; and the worker, instead of spending a fixed number of hours on his job, went on till he had finished his 'stint', and then stopped. In this case, there was a standard daily or weekly rate, as in time-working trades : in pieceworking trades there was usually none. Only much later did it become the common practice to demand for pieceworkers a 'guaranteed wage' by the day or week ; but the Lancashire weavers were already struggling for a minimum wage in the very early years of the nineteenth century. Samuel Whitbread had introduced before 1800 his Bill to provide for the fixing of minimum wages ; but he got little support.

Later in the nineteenth century some of the craft Unions, especially in the building, woodworking and metalworking trades, strongly opposed all forms of piecework as leading to 'speeding-up' and bad workmanship. But this attitude was never general. In other trades piecework was insisted on as fairer to the worker and as involving less driving by foremen and overseers. The Trade Union attitude differed mainly according to the conditions of the trade. Where a given effort could reasonably be expected to yield a corresponding output in most cases, piecework was preferred to time-work. Where, on the other hand, it was difficult to relate effort and output, as in building (owing to weather conditions) and in much metal-working and woodworking (owing to varying materials and the special nature of many jobs) the workers, and the Trade Unions, usually did their best to insist on payment by time, and therewith sought to establish standard weekly, or at least daily, rates of wages.

The struggle for standard time-rates in some trades and for standard piece-rates in others was one of the main preoccupations of the Trade Unions during the second half of the nineteenth century. While the engineers, the carpenters, the building trades, and many others sought to enforce standard time-rates for skilled craftsmen, the cotton operatives fought for standard piecework lists, and the miners both for pit lists of piecework prices and for standard or minimum wages for each shift of work. The skilled coal-hewers then usually demanded piecework payments, and were perpetually at battle with the 'contractor' or 'butty' system, under which the 'contractor' played the part of 'piecemaster', receiving payment by the ton, but paying the men under him a fixed day wage. The builders for a long time fought for a daily wage, but were defeated by the employers, who insisted on time-payment by the hour, and thus avoided payment when bad weather stopped work. The engineering trade had to accept piecework in some cases, but insisted that it should be worked only where the standard time-rate was also guaranteed.

The attempt to establish standard rates of wages had two main aspects. It was directed to establishing a common rate for all workers of the same craft in a particular factory; and it was also directed to securing that all the factories in a trade in one area paid this rate, and to extending this uniform payment to the surrounding country districts and smaller towns. Objection was not taken to an employer paying more than the standard rate, provided he paid it to all the workers in the grade concerned ; but objection was often taken to an employer paying men of the same grade at different rates, either in accordance with his view concerning their individual merits or for any other reason. This, it was held, led to favouritism and undermined the solidarity of the workers as a group. But in many trades there were some employers in a district who paid better than others, and this, far from being objected to, was welcomed as a lever for forcing up the rates elsewhere. In practice, different rates were quite often paid to different men in the same factory, by granting special bonuses or by promoting them to a superior grade. The Trade Unions used to object to this much more than most of them do nowadays ; but it was never easy to prevent an employer from paying *more* than the agreed rate.

The gradual extension of the standard wage-rates to more and more firms in a district, and to outlying areas, occupied a great deal of the attention of the craft Unions from the time when they began to grow strong almost to the present day. But in the main industries, and to a great extent in others too, the development of Trade Unionism and the enforcement of standard rates by law in times of war (and in times of peace too, where wages are regulated under statute) have made such matters much more automatic. To-day, most firms pay the standard rates for skilled workers almost without question, and the decisions made by collective bargaining are usually applied without much difficulty even to firms which do not belong to the employers' federation or association concerned. This does not make it the less necessary for Trade Unions to concern themselves with wage-rates : they need both to deal with changes in the standard rates and to give much more attention than used to be needed to the application of these rates in connection with the special bonuses and allowances paid by particular firms. But a good deal of energy that used to be spent in bringing pressure on one recalcitrant firm after another, in order to induce it to pay the standard rates, can now be applied to other purposes.

Standard wage-rates were established, during and before the nineteenth century, almost exclusively for skilled craftsmen and, in some cases, for 'labourers'. Indeed, no category of workers was usually recognised between the skilled man and the labourer, save in a few special cases, where a category of specialised 'mates', or 'skilled labourers', achieved recognition—e.g. plumbers' mates, fitters' mates, bricklayers' mates. There was indeed in most industries no considerable category of semi-skilled workers until mass-production under the factory system set in, especially in the metal trades in and around Birmingham. As the factory system spread to more and more industries the numbers of such workers rose rapidly ; but they remained for the most part unrecognised. The craft Unions would not accept them, and the general labour Unions, which later enrolled many of them, were not yet in the field. Accordingly, employers were able to pay them such wages as they pleased, provided only that they paid enough to attract the labour they wanted and did not pay less than the standard or customary rates for unskilled labour, where such rates existed. In these circumstances, each employer, or at any rate each large employer, tended to develop his own practices in paying and in grading his semi-skilled machine operators. Some of those nearest to the fully skilled craftsmen were fairly soon organised by the craft Unions, some of which agreed on rates for them at so many shillings a week below the standard craftsman's rate. But most of them continued to have no standard rate applicable outside the particular factory in which they worked ; nor did the general labour Unions, when they organised substantial numbers of them, usually attempt to introduce such rates. The craft Unions were more inclined to do this, where and when they opened their ranks to the less skilled ; but they found so many different works practices in being that it was very difficult to achieve any uniformity—above all where the less skilled workers were divided between them and the general labour Unions. This was one of the reasons why, as mass-production developed further, wage-bargaining for the less skilled workers had so often to be done firm by firm, as it is to-day in many types of work. Moreover, such bargaining with particular firms about the grading and payment of the less skilled workers necessarily reacted on bargaining about the wages of the more highly skilled, both because questions often arose of the payment to be made to craftsmen for setting-up and overlooking the machines operated by less skilled workers, and because, where groups of less skilled workers, especially on piecework, were able to earn high wages, the skilled men were led to demand more in order to keep their 'differentials' over the less skilled, or even to prevent the less skilled from earning more than they themselves could earn on time-work, or on skilled piecework jobs that could not be speeded up without loss of quality, if at all.

Thus, although changes in the standard rates, negotiated by collective bargaining (or laid down by arbitration or under statutory regulation) continued to be followed by movements of earnings throughout the trades or industries to which they applied, there came to be increasingly another element in earnings which depended on bargains made in a particular establishment or workshop—special gradings of jobs or of workers, special bonus payments to skilled workers who had no direct product of their own because they were engaged in setting up or maintaining machines, or in other 'oncost' work, special payments to toolroom workers, and special payments 'in lieu' of piece-rates to workers whose output could not be easily measured in relation to effort. Such matters could usually be regulated only in and for a particular factory or workshop, and could not be covered by bargains extending over a whole district or a whole trade. This, as we have seen, has been one of the reasons for the development of the shop steward system ; and it has also meant that the Trade Union representatives who take part in such bargaining need to have a growing amount of technical knowledge of processes and machines if they are to tackle their tasks efficiently.

The old-style craftsman normally worked alone, or with a mate, with a kit of tools or on a single machine, or shifting from one machine to another as he practised different parts of his craft. He hardly ever operated more than one machine at the same time. But the semi-skilled machine operator very often does this, when the machines are largely automatic and do not need continuous tending. Many craftsmen to-day supervise large numbers of machines, which are operated, several at a time, by less skilled workers. In these circumstances, it is common for some workers to operate more machines than others, partly according to the nature of the jobs in hand, and partly according to differences in speed and dexterity. Thus earnings may depend on the number of machines a single worker is able to operate, as well as on the output from each machine. Moreover, skilled workers supervising a number of operations may be paid a bonus depending on the total output of the machines for which they are responsible : so that in effect the payment for output is shared, in proportions that need to be fixed, between operators and craftsmen. This, again, gives rise to negotiation that has to be done mostly in a particular establishment.

Of course, some craftsmen, such as the plumbers and electricians on installation and maintenance work, continue to work largely under the old conditions. But in factories the work of the skilled craftsman becomes more and more, not direct production, but machine supervision and maintenance, making of special tools and jigs, fitting of parts which require nice adjustment, and other kinds of special work distinct from that of the ordinary machine operator.

Thus wage-bargaining tends to change its character as the technical conditions of production change. The days are gone, save in a very few occupations, when bodies of workers pursuing an exclusive craft skill could be satisfied with endeavouring to establish a standard wage-rate, almost regardless of the less skilled workers—though not, of course, of the rates paid to cover bodies of skilled workers whose skill was thought of as on a par with theirs. There was a strong tendency, under the old conditions, for the wage-rates of skilled craftsmen to be not very different over a wide range of trades. In the eighteenth century, compositors tended to get rather more than most others, presumably because of the high literacy required of them ; and so did gold-beaters and silversmiths, and others who worked on expensive materials—perhaps because they were required to resist stronger temptations. Different types of building operatives were paid rather differently because of the intermittent nature of their work. Silk weavers tended to be paid very badly, in relation to other craftsmen, because of foreign competition. But these were exceptional cases : in the same town, as a rule, the wages of most of the different kinds of craftsmen were not very far apart. Wage-rates became much more differentiated in the early days of the factory system, largely because of the untrammelled competition among factory owners and of their constant search for cheap labour. Thus wage-rates in particular trades tended to become more uniform within a locality, as a result largely of Trade Union action ; and, as between areas, differences narrowed as the more backward were gradually pulled up nearer to the main centres. There was also some tendency for the 'relativity' of wages as between trades to re-assert itself ; but this tendency was not so strong, and was kept in check by differences in conditions of marketing—for example, between exporting trades and trades which produced for the home market, and between trades more and less liable to the effects of cyclical fluctuation. Wages fluctuated much more widely in some industries than in others—most of all in coal-mining, in which they represented a very high proportion of total cost, in iron and steel and in shipbuilding, which were much affected by ups and downs in economic activity, and in the woollen trades, which passed through endless short booms and slumps dependent mainly on overseas demand.

In the early years of the present century, growing foreign competition in many industries was reducing profit-margins and making employers more resistant to demands for wage advances. Real wages, measured by changes in the cost of living, began to fall, whereas they had been rising during the later nineteenth century as a result of cheaper food. Then came the first World War, of which one effect was to bring wages closer together. Flat-rate advances to meet the rising cost of living narrowed the real differences between skilled and less skilled workers in the same industries ; and at the same time a number of the worse paid industries secured larger advances than others, and there was a considerable levelling-up of low-wage areas in which living had been, or had been supposed to be, cheaper than elsewhere. As wage-rates were cut down during the post-war slump, some of these trends were partly reversed, but few entirely. Certain industries, however, lost ground, whereas others gained, as a result of the movement as a whole. After 1925 miners and shipbuilders underwent a heavy fall from their former eminence, whereas motor-car workers and at least the lower-paid railway workers improved their relative position. These trends continued, or were intensified, during the depression of the 1930s.

The second World War, like the first, reduced real-wage differentials between skilled and less skilled workers. But in the expanded industries—which also mostly remained at a high level after 1945—this trend was in general more than offset by special bonuses and allowances to skilled workers. In contracting industries, on the other hand, and in service occupations such as railways and public utilities, these offsets seldom occurred ; and the less skilled did relatively better. The mineworkers, after passing through very bad times, regained most of their losses ; and so, to a smaller extent, did the shipbuilding workers. What chiefly appeared in the 1950s, however, was the wide difference between earnings in different establishments within the same broad industrial group—especially in the highly diversified engineering and metalworking industries.

What has been said so far about relative wages applies chiefly to male workers. For women there was in general a marked improvement, relative as well as absolute. In October 1952, over the entire range of industries covered by the Ministry of Labour's periodical inquiries into wages and hours of labour, the average weekly earnings of adult women were 196 per cent, and those of adult men only 159 per cent above the earnings in October 1938, and hourly earnings of women 208 per cent, as against 158 per cent for men. Boys, and youths' earnings had risen more than men's, and girls' considerably more than women's. The averages for both sexes and all ages were an increase of 185 per cent weekly, and 188 per cent hourly. Hours worked were almost unchanged for adult men—about 47½ a week—but had fallen for the other three groups.

The relative rise in women's wages is, of course, in part only one aspect of the general narrowing of differentials between skilled and less skilled workers. But it goes beyond this, and must be partly attributed to more employment of women in the better paid occupations and partly to full employment—for the 'marginal' woman is harder to attract into wage-earning—or to hold there—than the 'marginal' man. Women are also now better organised than they were—though still badly ; but it may be doubted whether this is as much cause as result of the improvement in their conditions.

III. HOURS OF LABOUR

No less important than wage-bargaining, and intimately connected with it, is collective bargaining about standard working hours. Up to the introduction of gas lighting in the nineteenth century the hours of work were largely determined by the season, at any rate during the winter, though a good deal of work was done by candle-light when it had to be finished in a hurry. Gas-lighting, by removing the natural limits, encouraged the employers, especially in power-using factories, to prolong the working day to the utmost, in order to get all they could out of the expensive machines. Gas-light did not reach the private house—much less the worker's cottage—until much later, when a great deal of industry had passed to the factories ; and work in the home, or in small workshops, continued for a long time to be largely conditioned by the need for daylight. The hours often differed greatly from summer to winter ; and when the workers worked in their homes as pieceworkers there was no standard working day—as indeed there was none later in the sweatshops which continued well into the present century.

The Trade Clubs and Unions of skilled craftsmen in the eighteenth and early nineteenth century—those whose members worked on the employers' premises—fought to maintain a standard working day, and on the whole succeeded fairly well. But in the factories terribly long hours were worked, by women and young children as well as by men. The greatest agitations of the textile workers from 1815 onwards turned on this issue : the Unions fought to secure a limitation of the working day both by industrial action and by demanding legislation restricting the length of shifts and the hours during which factories could remain open. There was no chance of Parliament agreeing to limit by law the working day of adult men : that would have been regarded as too great a breach of the principle of 'freedom of contract'; but from 1819 onwards, as the result of the combined efforts of the workers' movements and of upper and middle class helpers, Parliament was induced to limit the hours first of children and then of young persons and women, and to restrict the hours of opening of textile factories in which such persons were employed. The legislation was confined at first to cotton, then extended (in 1833) to other textile factories, and at length (in 1867) to other factories using power. The first proposal for a general limitation came from Robert Owen : the first Acts were passed with the aid of the elder Sir Robert Peel : Lord Shaftesbury played a leading part in promoting the Acts of the 1830s and 1840s. The Ten Hours Act, for textile factories only, became law in 1847, but was modified, with improved enforcement, to a Ten and a Half Hours Act three years later.

It is not possible to disentangle the respective parts played by the Trade Unions and by the philanthropists in securing this legislation. The workers' Short Time Committees co-operated with friendly employers, Members of Parliament, and friends such as Richard Oastler, the 'Factory King', in a sustained series of agitations. The adult male workers in practice got the advantage of the Acts, though they applied directly to women and young persons only, partly because of the requirement that the hours of factory opening should be limited where such persons were employed, but also because they followed up the legislation with demands made on their own behalf. Throughout the first half of the nineteenth century the great cry was for the 'Ten Hours', though in 1834 Robert Owen and some of the Trade Unionists put forward a plan for a concerted refusal to work more than eight hours. After 1850 nothing much happened for a time; but in the 1860s the demand for a Nine Hours day began to take shape, especially in the engineering and building industries. Towards the end of the 'sixties, the textile workers began an agitation for the Eight Hours Day. The Factory Act of 1874, however, did no more than reduce the maximum working week from 60 to 56½ hours in textile, and in other factories the maximum remained at the 60 hours laid down in 1867.

The engineering and shipbuilding workers won the Nine Hours Day as a sequel to the great Nine Hours Movement which paralysed the North-East Coast in 1871; and the builders were also successful in winning a similar reduction in one area after another. But these successes owed nothing to legislation: even the textile workers had thereafter to rely on their own efforts to get the working week reduced below 56½ hours, and to establish the full half-holiday on Saturdays, which was gradually extended from trade to trade during the rest of the century. The next round began with the Eight Hours Day as the main objective. This became a great popular cry in the 1890s, and was taken up by the New Unionists and Socialists, who urgently demanded an Eight Hours Law. But Parliament would do nothing; and at the outbreak of the first World War in 1914 normal working hours remained at 52 or more in the great majority even of highly organised industries. The mineworkers, indeed, obtained an Eight Hours Act in 1908; but no other legislative change was made. Only after 1918 was there a fairly general reduction of the working week to 48 hours—or fewer in some cases; and even then the Government refused to ask Parliament to ratify the

Forty-Eight Hours Convention which was the first International Convention to be drafted by the newly formed International Labour Organisation.

At the close of the first World War there was a widespread demand for the Forty Hours Week, or at least for the Forty-Four Hours Week, and unofficial strikes of shipbuilders and engineers on the Clyde and at Belfast were called on this issue, but were defeated. These industries were however granted by negotiation a working week of 47 hours ; and at about the same time the iron and steel workers, many of whom had been working twelve-hour shifts, secured the eight-hours shift by collective bargaining. The mineworkers, before the Sankey Coal Commission, demanded the six-hours shift, and were given by legislation a shift of seven hours, with a promise of six hours to come when conditions had settled down. Instead of this, they were put back to eight hours after their defeat in the post-war slump, and then the Labour Government of 1929 put the shift at seven hours and a half. In most industries the working week remained at or near 48 hours right up to the second World War. Meanwhile, in the 1930s, both France and the United States had established a normal working week of forty hours—usually five days of eight hours, with a free Saturday, except for overtime.

The questions of overtime payment and of the conditions under which overtime is to be worked are, of course, closely bound up with that of the normal working day, or shift, or week. Many Trade Unions have taken, over a very long period, strong objection to 'systematic' overtime working, and provisions against it have been included in some collective agreements. The objection has been particularly strong at times when unemployment has been rife, the Unions arguing that more men ought to be taken on, and the work shared. In recent years, because of full employment, this argument has applied only in exceptional cases ; but it is still deeply based in the sentiment of Trade Unionists. No objection is usually taken to overtime in cases of emergency ; and since working hours were reduced, there has been more tendency to welcome a moderate amount of overtime, especially at week-ends, in order to earn more money.

Collective agreements about wages usually lay down that payment for overtime shall be at more than the ordinary wage-rate. Sometimes overtime is paid for at a fixed rate for all hours worked (from 'time-and-a-quarter' at the lowest to 'time-and-a half') : sometimes a difference is made between the first hour, or two hours, and subsequent hours : sometimes the ratio varies with the total amount of overtime worked during a week, or even over a longer period. In some trades each day stands by itself for purposes of reckoning overtime : in others overtime rates are payable only when the full normal weekly hours have been worked. Higher payments than for ordinary overtime are usually made for work on Saturday afternoons, on Sundays, and during holidays—often at twice the normal daily or hourly rate. Work on nightshift is also paid for in many cases at special rates. In cases where duties are, or may be, discontinuous, as in many forms of transport, there are special agreements regulating the 'spread-over' of work and providing for special allowances in such circumstances as absence from home overnight or for more than a certain number of hours—e.g. for railway engine drivers.

Most major collective agreements now make provision for paid holidays ; and statutory Wages Councils and similar bodies are also empowered to make such payments compulsory. The holidays allowed with pay are sometimes for a fortnight, sometimes for only a week, in addition to normal holidays. A fortnight is tending to become the normal thing, with a shorter allowance to workers who have been in the same employment for less than a year.

In October 1952, the average hours actually worked in the industries covered by the Ministry of Labour's enquiry into Earnings and Hours were 46.1. Adult men averaged 47.7 hours, adult women 41.8, boys and youths 44.4, and girls 42.7. In 1938 the corresponding averages were 46.5 for all workers, 47.7 for men, 43.5 for women, 46.2 for boys, and 44.6 for girls. It is not possible to say how much of these hours was overtime, as the standard working week differs from trade to trade, as well as by sex and age. It is, however, safe to say that women and juveniles work much less overtime than adults, and in many cases none at all.

IV. GRADING AND CLASSIFICATION OF WORKERS—PROMOTIONS

In many of the older industries there used at one time to be only three recognised grades of workers, apart from supervisors, managers and clerks. These were journeymen, apprentices and labourers. The journeyman was a skilled worker who had passed through his apprenticeship ; the labourer started as a boy, without apprenticeship, and was not supposed to have any prospect of becoming a journeyman, though in practice some did, by going to work in country areas and picking up a skilled trade. In some trades there was a fourth grade—improvers, who were apprentices recently out of their apprenticeship, serving a period of probation before being recognised as full craftsmen.

This simple structure was seldom found in factory industries : it belonged to the age of small workshops and work done at home. In the cotton industry, for example, when it passed under the factory system, there were various kinds of workers possessing and needing different degrees, as well as different types, of skill. There was no system of apprenticeship : the required skills and dexterities were picked up. The mule spinner, who was highly skilled, learnt his job first as a little piecer and then as a big piecer, assisting the spinner. The weavers were of widely varying degrees of skill—from plain weavers of coarse stuffs to weavers of fine fabrics or of delicate patterns on a jacquard loom. The workers in the preparing branches—card and blowing room operatives, makers of rovings, etc.—needed relatively little skill—only a certain dexterity that was soon acquired. There were few entirely unskilled workers : there was no separate class of labourers such as existed where craftsmen and apprentices formed a class apart.

In engineering factories, on the other hand, there was for a long time a sharp division between craftsmen and apprentices on the one hand and labourers and unapprenticed boys on the other. Then, spreading from Birmingham light metal trades, there appeared, as we have seen, an ever-increasing body of semi-skilled, and even of almost unskilled, machine-minders, many of them working under the supervision of skilled men. Their arrival broke down the sharp division between craftsmen and labourers, and introduced many intermediate groups. But because no Trade Union made it its business to establish standard classifications or wage-rates for most of these workers, actual gradings and rates of pay differed widely from factory to factory, and indeed still do to-day, though some approach to systematisation has been made as a result of a long series of collective agreements and arbitration decisions each dealing with a particular case. As long ago as the period of the first World War I was concerned with an attempt to discover means of introducing some order into this chaos. Proposals were made for an attempt to rate the various machines according to the skill needed for working them, and to draw up a classification of machine types with an appropriate wage-rate attached to each. This, however, cut across the rival principle of rating the worker according to his personal skill, irrespective of the machine he operated ; and no way was found either of reconciling these two principles or of deciding between them. So nothing happened, or has happened since, though the matter has been repeatedly discussed. It would be even harder to tackle to-day, as each firm tends to have its own system, embodied in a host of workshop practices and agreements.

After the first World War, the very numerous separate railway companies were amalgamated into the four main systems which remained in being till they were nationalised after 1945. It was found, when the four groups were formed, that each railway taken over had its own different system of grading its employees, often under different names and with varying allocations of duties. There were in all several thousand groups, or separate names of grades ; and immensely complicated negotiations were needed to reduce them to a more manageable number, so as to allow uniform conditions of payment to be introduced. They were got down to about 300 ; and even then there remained differences of practice which were not straightened out until the railways were unified under public ownership.

A similar diversity still exists in the coal-mining industry. Each coalfield has not only its own names for particular kinds of workers, but also its own way of allocating tasks between the different grades. The Mineworkers' Union and the National Coal Board have been engaged for some time in trying to work out a uniform national system of grade-names for the purpose of settling rates of payment, and therewith in some cases a reallocation of tasks. There is to be, it is announced, a 'new wage system' for coal-mines, which will remove many of the present anomalies ; but clearly the working out of such a system is no easy task.

Conditions in the Civil Service are based on a detailed and elaborate grading system. This is relatively easy where there has always been a single employer ; but even so a lot of work went into the making of the present system—for example, in the Post Office. In industries where the firms are many, uniform grading is much harder, and may be impossible ; but it is bound to be demanded wherever an industry is unified under a single control. In practice, even where employers are numerous, the question of grading may play an important part in Trade Union negotiation ; and it is bound to arise in any industry for which the State sets up compulsory machinery for the fixing of minimum wage-rates. In tailoring, for example, grading plays an important part in the work of the Wages Council, as it did previously in that of the Trade Board set up under the Act of 1909.

In a few exceptional cases, the practice is to grade the individual worker rather than his job. The best-known example is that of the Birmingham brass trade, where the grading is done by the local Technical College on a basis of tests of skill. There have been somewhat similar methods in some branches of the furniture trades. Of course, where formal apprenticeship exists, passing through this training qualifies the apprentice as a skilled craftsman. In some trades—tailoring is again an example—there are formal provisions for learnership as distinct from full apprenticeship of the normal sort.

The question of promotion is closely associated with that of grading, especially in the public services. When employment is normally lifelong, the employee normally expects to pass, almost of right, through a series of grades in the course of his life ; and he can, subject to good conduct and tolerable efficiency, be assured of this in cases in which promotion is by seniority. On the other hand, where it is by 'merit', as assessed by supervisors, he may be passed over again and again. Promotion by seniority is unobjectionable when it is simply a matter of getting a higher salary, without change of duties ; but where it involves taking on more responsible work, and perhaps supervision of former colleagues, the question of 'merit' necessarily arises. Trade Unions in the public services, and elsewhere if similar conditions exist, have usually been inclined to insist on the importance of seniority in determining claims to promotion ; but the higher officials have been disposed to insist on 'merit', which is indeed the only principle recognised for the higher posts. At lower levels seniority has often counted for a good deal, but seldom as the sole criterion. In recent years the Post Office has introduced for certain supervisory posts at the lower levels a system of consultation with the representatives of the staffs concerned ; and, as this may well provide a precedent for imitation elsewhere, it seems worth while briefly to describe the procedure. It applies only in the provinces, and only to certain grades.

In each area there is a Promotion Board, consisting of senior officials, without Trade Union or staff representation. This Board draws up each year for each grade an 'acting list' of persons who are to be given a chance of performing as substitutes for officers absent ill or on holiday the duties of a higher grade. The Staff side of the local Post Office Whitley Council, which is the negotiating body within the service, can nominate persons to serve on this 'acting list'. So can senior officials. Every person on the list is given as nearly as possible an equal chance of performing the higher duties, and is reported on by officials belonging to a still higher grade. When a vacancy occurs, the Staff Side can put forward a nomination for filling it, to be considered by the Promotion Board together with any name or names submitted by the higher officials concerned. The Board then appoints whomever it thinks best ; but a senior man who is passed over for appointment to the 'acting list', or for promotion, has a right to appeal for his case to be considered. Actually, there is some tendency for the Staff Side to put forward the name of the most senior person eligible, and thus to defeat the purpose of the procedure ; for if this is regularly done, no notice is likely to be taken of the staff nominations. Recently, as an outcome of pressure from the Trade Union side for representation on the Promotion Board or for some alternative way of increasing staff influence, an experimental new procedure was introduced in a few selected areas. The new feature is that the Staff Side is entitled, not only to submit a nomination for a vacancy, but also to argue its case with the Promotion Board, whereas previously it was allowed only to make representations, in writing or orally, without discussion. The Board, if it rejects the staff's nomination, has to make a report of the discussion for confidential use by the Staff Side, and an appeal is allowed to the Regional Director of the Post Office—that is, to a still higher level.*

In industry generally, it is rare to find any arrangements for consulting the workers or their Trade Unions when promotions are being considered. There is in most industries no regular system of promotion from grade to grade, such as exists in the public services ; nor is it usually expected that more than a few workers will remain in the service of the same employer all their

*See *Promotion Procedure in the Post Office*. Union of Post Office Workers, 1949.

lives. Promotion is usually regarded as exclusively the firm's business, though a few firms with exceptionally wide arrangements for joint consultation do use it on occasion for this purpose. Promotion is evidently one of the matters to which joint consultation, as it develops further, is most likely to be regularly applied, not only in the nationalised industries but also in large private firms.

V. OTHER CONDITIONS OF EMPLOYMENT—JOINT CONSULTATION

The foregoing sections have dealt with most of the major matters that are ordinarily bargained about by Trade Unions and employing bodies. But there are a host of secondary issues that may come up, either at the factory or workplace level or at higher levels. Most of these, however, arise out of the special circumstances of particular industries and do not lend themselves to general treatment. A few random examples must suffice.

In some occupations, questions of physical fitness for the job are of great importance—for example, eyesight in the case of engine drivers. Men considered for promotion to the rank of drivers—and still more, for driving express trains—have to submit to special eyesight tests. Failure to pass the test may destroy a man's prospects for life. Therefore, the Associated Society of Locomotive Engineers and Firemen for many years pressed to be consulted about the tests and to bargain about them if it thought them unfair. Incidentally, this was one of the main reasons given by the engine drivers for insisting on maintaining their separate Trade Union, instead of joining forces with the National Union of Railwaymen on its formation.

Where uniforms are worn, as by postmen and railwaymen, or where work is particularly dirty and overalls are provided, the extent and conditions of such provision normally become a matter for bargaining. Thus, at the Annual Conference of the Union of Post Office Workers, questions about uniforms usually occupy quite a considerable time.

In dangerous occupations, such as coal-mining, or where industrial diseases are common, safety measures often come up in negotiation, and are sometimes entrusted to a special joint body. The Coal Mines Regulation Acts and the Factory Acts contain numerous compulsory requirements designed to promote safety—e.g. concerning ventilation and fire-prevention in mines, and concerning the fencing of machinery in factories ; and joint discussion often turns on the means of making these provisions effective. But it can also go beyond the legal requirements, and have for its object the promotion of a 'safety first' attitude. In the past, employers were often exceedingly callous about dangers to their employees, where they could save money by omitting desirable precautions. Notorious examples are to be found in the history of the shipping industry in the days before Samuel Plimsoll's successful agitation against 'coffin-ships', which led to the Merchant Shipping Act of 1875 ; and there are also a great many instances of preventable accidents in coal mines and in factories. Something was done to make employers less careless by the enactment of the Employers' Liability Act of 1880, which made employers liable to damages for accidents caused to their employees by their own or their agents' negligence, including that of fellow-employees. The Workmen's Compensation Acts, from 1896 onwards, extended the workers' claim to cover compensation on a restricted scale for injury even when it was not the employer's or his agent's fault. These Compensation Acts were replaced by the Industrial Injuries Act, as part of the general plan of Social Insurance introduced after the Beveridge Report by the Labour Government of 1945. Most substantial employers are now prepared to co-operate in taking proper precautions against accidents or certifiable industrial diseases ; but much remains to be done in obsolete factories and in small workshops ; and such matters are now often discussed at the factory level, as well as higher up.

Holiday relay arrangements are another matter that may come up for joint discussion. So may arrangements for factory canteens, sanitary provision, clocking on or off, and a host of other questions affecting the amenity of the job. Other matters, much more important formerly than to-day, are those of fines or locking-out for late attendance, fines for spoilt work, or for disciplinary offences, demotions or suspensions for the same reasons, regulations about talking or singing at work, restrictions on the rights of shop stewards to move about the department or to inspect Trade Union cards on the factory premises, and so on.

Some of these matters fall well within the normal field of Trade Union bargaining. Others are on the borderline between Trade Union matters and matters which fall outside the range of normal negotiation. Before Joint Consultation came into vogue under that name, some employers had set up joint Works Committees, not for Trade Union bargaining, but for common discussion, and in some cases joint action, on matters which were regarded as falling outside the negotiable terms of employment. Canteens were often managed by such Committees, and some firms had sports clubs and other social activities which were dealt with either by or through the Works Committee or by a number of separate committees for different purposes. Some employers, again, had pension schemes managed by joint bodies. Where such Works Committees, special or general, existed, there might be in the same works one or more Shop Stewards' Committees concerned with Trade Union matters, but entirely separate from the Works Committee, though often with overlapping members. Works Committees dealing with 'social' matters were commonly elected by all the employees, including non-Unionists, whereas Shop Stewards' Committees normally represented only Trade Union members.

No sharp line can be always drawn between matters that belong to the field of Trade Union bargaining and matters that do not. The scope of Trade Union bargaining is not fixed : it tends to grow wider as the power of the Trade Unions increases. At any stage, there are bound to be borderline cases.

This appeared plainly when Joint Production Committees were set up in many war factories to aid the effort at higher production. These committees were precluded by their constitution from encroaching on collective bargaining functions ; but they could not always avoid doing so, nor was it always agreed what such functions were. Trouble arose in particular when employers attempted to get Joint Production Committees to deal with individual cases of absenteeism, so as to act as disciplinary bodies. Such action was usually objected to by the Trade Unions. The Committees were not supposed, either, to deal with questions of wages ; but where such matters as conditions of piecework or bonus payments arose in close connection with proposals designed to increase output, it was not easy to keep the two apart, and very close interworking between J.P.C.s and Shop Stewards' Committees was needed for the avoidance of confusion.

When, after the war, the surviving J.P.C.s were reconstituted as Joint Consultative Committees and when consultative machinery was established at all levels throughout the nationalised industries, these overlaps of functions to some extent persisted : they are still in process of being sorted out. In some industries under public management, notably the Post Office, the distinction does not exist. The Post Office Whitley Councils deal both with conditions of employment and with matters of joint consultation. A somewhat similar state of affairs exists in the railway industry—and did, even before public ownership came into force.

The Whitley scheme indeed, on its introduction after the reports of the Whitley Committee in 1917, was explicitly intended to improve industrial relations by providing special machinery for the discussion of matters falling outside the scope of ordinary Trade Union bargaining. The Whitley Joint Industrial Councils were not meant to supersede or interfere with the arrangements between Trade Unions and employers for negotiating about wages, hours of work, and similar questions. In practice, however, where the Councils were established and survived, the distinction broke down, and they turned into collective bargaining bodies differing from other such bodies only in having explicitly wider terms of reference, including joint consultation on any matter of common concern that both sides were prepared to discuss.

Reference has been made in a previous section to the development of joint consultation at the workplace level both in the nationalised industries and elsewhere. It is necessary here only to add a little about joint consultation at the higher levels and its relation to joint consultation in the workplace. Nationally, and at regional and local levels, joint consultation, where it exists, takes place between representatives of Trade Unions and employers' associations, and is mainly conducted, on the Trade Union side, by full-time officials and Executive members. The Joint Consultative Committees in the particular workplaces are not represented as such : there is no building up of a consultative hierarchy on the basis of the workplace bodies. In a few big firms, such as Imperial Chemical Industries, something of this sort does occur, in the form of conferences of delegates from local works bodies ; but nothing similar has occurred either in the nationalised industries or in private industries as wholes. It is, indeed, certain that the Trade Unions would object to any such development, as tending to establish a rival centre of power and to undermine Trade Union control of collective bargaining. We shall return to this question when we come to consider the conception of 'Workers' Control' in industry, or 'Industrial Self-Government', advocated by Guild Socialists but so far unwelcomed by the majority of Trade Union leaders—with the Union of Post Office Workers again a lonely exception.

CHAPTER V

CENTRAL ORGANISATION

I. THE TRADES UNION CONGRESS

IN each country in which Trade Unionism has reached any considerable development there exists some central body—sometimes more than one—which is designed to group the Trade Unions for the defence of their common interests, for the discussion of common policies, and for the furtherance of common aims. The relations of this central body to the separate Unions connected with it differ from country to country. In Great Britain, the existing central body began simply as a Congress of delegates from Trade Unions and from local Trades Councils (to which we shall come later) mainly for the promotion of industrial legislation and for the securing of the legal status of the movement, which was then under heavy attack. Thus, in Great Britain, Trade Unions existed in considerable numbers, and were already linked up locally through Trades Councils in a number of places, before the present central organisation came into being. In some other countries the centre was founded before more than a few Unions had been firmly established, save on a purely local basis ; and in such cases the central body took a larger part than in Great Britain in shaping the structure of the movement and was able to exert more power over the individual Unions. This was the case, for example, in Germany and also in Russia, where stable Trade Unions hardly emerged before the Revolution of 1917. In the United States, though the American Federation of Labor was not the first attempt to create a central organisation, it came into being at a time when American Trade Unionism was still very fluid, and was able to influence its development to a very considerable extent.

In the United States, as we have seen, there are at present two rival central bodies—the American Federation of Labor and the Congress of Industrial Organisations.* The older of these, the A.F. of L., was built up as a federation of Unions formed mainly, though not exclusively, on a basis of craft. Some of these existed before its establishment in 1886 : many more were set up later

*See page 83.

under its auspices. The A.F. of L.'s practice was, and is, to grant each Union admitted to it a 'charter of jurisdiction', defining the types of workers to be enrolled, and not to grant more than one Union a charter to enrol the same type of workers. The British Trades Union Congress has no similar practice. It can refuse to accept into affiliation a Union which it considers to be a pirate, endeavouring to steal members from other Unions ; but it has included from the first Unions which are competitors for the same workers, and it has never been in a position to enforce any rule that there shall be only one recognised Union catering for each kind. Indeed, when it was formed and for a long time afterwards, it was not thought of as having any jurisdiction over its affiliated bodies, or any function in relation to the forms of organisation. Its purpose was to mobilise Trade Union resistance to legal and political repression and to press for legislation in the workers' interests—not to organise for industrial purposes or to determine the lines of organisation—much less to engage in any sort of collective bargaining. Only in the 1920s was it given even the most rudimentary powers to deal with inter-union problems or to co-ordinate industrial action ; and as we saw these powers are narrowly limited even to-day.

The first Trade Union Conferences extending beyond quite small areas were held in Great Britain in the 1830s, in connection first with John Doherty's National Association of United Trades for the Protection of Labour (1831), and then with the Grand National Consolidated Trades' Union (1833-34), in which Robert Owen played an important part. After the collapse of these bodies, no further attempt was made until 1845, when a new National Association of United Trades was set up, but shrank almost to nothing after a few years. Ernest Jones, the Chartist leader, made some abortive attempts in the 1850s ; but nothing of significance occurred until, in 1864, the Glasgow Trades Council, acting in close conjunction with the recently formed Miners' Association led by Alexander Macdonald, called a Conference of Trade Unions and Trades Councils to consider means of securing the amendment of the law of Master and Servant.* This special Conference was the beginning of a movement for closer co-operation among the Trade Unions, especially in Scotland and the North of England. Two years later, a Conference called by the Sheffield Trades Council decided to set up a

*See page 173.

general federation for mutual defence against attacks on wages or attempts to worsen conditions ; but this body, the United Kingdom Alliance of Organised Trades, failed to get the support of most of the stronger Unions, and died out after a few years. The following year, 1867, was the beginning of the great struggle of the Trade Unions which followed the demands for repression arising out of the Sheffield Outrages and the legal decision in the case of *Hornby v. Close.** The London Trades Council,† which had been asked to summon a further Trade Union Conference that year, refused to do so ; but a Conference was called by a rival body, the London Working Men's Association, which was mainly political, and was trying to persuade the Trade Unions to put forward candidates for Parliament. (The second Reform Act, which enfranchised many of the skilled workers, was passed in 1867). The following year, it was the turn of the Manchester Trades Council to summon a Conference ; and at this gathering it was decided to make the Congress, as it was thereafter called, an annual affair. In 1869 the Congress, held in Birmingham, decided to elect a Parliamentary Committee—the name is significant of its purpose—to act for it between Congresses ; and thereafter this Committee was re-elected at each Congress until it was replaced by the Trades Union Congress General Council in 1921. The Parliamentary Committee played an important part in the 1870s in the struggle over the Labour Laws. Into it was in effect merged in 1871 a separate body, the Conference of Amalgamated Trades, which a few of the principal craft Unions had set up in 1867 to fight their own battle before the Royal Commission on Trade Unions, appointed in that year.

The Trades Union Congress officially dates its foundation in 1868, taking no account of the Conferences which led up to it. Until 1895 it represented the local Trades Councils as well as Trade Unions ; but in that year the Trades Councils were excluded, nominally on the ground that their membership duplicated that of the national Trade Unions, but actually because their delegates were apt to represent points of view well to the left of those of the national Union leaders, who were then mostly hostile to the developing Socialist and 'New Unionist' movements. Thereafter the Congress represented only Trade Unions, including some that were merely local : it was dominated by the larger national Unions—miners, textile workers, engineers, and a few

*See page 167. †See page 135.

others. Its affiliated membership fluctuated a great deal. In 1868 it was only 118,000, and in 1872 only 255,000. Then, amid the heat of the struggles and under boom economic conditions, it leapt to 750,000 in 1873 and to 1,192,000 the following year. By 1881 the slump had brought it down to 463,000 ; but thereafter it rose gradually, and towards the end of the 'eighties by leaps and bounds, reaching 1,470,000 in 1890, the year following the London gasworkers' and dockers' strikes. From that peak it fell to 900,000 in 1893 (affected by meeting in Belfast) and did not reach the 1890 figure again until 1903, when it was 1,500,000. Thereafter it again rose fast. In 1915 (which gives the actual membership for 1914) it was 2,682,000, and by 1920 it had reached 6,505,000. Then came the post-war slump and on top of it the General Strike of 1926, and by 1929 it was down to 3,673,000. After a slight recovery, the depression of the early 1930s brought it down to 3,295,000 in 1934; but by 1940 it was back to 4,867,000 and by 1946 to 6,671,000. By 1952 it exceeded 8 millions. These figures are a little affected by certain special factors—the exclusion of the Trades Councils in 1895, the removal of a few Irish Unions after the establishment of the Irish Free State, the forced resignation of the Civil Servants' Trade Unions in 1927, and the return of some of them after the repeal of the 1927 Trade Unions Act in 1946. But in the main they show the combined influences of certain great forward movements—after 1889, after 1906, and during both the World Wars—of trade recessions—in the 1890s, in the 1920s, and again in the early 1930s—and of the adhesion of new groups of non-manual as well as of manual workers.

Until after the first World War the Trades Union Congress and its Parliamentary Committee had hardly any staff beyond its salaried Secretary. Even in 1918 there was only one assistant in the office. The Congress was not intended to do more than pass resolutions, or the Parliamentary Committee, which consisted mainly of busy Trade Union secretaries, to do more than go on deputation to Ministers or Members of Parliament in connection with proposals for legislation or administrative reform. Sometimes, inter-union quarrels came up, and it had to attempt mediation ; but it had no authority to issue any orders. From an early stage, the question arose whether the Trade Unions ought to take part in politics in any further ways. In the 1860s the struggle for the Reform Bill was over before the Congress took shape, and the Trade Unions took part in this struggle through specially constituted bodies, such as the Trade Union Manhood Suffrage and Vote by Ballot Association (1862), which turned into the National Reform League. A section of the London Trade Unions supported the London Working Men's Association (1866), which after the Reform Act of 1867 attempted to organise a national movement for putting forward workers' candidates for Parliament. A number of seats were fought unsuccessfully in 1868; and in the following year the Trade Unions set up the Labour Representation League to organise the movement. Two Trade Union candidates, both miners—Alexander Macdonald and Thomas Burt—were elected to Parliament in 1874; but thereafter the League petered out in the slump.

In the early 1880s there was an attempt at revival; and the Trades Union Congress was invited to take the lead. In 1886, as a sequel to the Reform Acts of 1884 and 1885, which had greatly extended the franchise and re-distributed seats to the advantage of the industrial areas, the Congress agreed to set up a Labour Electoral Committee to promote working-class candidates; but the following year this body, re-named the Labour Electoral Association, was separated from Congress and thereafter held its own separate Conferences of local Labour Electoral Associations, which were mostly supporters of the policy of a Liberal-Labour alliance and hostile to Socialism. The Trades Union Congress thus washed its hands of the movement, not because it was against it, but as falling outside its proper sphere. Within the next few years, however, a powerful movement developed, under Socialist leadership, for Labour representation independent of all other parties, and some of the local L.E.A.s went over to this movement, which led to the foundation of the Independent Labour Party, under Keir Hardie's leadership, in 1893. A new demand then began for the Trade Unions to rally behind the movement for independent Labour representation; and for the rest of the 1890s the Socialists in the Trade Unions were continually pressing the Trades Union Congress to endorse this development. At length, in 1899, they induced the Congress to instruct the Parliamentary Committee to call, in conjunction with the Socialist bodies, a conference with this end in view; and in 1900 this conference set up the Labour Representation Committee, which took the name, Labour Party, in 1906. Again, it will be seen, the Trades Union Congress, instead of taking up parliamentary action itself, transferred the task to a specially constituted body.

The account of the Trade Unions' relations to the Labour Party will be found in a subsequent chapter. What I have been trying to show here is how narrowly the Trades Union Congress conceived of its functions, as excluding both electoral politics and control of industrial policy. This is further illustrated by the handling of the demand, which was also renewed in the 1890s under the influence of the New Unionism, for co-ordinated means of meeting the risks and costs of industrial disputes. Blatchford's *Clarion* took the lead in calling for a General Federation of Trade Unions, with a central fund for financing Trade Unions involved in strikes or lock-outs ; and this demand, like that for parliamentary action, was carried to the Congress. It was handled in the same way. The Trades Union Congress agreed to call a special meeting of interested Unions ; and as a result a General Federation of Trade Unions was founded as an entirely separate body. Each Union that agreed to join it paid in contributions at a rate proportionate to membership, and was promised in return fixed grants which it could use to supplement dispute pay provided out of its own resources. By no means all the Trade Unions joined the new body ; but a number did, including the Dockers and a good many of the Unions in the textile trades. The G.F.T.U. also attracted a considerable number of small Trade Unions, many of which did not belong to the Trades Union Congress. It was fortunate that most of the biggest Unions did not join ; for its finances would have been quite unequal to meeting the strain of a national stoppage in a major industry.

For a time, however, many Trade Unionists hoped that the G.F.T.U. would develop into the central co-ordinating industrial body for the whole movement that the Trades Union Congress showed no will to become. In 1901, mainly on the initiative of the German and French movements, an International Federation of Trade Unions was established with headquarters at Berlin. The British Trades Union Congress showed no interest in this move ; but the G.F.T.U. joined it as the British Section, and continued to hold this position right up to the first World War, when the International fell to pieces. On its reconstitution in 1919, the T.U.C., already beginning to take a wider view of its responsibilities, pushed the G.F.T.U. aside and took its place in the new International Federation, which lasted until it was reconstituted again, as the World Federation of Trade Unions, with Russian participation, at the end of the second World War. The affairs of the Trade Union Internationals are discussed in a later section : at this point I am again only illustrating the long-continued reluctance of the Trades Union Congress to advance far outside the very limited functions for which it had been originally set up.

After the first World War a change occurred. Just before 1914 the Miners' Federation, the newly established National Union of Railwaymen (1913), and the numerous Trade Unions loosely grouped in the not much older Transport Workers' Federation (1910-11), had created a joint body called the Triple Industrial Alliance. The idea underlying this move was that each of the three groups should arrange for its collective agreements with the employers to come to an end at the same date, that each should prepare its programme of demands, and that they should all agree, if these were not met, to strike together, and not to return to work until all three had been satisfied. This was by no means a simple plan ; for the employers were most unlikely to wish to make agreements that would would end simultaneously. The outbreak of war, however, both prevented the plan from being tried out at once and gave rise to an interval during which the agreements in question did all expire, leaving the Unions free to advance new demands as soon as hostilities were over. Thus, in 1919, all the partners in the Alliance were in the field with new programmes. But, even so, matters did not proceed according to plan. The Miners were persuaded to allow their claims to be referred to a Royal Commission under Mr. Justice Sankey, which speedily granted their demands for higher wages and shorter working hours. They accepted without waiting for their partners. The Railwaymen's claims came up in the summer of 1919 ; and after a strike, in which their partners played the part of mediators, but were not asked to join the stoppage, a settlement was reached in this case too. The Transport Workers also secured some advances, though not by any means all they wanted; but it was clearly impracticable, even if they had so wished, to call on their partners to strike on their behalf just after they had got their own claims settled. Consequently, the Triple Alliance was not called upon to act. The following year, however, the Miners, this time alone, became involved in a further wage dispute, and called on the Railwaymen and Transport Workers for help. This dispute was patched up without a strike ; but early the following year, 1921, the Government suddenly decontrolled the mining industry and handed it back to the colliery owners. As the post-war slump was then setting in, and coal prices were falling fast, the owners announced large wage-reductions and an extension of working hours. The Miners' Federation rejected these terms, and again called on its partners for support.

The question then arose whether, if the Railwaymen and Transport Workers agreed to strike in sympathy with the Miners, the Miners' Federation would agree to hand over to the Triple Alliance the power to settle on its behalf on such terms as their partners considered to be expedient in face of the slump. To this the Miners would not agree ; and the other Unions, after actually issuing strike notices, called them off on this ground at the last moment, leaving the Miners' Federation to fight alone. The day on which this was done came to be known in the Labour movement as 'Black Friday'. It was the end of the Triple Industrial Alliance, though a half-hearted attempt to resuscitate it was made at a later stage. Meanwhile, the Miners went down to inevitable defeat.

At this point it is necessary to go back to the situation which existed at the end of the war in November 1918. Almost every Trade Union had been preparing a programme of demands for presentation as soon as the fighting was over ; and the Government saw itself threatened with strikes in many industries besides those included in the Triple Alliance. In these circumstances Lloyd George summoned, early in 1919, a National Industrial Conference, to which all Trade Unions and employers' associations were invited, to consider general terms of settlement for industry as a whole. The Unions included in the Alliance, and also the Engineers, refused to take part ; but most other Trade Unions and most of the employers' bodies accepted. The Trade Unions represented set up a Committee to negotiate with a committee of employers : Arthur Henderson became chairman, and I secretary, of this body.

Thus, by the autumn of 1919, there were two other bodies in being, besides the Parliamentary Committee of the Trades Union Congress, which were representing important sections of the Trade Union movement and attempting to deal with matters of national policy. These were the Trade Union Committee of the National Industrial Conference and the Mediation Committee set up to handle the national railway strike—this latter being based mainly on the Unions of Railwaymen and Transport Workers. It had become evident that either the Trades Union Congress would have to take over at least some functions of industrial co-ordination, or a new body, designed for this purpose, would have to be set up. Discussions which followed between the three bodies resulted in an agreed plan, under which the Trades Union Congress was to be given wider functions and powers and its Parliamentary Committee was to be replaced by a General Council more fully representative of the main industrial groups. This plan, which I largely drafted on behalf of a joint committee of the three bodies, was accepted in a modified form by the annual Trades Union Congress of 1920, but did not come into force till the autumn of 1921—too late to affect the events arising out of the coal dispute of that year.

From 1921 onwards, the Trades Union Congress had, then, a General Council elected by the whole Congress by groups in the main industries and occupational categories. This meant that each leading Union was practically certain of being represented—whereas for the old Parliamentary Committee the election had been by the whole Congress, without any division into groups. In practice, the new plan gave the leading figures in the big Unions what were virtually safe seats. At the same time the General Council split up, for certain purposes, into a number of groups representing broad occupational categories. Two seats on the Council were specially reserved for women workers.

The Council, thus reconstituted, was given only very limited powers—much less than had been contemplated in the original draft scheme. The separate Unions were not prepared to surrender into its hands any power to prescribe or co-ordinate policies. Each Union, or Federation of Unions in a particular industry or occupation, reserved its right to frame its own policy, to conduct its own negotiations, to decide when to strike or not to strike. The General Council was given no power to negotiate—much less to call a strike ; and no provision was made for organising any form of sympathetic action under its auspices. The only new power it acquired—and that only in 1924—was that of adjudicating in disputes between Unions ; and even then it was armed with no sanctions except the power to recommend to Congress the exclusion of a Trade Union which refused to accept its decision. The Council did, however, acquire new functions, without corresponding powers. Its scope was widened to include such matters as the conducting of research, the drawing up of a 'charter' of working-class industrial demands, and the general consideration of matters of common economic policy. In effect, despite its limited powers over the affiliated Unions, the Council became a much more influential body than the Parliamentary Committee had been.

Its value was soon put to the test. In 1925 the Miners' Federation, again faced with a crisis arising out of depression following on the unwise return to the gold standard at the pre-war parity, made a renewed appeal for help, this time not to the defunct Triple Industrial Alliance but to the General Council. Under strong pressure from Trade Union opinion, the Council felt compelled to rally to the Miners' support ; but it had no power to call anyone out on strike. In these circumstances, it resorted to a method which had been already used for a political purpose in 1920, to stop the danger of Great Britain going to war against the Soviet Union in support of the Poles. In that case, the Trade Unions and the Labour Party had acted together, forming a Council of Action and threatening to call a General Strike unless Lloyd George abandoned his war plans. Supported by the main body of public opinion, the Council of Action had been remarkably effective, and no strike had needed to be called. In face of the mining crisis, the General Council decided, not to issue strike notices itself, but to summon a Special Conference of Trade Union Executives and place upon them the responsibility of authorising it, if they thought fit, to issue a call to strike. For the time being, in 1925, the crisis passed. The Government made temporary concessions to the Miners' Federation, in order to allow itself time to make preparations for resisting the strike threat. But the crisis recurred in 1926 ; and this time the Conferences of Executives, meeting again, actually issued the call to which the workers responded with the 'General Strike'.

The 'General Strike' was not in fact general, or meant to be. The Trade Unions called it a 'National Strike'; but the name 'General Strike' stuck. Actually, the groups called out in support of the Miners were, at first, only railwaymen and other transport workers, iron and steel workers, builders and printers. A few more groups were called out just before the end.

Although the General Council had not called the strike on its own authority, it had to take charge of it ; for there was no other body available.* No sooner had it begun than the very same issue as had wrecked the Triple Alliance arose. Who was entitled to arrive at a settlement ? The only question at stake—except those connected with the legal and political aspects of the conflict—was that of the terms under which the miners were to work. Was this still a matter on which the Miners' Federation was entitled to have the final word, or were the Unions whose members had struck in the miners' support now entitled to decide on what terms the coal dispute should be ended ? Throughout the ten days the General Strike lasted this was being argued about behind the scenes. The General Council insisted on its right to act on behalf of the entire movement : the Miners' leaders insisted that they were responsible solely to their own Delegate Conference, and could not go against its wishes. Neither side would budge ; and in the end this was the ground on which the General Council called off the strike, leaving the Miners to fight on alone. No doubt, most of them were glad to find an excuse ; for when the Government had clearly decided to fight to a finish it was evident that victory could not be achieved without revolution, than which nothing was further from either leaders' or strikers' thoughts. The Government, indeed, had quite deliberately forced a 'show-down' by breaking off negotiations on a flimsy pretext before the strike began ; and the General Council, which had never expected to be forced into it, was always at a loss how to handle the situation.

Thus, the General Council, though Congress had given it no negotiating powers, had to demand them from the Miners when it had taken over the conduct of the strike which the Conference of Trade Union Executives had authorised ; but it was in a weak position *vis-à-vis* the Miners because it had no formal authority to do what it was claiming. The Miners, for their part, were unreasonable in expecting the other Unions to strike in their support without being allowed any part in deciding on the terms of settlement. Of course, the question ought to have been cleared up in advance, especially after the experience of 1921. That it was not is pretty strong evidence that the General Council did not expect to have to implement the threat to strike.

After 1926, this question of the General Council's powers in a general or sympathetic strike receded into the background.

*The Conference of Trade Union Executives, which authorised the General Council to act, had no permanent organ of its own.

Strikes of the kind at issue were outlawed by the Trade Unions and Trade Disputes Act of 1927;* and in any event the Trade Union movement was in no mood to repeat its experience. But a new issue almost at once arose; for in 1927 a group of big employers headed by Sir Alfred Mond (later Lord Melchett) of Imperial Chemical Industries approached the General Council with a proposal for a general discussion of relations between Capital and Labour; and the General Council accepted the invitation, though it came not from the recognised central employers' bodies—the Federation of British Industries and the National Confederation of Employers' Organisations—but from an unofficial group. The defeat of the General Strike—and subsequently of the Miners—had left the Trade Unions weak and in fear of a general attack on established standards; and the General Council leapt at the chance of coming to terms with a powerful group of employers who preferred industrial peace to an attempt to rout the Unions in an all-out conflict.

The discussions which followed are commonly known as the 'Mond-Turner' conversations (Ben Turner, the leader of the woollen workers, was Chairman of the General Council when they began). The Council was criticised for taking part in them, both on grounds of policy (especially by Arthur Cook, the Miners' leader) and on the ground that its action was *ultra vires*. Actually, in the end, little came of the talks—little, that is, in concrete arrangements, but a good deal in preventing head-on conflict from being precipitated by the more militant employers' groups. Reports were produced, proposing the establishment of a joint council representing the General Council and the big employers' organisations—a project which had been advocated by Arthur Henderson at the time of the National Industrial Conference of 1919—and also recommending certain reforms in the handling of unemployment. But when it came to the point, the Federation of British Industries and the Employers' Confederation were not prepared to accept the plan; and all that resulted was a very vague arrangement for consultation, of which little use was made. The whole affair did nevertheless have a substantial effect in turning the General Council into a body more regularly concerning itself both with general matters of industrial relations and with wider issues of economic policy; and during the 1930s its development in these fields went practically without challenge,

*For the legal position as a whole, see Chapter VII.

and its influence expanded without change in its constitutional powers. The way was made smooth for the big developments of joint consultation at the national level which came about during the second World War.

These developments differed from the 'Mond-Turner' proposals in that the initiative was taken by the Government—mainly after the Labour Party entered it in 1940. The 'Mond-Turner' plan had involved a joint body of employers and Trade Unionists to consider industrial and economic questions apart from the Government, and with a view to bringing joint pressure upon it. The plan was announced as a step towards 'industrial self-government', designed to allow industry to issue orders to 'politicians', rather than *vice-versa* ; but the joint consultation which grew up during the second World War took the form of Joint Councils formed under government auspices to advise the Government and its departments, with government representatives playing an active part at every stage. The difference was no doubt largely due to the fact that the nation was at war and its industry under state control directed to the war effort. The effect in any case was to establish a form of consultation much less dangerous than if employers' associations and Trade Unions had come together in a joint pressure group directed against the Government—and perhaps against the consumers.

War conditions led to a further rapid expansion in the work of the General Council, which was responsible both for the Trade Union side of the general consultative machinery that was set up and also for co-ordinating the work of the special Joint Advisory Councils attached to each main department and of the regional and local bodies working with the Ministries of Labour, Production, Supply, and other economic services. As a large part of this machinery was continued into the post-war period, and became part of the regular machinery of post-war economic planning, the General Council found itself with a permanently expanded range of functions, requiring a steadily expanding staff of specialists. It is a far cry from the two rooms, occupied by one secretary and an assistant, of the Trades Union Congress of 1914 to the complex organisation and considerable staff of the T.U.C. of to-day.

Yet, as we shall see later, the General Council—and indeed the Trades Union Congress itself—still falls a long way short of acting as an agency entitled to formulate a common policy in any way binding on the affiliated Unions. Nor has the General Council expressed any wish to be endowed with the powers that would authorise it to act in this way. It has, for example, again and again expressed its disapproval of proposals to give it power to formulate a common wage policy (often called a 'national wages policy') for the entire movement ; and Congress has rejected resolutions demanding such a policy. The General Council has repeatedly affirmed its faith in the advantages of the method of negotiating about wages separately, industry by industry or trade by trade. It has accepted the traditional structure which leaves each Union the master of its own affairs, in accordance with its own constitutional arrangements for consulting its members. The growth of its powers has been much more advisory than compulsive, much more politico-economic than industrial. The experience of the General Strike, far from making for greater centralisation of power, caused the Trade Unions to shrink back from it, as having all too dangerous potentialities.

II. TRADES COUNCILS

In each town or substantial industrial area there is normally a federal body, called a Trades Council, or sometimes a Trades and Labour Council. This body links together most of the Trade Union branches in the area, and also local Unions, where they still survive. There is no compulsion on any branch to join ; and in fact the total paid-up membership of Trades Councils recognised by the Trades Union Congress in 1952 was only three millions as compared with a T.U.C. membership of eight millions. This big difference was accounted for mainly by three factors—failure of branches to affiliate, payment of fees on less than the full membership on the books, and the non-inclusion of Scottish and Northern Irish Councils, which are separately affiliated to the Scottish and Irish Trades Union Congresses. Other factors were the absence of Trades Councils in scattered areas, and the existence of some Councils not recognised by the T.U.C.—usually because of alleged Communist activity on their part. Recognised Trades Councils making returns to the T.U.C. numbered 531 : the number of Trade Union branches affiliated to these Councils was 15,561.

Trades Councils go back a long way ; but few of them can trace a continuous existence further back than 1860, when the present London Trades Council was set up. Before that date, they went by a variety of names—in London, at one period, Metropolitan Trades' Committee ; in Glasgow, Trades' Guardian Association. In the first half of the nineteenth century they usually came into being as special joint committees to support a particular strike or agitation, and often went out of existence when the immediate job was done. In the great Trade Union wave of the 1830s, in addition to local Councils, there were created a number of County Trades' Associations, based partly on Trade Unions and partly on local Councils ; but these were swept away during the collapse of 1834. New local Councils, or Committees, were continually being founded and going out of existence in the 1840s and 1850s ; but a new epoch began with the formation of the London Trades Council as the outcome of a special joint committee set up to aid the builders in their struggle of 1859.

From 1860 until the Trades Union Congress Parliamentary Committee took over some of its functions ten years later the London Trades Council played an important part in the national Trade Union movement as well as locally. A number of the principal Unions—especially such 'Amalgamated Societies' as those of the Engineers and Carpenters—had their head offices in London ; and the national leaders of these bodies took the London Trades Council seriously, and used it for a number of purposes for which no national body existed. The L.T.C. compiled and published the first national Trade Union Directory : It established regular correspondence with Trades Councils in other areas, and advised on the constitution of new ones. Most important of all, it became the body to which any Trade Union involved in a strike or lock-out which it could not carry through with its own resources appealed for help, both in the form of money and in that of circulars urging Trade Unions everywhere to come to the rescue. The London Trades Council was not prepared to give such help to any Trade Union that asked for it. On the contrary, it scrutinised each appeal closely and, refusing many, constituted itself a sort of censor of the legitimacy of strike action. Dominated by the moderates at the head of the Amalgamated Societies and by their friends such as George Odger, the L.T.C. got itself disliked, not only by the entire left wing, but also by some of the Trade Unions in the North, which resented the pretensions of the Londoners. Nevertheless, it did an important piece of work, and was in some respects a much more efficient co-ordinator than the Trades Union Congress which took its place in this field.

The London Trades Council was a political almost as much as an industrial body. It was the centre for organising demonstrations of the London workers and for taking up any current issue that aroused widespread working-class interest. Sometimes it did the job itself: sometimes it took part in setting up a special agency or committee—for example to welcome Garibaldi. It had a rival in the London Working Men's Association, formed in 1866: as we saw, this body convened the national Trade Union Conference of 1867 when the L.T.C. refused. But the L.T.C., and not the L.W.M.A., was the body most closely associated with the International Working Men's Association of 1864 and with the agitation for the Reform Act which became law in 1867. Its connection with the I.W.M.A. developed out of its recognised function of acting as host to foreign workers' delegations visiting London: for it was out of the visit of the French delegates to the London International Exhibition of 1862 that the I.W.M.A. arose.

When the great struggle for legal recognition of the Trade Unions began, the L.T.C. suffered some decline in importance; for the Amalgamated Societies in London decided to conduct their campaign through a specially constituted joint body—the Conference of Amalgamated Trades—which excluded most of the London Trade Unions. It remained, however, an important auxiliary, and played its part in getting more Trades Councils set up to participate in the struggle, and also in helping Unions involved in strikes during the boom period of the early 'seventies. It maintained its pre-eminent position in the Trades Council movement and as the only common agency of the London trades—for the L.W.M.A. soon disappeared. In 1895, in common with other Trades Councils, it was expelled from the Trades Union Congress; but before this its political importance had begun to decline as new agencies were set up for carrying on the campaign for independent Labour representation in Parliament and on local government authorities. The L.T.C. gave only small help to the London dockers in 1889, when it was still dominated by the old craft Unions. But the effect of the Dock Strike and of the New Unionism was to bring in a flood of new members and of new societies, headed by the branches of the Dockers' Union.

The New Unionists soon began to play a leading part in the Trades Councils, not only in London but also in many other areas ; and under their influence, a good many became Trades and Labour Councils, admitting local Socialist and other working-class bodies as well as Trade Union branches. As early as 1891 the L.T.C. decided to raise a fund for running candidates in national and local elections ; but the work was handed over to a separate Labour Representation League, and went out of the Council's hands.

Already, in the 1890s, the L.T.C. was being faced by a further problem. Separate Trades Councils were beginning to come into existence round the edges of the Metropolitan area and to divert members from it. The L.T.C. considered, but rejected, a proposal to form local Sub-Councils under its control ; and the number and importance of the separate Councils continued to grow to its detriment. In 1900, when the national Labour Representation Committee was formed, the L.T.C. did not at once join, but set up a separate Political Committee of its own. In 1903, it changed its mind and joined the L.R.C., but great confusion developed because it maintained its own Political Committee without any co-ordination with the increasing number of local L.R.C.s and Trades and Labour Councils in the London area. The mess was not cleared up until 1914, when the London Labour Party was established as a body entirely separate from the L.T.C.

There were similar confusions in other areas. Right up to 1918 the Labour Party worked largely through local Trades and Labour Councils, which performed both political and industrial functions. In some areas there were two bodies—a Trades Council and a local L.R.C.: in some, even two rival Trades Councils, one purely Trade Unionist, and the other a Trades and Labour Council, combining industrial with political functions. Then, towards the end of the first World War, the Labour Party began, under its new constitution, to set up local Labour Parties in every parliamentary division throughout the country, transforming, where it could, the local Trades and Labour Councils into Labour Parties. This led to the formation of a large number of new Trades Councils, made up entirely of Trade Union branches; and thereafter, almost everywhere, the Trade Union branches found themselves called upon to join both a Trades Council and a Labour Party. In some big towns central Trades and Labour

Councils continued to exist for the whole town, while local Labour Parties were set up in the constituencies within it. In other cases the central Councils became Central Labour Parties, and new Trades Councils were set up. The general effect was that the Trades Councils lost their political functions and were left without any central body to co-ordinate or direct their activities ; for the Trades Union Congress, since their expulsion in 1895, had ceased to have any formal connection with them or to take any responsibility for their affairs, whereas the growing Labour Party had made great use of them until it was ready to establish separate local machinery fully under its own control.

In the 1920s the Trades Councils had a reputation for 'leftness'. They came into their own during the General Strike, when most of them set up Councils of Action to take charge of strike affairs, and many showed excellent organising capacity while the strike lasted. This episode drew attention to their importance ; and the Trades Union Congress General Council, partly in order to use them as its local agents in recruiting and propagandist campaigns and partly in the hope of keeping them out of Communist hands, began to take more notice of them. Actually, from 1925, the General Council has organised an Annual Conference of Trades Council representatives ; and this Conference elects a Trades Councils Consultative Committee, whose advice, like that of the Conference, the General Council can accept or reject as it thinks fit.

Trades Councils are narrowly limited in what they can do because they have very little money. In 1951 the total income of 531 recognised Councils from affiliation fees was only £32,000—about £60 a Council—barely enough to pay for meeting places and stamps for a Council of average size. A little more came from special effort funds and donations, but only a little. The Councils, save very few, could undertake nothing that cost money unless the cost was met by some other body, such as the T.U.C.

In these circumstances, the Trades Councils can be no more than meeting-places for local Trade Union delegates. Moreover, they suffer from the further weakness that they represent only branches of Trade Unions, and not Districts, though in many Unions the real local authority rests, in industrial matters, with the District rather than with the branch.* Trades Councils can debate local issues (or national issues for that matter) ; they can

*See pages 35ff.

pass resolutions ; they can send resolutions or deputations to the local authority or to one of its departments ; they can try to raise funds or give other help in local strikes ; and they can, with national help, conduct local Trade Union recruiting campaigns or organise public meetings in connection with current national movements or agitations. But more than this they cannot in most cases do, save in a quite exceptional emergency. They have no control at all over local industrial policy, which is in the hands of the separate Unions, although of course they can become involved in unofficial strike movements, usually at the cost of bringing down on themselves the displeasure of the General Council.

In many areas there are Federations of Trades Councils, often on a county basis. But these bodies suffer at least equally from financial weakness, as they depend on affiliation fees paid by the local Councils out of their exiguous incomes. Most of them are in practice no more than occasional conferences of delegates for the passing of resolutions and the discussion of regional organising problems.

Despite the limitations of the Trades Councils, their usefulness is undoubted. They bring together representatives from the different Trade Unions in an area, and provide a valuable centre for learning about the wider problems of the movement. Many a Trade Union leader has served part of his apprenticeship in Trades Council work. Without them, local contacts would exist only on the political side of the movement, through the local Labour Parties, which have usually larger resources. This would be unfortunate ; for common industrial problems also need attention. It is very regrettable that the extreme centralisation of British Trade Unionism leaves them with so little scope or power. It is, however, unlikely that anything much will be done in the near future to alter this situation. The leaders of the Trade Unions do not want to be faced with any alternative focusing-point of Trade Unionist sentiment and power. Ever since the rise of the New Unionism in the 1890s led them to expel the Trades Councils from the T.U.C. they have been suspicious of them as potentially left-wing irresponsible bodies, which, if they were stronger, might make the system of centralised national collective bargaining unworkable. Since the advent of Communism all their suspicions have been renewed and strengthened, and they have been determined, though they now see the need to recognise and help the Trades Councils, to keep a tight hold over them—which is the easier because they are so poor and can do so little without help.

A sharp contrast to this situation is presented by the development of Trade Unionism in France. There the movement grew up mainly round the local Councils (*Bourses du Travail*). There were few national Trade Unions : the usual structure was made up of independent local Unions (*syndicats*) federated simultaneously in the local *Bourses* and in national industrial or craft federations. The whole movement had very little money ; but what it had was mostly in the local *syndicats*, not in the national federations. Thus the local *syndicat* could finance a *Bourse* as easily as a federation ; and the French equivalent of the General Council was made up of equal groups of representatives of the federations and of the localities. More recently, since the rise of Communism, the French General Confederation of Labour has become a more centralised body ; but the power has gone straight to the Confederation more than to the national Unions or federations, and it has still to be exercised with much regard to the final ability of the local *syndicat* to go its own way.

Even in the United States, though Trade Union centralisation is high in comparison with the position in France, State Federations of Labor and even local federations have much more power and are much more active than Trades Councils or Federations of Trades Councils in Great Britain, mainly because they have much more money. This is the case also partly because the country is so large, and partly because it is divided into separate States, each with its own laws and politics ; but it is largely because American Trade Unionists are prepared to pay much higher dues. In Great Britain, the maintenance of national Trade Union organisation costs nearly all the money Trade Unionists are apparently willing to pay, leaving very little for local work. This means that Trades Councils have to go short.

III. THE SCOTTISH AND IRISH TRADES UNION CONGRESSES

Scotland has its own separate Trades Union Congress, which has met annually since 1897, except that no meeting was held in 1915. In 1951 the affiliated membership of the S.T.U.C. was about 750,000, drawn from 87 Trade Unions ; and there were also affiliated 50 local or area Trades Councils, a few of which had local subsidiaries in particular places within their areas. Of the affiliated Trade Unions, about twenty, with about 75,000 members, were Scottish Unions ; the remaining nine-tenths of the membership was made up of the Scottish Districts of Trade Unions operating throughout Great Britain. Most of the larger Scottish Unions are also affiliated to the British Trades Union Congress—the only considerable exception being the Scottish Transport and General Workers' Union, with about 6,000 members—a body which arose out of a dispute within the Transport and General Workers' Union at the Clyde docks. The largest entirely Scottish Unions in 1952 were the Scottish Horse and Motormen's Association (20,000), which refused to join the Transport and General Workers at the time of the great amalgamation after the first World War, the Scottish Bakers' Union (15,700), and the Scottish Typographical Association (7,300).

The fifty Trades Councils, and the 15 local Committees covering parts of the areas of four of them, are spread widely over most of the country, except that there are few of them in the Highlands or in mainly agricultural areas. The Scottish Farm Servants' Union, long an independent body, became in the 1930s a section of the Transport and General Workers' Union, but still maintains some degree of autonomy. The agricultural workers are not, however, highly organised.

The Scottish Trades Union Congress is divided into occupational groups on much the same lines as the British T.U.C. It elects a General Council ; but the members of this body are chosen by vote of all the delegates and not, as in the British Congress, by separate group voting. Trades Council representatives are eligible ; but in 1952, out of 12 members, only one was from a Trades Council (Edinburgh). Two others represented Scottish Trade Unions : the rest Scottish sections of British Unions. Four other Trades Council nominees were defeated.

Debates at the S.T.U.C. range over a wide field, including international and British as well as peculiarly Scottish affairs. Formally, the Scottish Congress is entirely independent of the British, and can adopt such policies as it pleases. In practice, its resolutions, when they deal with international or British affairs, are usually kept in line with British Trade Union and Labour Party policy. The Scottish General Council sometimes adjudicates on inter-union disputes, but usually when at least one of the parties is a purely Scottish Union. It attempts to prevent poaching by one Union on another, with a reasonable amount of success. It has a Women's Advisory Council, representing in 1952 about 131,000 members, and also a Youth Advisory Council, which was then attempting to persuade the affiliated Unions to make an intensive effort to organise juvenile workers. Like the British T.U.C., the Scottish Congress recognises both the Workers' Educational Association and the National Council of Labour Colleges : it also does a small amount of educational work of its own, by holding Summer Schools on Trade Union affairs. It is represented on the Council of Newbattle Abbey, the Scottish College which is the nearest equivalent to Ruskin College, but is not, like Ruskin, controlled exclusively by Trade Union and Co-operative representatives. So far (1953), Newbattle has received rather little Trade Union support, and has been saved from collapse only by the use of part of its premises by the Scottish Coal Board for its training courses.

In 1951-2 the General Council of the S.T.U.C. found itself involved in legal difficulties arising out of a dispute with the Glasgow Trades Council. This old-established body, like the London Trades Council,* had fallen under Communist influence, and had been adopting and publicising resolutions, dealing with international affairs, which ran counter to the policy of the S.T.U.C. The Scottish General Council not only disaffiliated the Glasgow Trades Council, but also attempted to transfer its assets to the control of a new provisional Executive set up by a specially summoned conference of Glasgow Trade Union delegates. The old Trades Council thereupon appealed to the law courts and procured an order forbidding the S.T.U.C. to interfere with its assets or to take over control. This did not prevent the Scottish General Council from proceeding with its plans to set up a new Trades Council ; but it left the disaffiliated Council still in being, and a contest for support then occurred between the two bodies. The S.T.U.C. also altered its rules in consequence of the outcome of the legal proceedings, in order to strengthen its powers to enforce compliance with its decisions on the Trades Councils affiliated to it. It may have been a consequence of this legal case that the British General Council, when it disaffiliated the London Trades Council in 1952, made no attempt to take over the assets or the control of the old Council.

*See page 135.

In Ireland there are two rival bodies seeking to act as central co-ordinating agencies for the Trade Union movement. In Northern Ireland the workers are organised mainly in Trade Unions which have their headquarters in Great Britain ; and the British Trade Unions have a substantial membership in the Irish Republic also. The Irish Trades Union Congress includes all, or nearly all, the Irish Sections of such Trade Unions, and also a number of separate Irish Unions, of which the largest is the Workers' Union of Ireland (25,000), led by James Larkin, son of the James Larkin who was the leader of the Irish Transport and General Workers' Union in the great Dublin strike shortly before the first World War. The Irish Trade Union Congress sets out to cover both the Irish Republic and Northern Ireland : in 1952 it had a total affiliated membership, excluding local Trades Councils, of about 215,000, and of these 153,000 were in Trade Unions with headquarters in Great Britain, and about 62,000 in purely Irish Unions, including a few confined to Northern Ireland. The largest membership in British Unions came from the Transport and General Workers (40,000), the Amalgamated Engineering Union (21,000), and the Amalgamated Society of Woodworkers (16,000). The National Union of Railwaymen was in process of transferring its Irish membership to a separate Irish Union. The largest of the purely Irish Unions, after the Workers' Union of Ireland, were the Irish National Teachers' Organisation, the Irish Women Workers' Union, the Post Office Workers' Union, and the Irish Bakers' Amalgamated Union (all between 8,000 and 5,000).

The chief rival of the Irish Trade Union Congress is the Congress of Irish Unions, which consists entirely of Unions with their headquarters in the Irish Republic. The Congress of Irish Unions takes a more definitely nationalistic attitude than the Irish T.U.C., and attempts to promote unity have repeatedly broken down. The Congress of Irish Unions is dominated by the Irish Transport and General Workers' Union (about 135,000), which is the largest Union in Ireland. This one Union accounted in 1952 for more than three-quarters of C.I.U.'s total membership of about 175,000. This membership was in effect confined to the Irish Republic, in which the C.I.U. had a larger following than the Irish Trade Union Congress. The only other Trade Union with more than 5,000 members belonging to the C.I.U. is the Irish Union of Distributive Workers and Clerks (about

15,000). The remaining membership is scattered among a number of small societies, mostly in direct competition with British-based Unions affiliated to the Irish T.U.C. The latter body has 11 affiliated local Trades Councils, 5 of them in Northern Ireland : the C.I.U. has only 5, all in the Republic. Dublin, Cork, Dundalk and Waterford all have rival Trades Councils attached to the two central bodies. These divisions are obviously a great source of weakness to the movement. It is difficult to overcome them because the desire to establish a nationalistic Trade Unionism in the Republic runs counter to the desire to maintain Trade Union unity between the Republic and Northern Ireland.

In 1953 there were in all over half a million Trade Unionists in Ireland, including about 42,000 in Trade Unions affiliated to neither the I.T.U.C. nor the C.I.U. Nearly 320,000 were in the Irish Republic, and about 194,000 in Northern Ireland. Of those in the Republic, about 273,000 belonged to Trade Unions with headquarters in the Republic, and 46,000 to Unions with headquarters in Great Britain. In Northern Ireland, on the other hand, 175,000 belonged to British-centred Unions, and about 10,000 to Unions with headquarters in Northern Ireland, and a mere 8,000 to Unions with their head offices in the Republic.

IV. INTERNATIONAL ORGANISATION

International Trade Union organisation began with the International Working Men's Association, founded in 1864 by British and French Trade Unionists as the sequel to meetings held during the London International Exhibition of 1862. The 'First International' was at the outset essentially a Trade Union body, based on the Trade Unions of London and Paris. The English participants were the leaders of the Trade Unions with headquarters in London—mainly the growing Amalgamated Societies: the French were Parisian craftsmen, representing a variety of small-scale skilled trades. Trade Unionism in France was only just beginning to emerge from a period of active repression, and was still barely tolerated. In Great Britain it was already well established, but was about to plunge into a great struggle for legal recognition. From this it was destined to emerge victorious ; but in France Trade Unionism was soon to be almost destroyed in the repression that followed the defeat of the Paris Commune in 1871.

From its foundation until 1870, when the outbreak of the Franco-Prussian War arrested its advance, Trade Unionism leapt forward in Western Europe ; and in a number of countries the workers' organisations became Sections of the International. This was the case in France, in Belgium, in Switzerland, and in parts of Italy and Spain, but never in Great Britain, where the Trade Union leaders, though personally active on the Council of the International, kept their organisations quite apart from it. Consequently, when the International collapsed in the 'seventies, its dissolution had no appreciable effect in Great Britain. International contacts, never made except by a few leaders, simply ceased ; and nothing occurred to renew them until continental Trade Unionism began to recover from its eclipse, and to feel out for renewed contacts. These were made largely under Socialist auspices, with some admixture of Anarchist influences, in a series of partial movements which led up to the calling of the two rival International Labour and Socialist Congresses held in Paris in 1889. Further Congresses followed, in the course of which the Anarchists were driven out ; and in 1900 the Socialists set up an International Socialist Bureau to arrange future Congresses and to take charge between them. This was the 'Second International'. The following year, largely on German and French initiative, a quite separate International Federation of Trade Unions was founded, with headquarters in Berlin ; but the British Trades Union Congress, instead of joining this body, continued to send delegates to the Congresses called by the International Socialist Bureau ; and, as we have seen, the much less representative General Federation of Trade Unions* became, and remained till after the first World War, the British Section of the I.F.T.U. This meant, in effect, that the British movement played little part in the I.F.T.U.—or indeed in the international movement as a whole ; for the Trades Union Congress took no regular part in the work of the Second International. Soon, however, distinct Trade Internationals began to be set up for particular industrial and occupational groups ; and a number of British Trade Unions, including the Miners and Textile Workers, and later the Transport Workers, played an active role in these specialised Internationals, which, up to 1914, were mostly centred in Germany.

International Trade Unionism was disrupted by the first World War ; but after 1918 both the I.F.T.U. and the Trade

*See page 126.

Internationals were speedily reconstructed, and a number of new Trade Internationals were set up. At this point, the movement had to meet the challenge of the Russian Revolution. Under the leadership of the new Soviet Trade Union movement, a rival body was established—the Red International of Labour Unions—made up, apart from the Russians, chiefly of Minority Movements in the non-Communist countries in rebellion against the official Trade Union leadership. This movement never got any substantial hold in Great Britain, and presently the Soviet Trade Unions and the British Trades Union Congress formed a joint committee in the hope of being able to work together, and the British took the lead in trying to arrange an accommodation which would bring the Soviet Trade Unions into the I.F.T.U. This attempt failed ; and presently relations between the British and the Russians became more strained. Meanwhile the French Trade Unions had split into two rival bodies, one Communist and the other not ; and the German Trade Unions had been almost disrupted by the struggle between the rival tendencies. The I.F.T.U. was in these circumstances largely ineffective—the more so because the American, Canadian, Australian, and other non-European movements stood aloof. The Nazi victory in Germany destroyed the German Trade Unions, as Fascism had previously destroyed the Italian. International Trade Unionism shrank up into a very small affair, though a few of the Trade Internationals—above all, the International Transport Workers' Federation—managed to maintain a lively existence. Transport, of course, lends itself particularly to international organisation because of the position of seafarers and their relation to workers at the ports.

The I.F.T.U. maintained a shadowy existence through the second World War. Thereafter, in 1945, it was superseded by a World Federation of Trade Unions set up at a Conference attended by the Soviet Trade Unions and their allies, and also by the American Congress of Industrial Organisations, as well as by the bodies which had belonged to the I.F.T.U. between the Wars. But this attempt to bridge the gulf between Communist and non-Communist Trade Unions was short-lived. The American Federation of Labor refused to take part in it ; and by 1949 both the British Trades Union Congress and the American C.I.O. had had enough. The headquarters of the W.F.T.U. had been placed in France, where the Communists had captured the reunited

Trade Union movement ; and its secretary was a Communist. The British and Americans accused him and the Executive majority of using the W.F.T.U. for Communist propaganda. They withdrew from affiliation, followed by a number of other national bodies, and set up a new organisation—the International Confederation of Free Trade Unions—which the American Federation of Labor was also induced to join. The French Trade Unions split again, and a small section (*Force Ouvrière*) joined the I.C.F.T.U., the majority remaining with its rival. A similar situation developed in Italy. The West Germans came into the I.C.F.T.U., while the East Germans remained with the W.F.T.U. As we have seen, a struggle then developed between the two bodies for the adhesion of the developing Trade Union movements in Africa and Asia.*

The situation was complicated by the existence in certain countries of separate Christian Trade Union movements, which formed an International of their own, and could not be induced to merge with the I.C.F.T.U. But this separate movement exists only in a few countries,† though in Italy the non-Communist Trade Union movement is largely under Christian influence.

After 1949, the I.C.F.T.U. and the W.F.T.U. both tried to capture the sectional Trade Internationals, which had been refusing to sink their identity entirely in the W.F.T.U. The outcome was that in many industries there arose rival Trade Internationals (or Secretariats) attached to the two main contending bodies. The W.F.T.U., on its foundation, had succeeded to the recognition formerly given to the I.F.T.U. as a consultative agency for the inter-governmental International Labour Organisation ; and it was given a similar status in relation to the new Specialised Agencies of the United Nations, such as the Food and Agriculture Organisation. After the split, this recognition was not withdrawn from the W.F.T.U., but was extended to the I.C.F.T.U. and to the I.F.C.T.U. (the Christian International) as well. In practice, however, the W.F.T.U. ceased to have any close connection with either the I.L.O. or the other United Nations agencies.

The I.C.F.T.U. has been giving considerable attention to the development of Trade Unions in the backward countries—especially in colonial or former colonial areas. The British Trades Union Congress and the C.I.O. in particular have voted large

*See pages 30ff. †See page 32.

sums for this purpose. Missions have been sent to help in organisation ; office equipment and literature, and also films and filmstrips, have been supplied ; and more recently regional conferences have been held, and Trade Union educational centres established to train officers in the backward countries in administrative and organising work. A College of this kind was opened in India in 1952.

These forms of help are inevitably mixed up with the struggle against Communism. The I.C.F.T.U. is endeavouring to guide the movements in the less advanced countries along the lines which Trade Unionism has followed in the Western democracies, and to prevent it from becoming either an agency of Communist propaganda or a mainly political movement dominated by the nationalist politicians of the countries concerned. The W.F.T.U. on the other hand has been taking the part of colonial nationalism in its attempt to win the Trade Unions to its side. The American Federation of Labor, outdoing the rest of the I.C.F.T.U. in anti-Communist fervour, has been conducting an independent campaign of its own in the backward countries, and in Japan, instead of co-operating with its partners in the I.C.F.T.U.

The Communist theory of democratic centralism involves central control in every sphere, as far as it is practicable ; and this applies to the W.F.T.U., though modified by tactical considerations. The constitution of the I.C.F.T.U., on the other hand, guarantees the independence of each affiliated national body, and is so drafted as to prevent domination by the larger movements. Its Executive is chosen on a regional basis—5 from continental Europe, 2 from Great Britain, 4 from North America, 2 from Latin America, 1 from the West Indies, 3 from Asia and the Middle East, 1 from Australia and New Zealand together, and 1 from Africa. The I.C.F.T.U. Constitution also provides for the setting up of Regional Organisations in the main areas of the world ; and such machinery already existed in 1952 for Europe, Asia, West Africa, the Near and Middle East, and Latin America, and was in preparation for East Africa. In Europe, the I.C.F.T.U. is badly hampered by its weakness in France and Italy, by divisions in Holland and Belgium, and by the eclipse of Trade Unionism in Spain under the Franco régime. The Trade Unions in the satellite countries are, of course, wholly under Communist domination : the Yugoslav Trade Unions became independent of both Internationals after the rupture with the Soviet Union. As against these deficiences, there has been a vigorous revival in Western Germany ; and the Scandinavian Trade Unions retain their undivided strength.

The British Trade Unions are to-day much more internationally minded than they have been in the past. In this they are not peculiar ; for in Great Britain the ordinary person has been shaken sharply out of his former insularity by the change in the world position of the British economy as well as by the threat of war destruction beyond all previous imagination. But they are uncomfortable in their new-found internationalism. Their leaders find it a good deal easier to get on with the Americans of the Congress of Industrial Organisations than with any 'foreigners' who speak a different language ; and the capture of most of the French Trade Unionists by Communism removes the continental group with which it would be most natural for them to co-operate closely. The Germans are only now (1953) coming back into full association with the West, and are still subject to some suspicions—though in practice British and German Trade Union leaders appear to get on well. The I.C.F.T.U. depends too much on the British and the Americans of the C.I.O. acting closely together to be altogether at home in tackling the problems either of European Trade Unionism or of the newest movements in the colonial countries.

On the other side of the 'curtain', Trade Unionism in the Soviet Union, in China, and in the satellite countries is definitely part of the Communist-dominated State machine ; and it is very difficult for the Unions of the Western, 'democratic' group to arrive with them at any common language. The clash occurs chiefly in France and Italy and in the countries in which the West and the Soviet Union are contending for mastery of the rising forces of democratic nationalism—for example, India, Malaya, and Japan. This struggle is being fought out both politically and industrially, in the international Socialist movement as well as in the Trade Unions ; and at present (1953) it would be foolish to prophesy the outcome. It is indeed a race between the ability—and the willingness—of the developed countries of the West to bring aid for the technical and economic development of the backward countries, without attaching political 'strings' that offend nationalist sentiments, and the operation of forces which drive the peoples of these countries into a despairing revolutionism that excellently suits the book of Communism. The danger is that, in attempting to build up anti-Communist Trade Union movements, the Trade Unions of the West may come to appear as the allies of imperialism against national aspirations and may antagonise the workers whom they are seeking to help towards independent forms of economic organisation. This danger especially besets the American Federation of Labor ; but it is not absent from the well-meant attempts of the I.C.F.T.U., especially where, as in the French colonies, the French Trade Unions belonging to *Force Ouvrière* have close connections with the French civil servants (*fonctionnaires*) and settlers and with the groups that have been most affected by the French policy of 'assimilation'. But the danger exists also in British colonies—in Malaya and in East Africa, above all.

CHAPTER VI

TRADE UNION FINANCE

THERE are no particulars concerning the financial affairs of all Trade Unions; but nearly all the big Trade Unions and many of the smaller are registered under the Trade Union Acts, and the Chief Registrar of Friendly Societies publishes an annual statement dealing with their finances. For 1951 the statement covered 413 Trade Unions, with 8,287,000 members, out of a total of 704 Unions, with 9,480,000 members, known to the Ministry of Labour. It can therefore be taken as fairly representing the general position of the movement.

During 1951, these 8,287,000 Trade Unionists paid to their Unions a total sum of £16,226,000, or not much short of £2, or about 9d. a week. The total income of the 413 Trade Unions, from all sources, including invested funds, was £18,246,000. Their accumulated funds at the end of the year amounted to £64,825,000—an increase of £2,675,000 over the previous year. Funds have been increasing steadily for many years past: in 1945 they amounted, for roughly the same group of Unions, to £42,417,000, and in 1941 to £27,525,000. Thus, in recent years, the Trade Unions have been living well within their income. They have, indeed, being doing this ever since 1933—that is, since the serious depression of 1931-33 came to an end. Even during those years the excess of expenditure over income was not great: the last year in which there was a serious fall in accumulated funds was 1926—the year of the General Strike. In that year, total funds fell from £12,556,000 to £8,478,000. At the end of 1938 the total had reached over £20,000,000.

The main source of Trade Union income is the weekly contribution paid by each member. A few of the non-manual workers' associations, which pay few or no benefits, have annual subscriptions; but the normal practice is to charge a weekly sum—though in many cases the members prefer to pay several weeks' contributions at a time. The rate of contribution differs considerably from one Union to another; and a good many Unions have several rates of contribution for different sections of their membership. For adult men the weekly rate, apart from a few exceptional cases, ranges from 6d. or 7d. to 2s. or 2s. 6d.—the lower sums being paid mainly by less skilled workers and the higher by skilled workers for a much wider range of benefits. For women members the contributions are usually much lower, from 4d. to 6d. a week; but a number of Unions allow women, if they choose, to pay at the men's rates and, by doing so, to qualify both for higher benefits and for full rights to hold office. In the Unions which have several rates of contribution, the right to hold the higher offices is often limited to members paying at the higher rates. There are usually rules which disqualify from standing for office members who are in arrears with their contributions, and also rules which disqualify from voting those more than so many weeks in arrears.

It is not possible, for reasons of space, to give more than a few examples of scales of contribution. The National Union of General and Municipal Workers had in 1952 for full members an entrance fee of 1s. and a weekly contribution of 7d. Women could join at these rates, or could become 'half-members', eligible only for some branch offices, at a rate of 6d. entrance fee and 4d. a week contribution. The Transport and General Workers had in 1952 the same rates of weekly contributions for adults, but raised them in 1953 to 8d. and 5d. But in the T. and G.W.U. there is in addition what is called 'quarterage'—a sum of 6d. for men and 3d. for women levied in the first week of each quarter and used to finance the Union's political expenses and also to provide benevolent funds for the branches to expend at their discretion. The N.U.G.M.W. does not levy this 'quarterage', but allocates most of the first week's contribution in each quarter to these purposes. The T. and G.W.U. has special rates of contribution for members under 18 years of age—5d. for boys and 4d. for girls (4d. and 3d. up to 1953). It also allows women or girls, if they prefer, to pay at the men's rates.

These rates can be taken as fairly typical of the lowest contributions charged by the Trade Unions of manual workers. At the opposite extreme stands the London Society of Compositors, composed exclusively of highly skilled workers and providing a very wide range of friendly benefits. The L.S.C. bases its rate of contribution on the earnings of its members: the rate ranges from 4s. 6d. a week for those earning under £5 for full-time work to 9s. 6d. for those earning over £9, with reductions for members who are employed for only part of the week. There is in addition a variable entrance fee of at least £1. There are special rates for apprentices, rising year by year from 9d. to 2s. a week for those who join at the beginning of their apprenticeship to as much as 5s. 6d. for those who become members only in the final year. Members who have left the trade pay 6s. 6d.; and there is a special provision for elderly members working only part-time to pay 1s. 6d., without getting rights to benefit or office. This is much the highest scale of contributions I know of in any Union in Great Britain ; but even higher scales exist in the United States, where the general run of contributions is much higher.

The Amalgamated Engineering Union can be taken as an example of a Trade Union which has a number of different rates for members of different degrees of skill. The Section I member of the A.E.U. pays at the rate of 2s. a week : membership of this Section is open only to skilled craftsmen who are actually getting the standard rate of wages for their craft, and each candidate has to be formally proposed and approved. Sections II and III need not be described, as they are survivals, no longer open to new entrants. Section IV consists of apprentices (but the apprenticeship need not be under a formal agreement). Members in this Section pay 3d. a week, or 5d. if they wish to qualify for unemployment benefit. Section V, described as the 'Industrial Section', is open to any male worker in the engineering industry, irrespective of skill : its members pay 1s. a week ; but there is also a Section VA, whose members pay only 8d., and are not eligible for unemployment benefit. Women form a separate Section, and pay 6d. if over 18 years of age, or 3d. if under 18. Qualifications for office vary from Section to Section ; and there are a number of special provisions for particular types of members—*e.g.* seagoing engineers.

Let us take finally another type of financial structure, in which rates of contribution vary from district to district. The Amalgamated Association of Operative Cotton Spinners is centralised only for certain purposes, such as general wage-negotiations and the general safeguarding of trade interests. It is made up partly of branches and partly of 'Provinces' which consist of a number of branches; each Province or independent branch fixes its own rate of contributions and provides its own range of benefits. The local or provincial weekly contributions for skilled spinners range from 2s. to 3s. (with one exceptional case of 1s. 6d.). Out of this 1s. is payable to the Amalgamated Association: the rest is retained by the branch or Province. The less skilled members—the piecers—pay from 6d. to 1s., sometimes with more than one rate in the same area. These sums are retained entirely by the Provinces or branches. There is a quarterly political contribution, except for those who 'contract out', of 8d., out of which 5d. goes to the central body, and 3d. is kept for local political purposes.

In most Trade Unions there are provisions which allow special levies to be added to the regular rates of contribution when funds run low. These levies are made chiefly by Unions which provide a substantial range of friendly benefits, especially superannuation benefit. But they are also sometimes used to supplement the central funds of Unions, such as the Spinners, which have only a fixed contribution to the centre and leave a substantial part of their funds in their branches or districts. This situation usually arises when what was formerly a mere federation of independent local Unions has been converted into a national Union without complete abolition of local differences.

Some Unions levy a separate contribution for political purposes, over and above the regular weekly payments. Others prefer to allocate the regular payment for certain weeks in the year to a Political Fund. Whatever the method of financing political expenditure, the Political Fund has by law to be kept separate from the Union's other funds, and contribution to it cannot be made a condition of membership.

How do the Trade Unions actually spend the sums which they receive from their members, or derive from interest on their substantial investments ? For the answer, we must again have recourse to the Table published annually by the Chief Registrar of Friendly Societies. The figures, which apply only to registered Trade Unions, are set out fully in Appendix 4.* Here we can be content with a broad summary.

During the six years 1946-1951, registered Trade Unions had an average annual income of almost £17,000,000, and spent on an average about £13,380,000. Of this total expenditure, nearly 57 per cent was accounted for by working expenses. Benefits of all kinds accounted for nearly 33 per cent. Political expenses, paid for out of the special Political Funds of the Unions, accounted for but 3 per cent of the total. The balance of nearly 7½ per cent was accounted for by grants for various purposes, payments to federal bodies such as the Trades Union Congress, educational work, and other miscellaneous expenses. Of all the benefits the

*See page 299

most costly was superannuation benefit, which, though it existed only in a few Unions of skilled workers, was responsible for nearly 13 per cent of total expenditure. Sickness and accident benefits came next, accounting for more than 8 per cent of the total. Funeral benefit cost 3½ per cent, unemployment benefit 1.7 per cent, and dispute benefit hardly more than 1 per cent of total outgoings. Other benefits, including legal aid and benevolent grants to members in distress, came to 5.3 per cent. Thus, of every £1 paid in contributions or derived from interest on accumulated funds, 11s. 5d. went in administrative and organising costs—largely the costs of negotiation and of working the Union machine; about 6s. 6d. was paid back to the members in benefits; rather more than 7d. was spent on political activities as defined in the Trade Union Act of 1913; and the remaining 1s. 6d. was spread over all other forms of expenditure.

This distribution of expenditure stands in sharp contrast to the ways in which Trade Union money was spent in the 1920s and 1930s. The following Table shows the contrast by comparing with the post-war average the actual expenditure in four selected years—1926, the year of the General Strike; 1933, the closing year of the serious depression of the early 1930s; 1935, a year intermediate between the depression and the rearmament boom of 1937; and 1938, the last pre-war year.

PERCENTAGE DISTRIBUTION OF TRADE UNION EXPENDITURE IN CERTAIN YEARS

	Working Expenses	*Superannuation, Sickness and Accident and Funeral Benefits*	*Unemployment Benefit*	*Dispute Benefit*	*Other Benefits*	*Political Expenses*	*Other Expenses*
1946–51 (average)	56.8	24.6	1.7	1.1	5.3	3.0	7.5
1926 ..	22.1	15.2	13.7	42.0	1.7	0.8	4.6
1933 ..	39.4	31.5	15.8	2.9	4.7	1.5	4.2
1935 ..	41.7	31.3	10.6	3.7	5.1	2.7	4.9
1938 ..	43.8	28.8	11.5	2.0	5.3	1.5	7.1

In 1951 registered Trade Unions spent in all nearly £16,000,000, spread over 8,287,000 members, or about 38s. 2d. a member. In 1935, which was a fairly typical pre-war year, they spent £6,321,000, on 3,795,000 members—or about 33s. a member. This means that in real terms, allowing for the change in prices, much less is being spent than before the war. Working expenses have increased from £2,633,000 in 1935 to £9,098,000 in 1951—that is, by 245 per cent ; but working expenses per member have risen only from about 14s. to about 22s.—that is by 57 per cent, which is much less than the rise in costs. Benefits cost in all £3,209,000 in 1935, and £4,803,000 in 1951—a rise of less than 50 per cent, though membership and average costs had both more than doubled. In effect, the sharp fall in the sums spent on dispute benefit and unemployment benefit had caused a sharp rise in the *proportion* of total expenditure accounted for by working expenses, but the real sum per head spent in this way had fallen with rising membership. Trade Unions had not in fact increased their paid staffs in proportion to the numbers needing their services. Either they were working their full-time officers harder, or less time was needed for each member as membership increased, or more of the work was being done for no payment or for very small payments, by shop stewards and local spare-time officers. In fact, all three things had happened; the full-time official had a harder job; the time taken per member decreased; and a good deal of negotiation had come to be carried on at the establishment or workshop level.

Trade Union benefits fall into five main categories, to which must be added a sixth miscellaneous group. Dispute benefit is provided by practically all manual workers' Unions and by some Unions of 'blackcoats', but is absent from such bodies as the Unions in the Civil Service, including the Post Office. Closely allied to it is Victimisation benefit, payable to workers discharged on account of their Trade Union activities. This benefit is usually at a higher rate than ordinary Dispute benefit—often at the level of full wages. It, like Dispute benefit, has become much less important since Trade Unions have achieved full recognition in the great majority of occupations. It is sometimes paid by 'blackcoat' Unions which make no provision for ordinary Dispute benefit. The sum involved is not large enough to appear separately in the Registrar-General's returns. Some Unions pay Dispute benefit as an addition to Unemployment benefit for members out of work through disputes; but it is usually entirely separate.

The second main kind of benefit is Unemployment benefit. This was never nearly so widespread as Dispute benefit, and its importance has waned greatly since State benefit under the Unemployment Insurance Scheme was raised to a level just sufficient for subsistence and since it was made possible to supplement the State insurance benefit by grants from the Assistance Board. Trade Unions were never able, save in a very few cases, to afford Unemployment benefits high enough to cover subsistence needs; and they now make no attempt to do this, merely providing a supplement to what can be had from the State and in certain cases filling in gaps which the State scheme fails to cover. Certain smaller benefits—Emigration and Travel grants, for example—are lumped with Unemployment benefit in the Registrar-General's returns ; but the sums involved are small.

The third category of benefits consists of Sickness and Accident benefits. These are provided mainly by Unions of skilled workers, with relatively high contributions. They, too, have become a good deal less important since State benefits were raised to a level nearer to meeting full needs. They are payable only for a limited number of weeks, often varying with length of membership or number of contributions paid. Like Unemployment benefit, they are now only supplementary to what is paid under the National Insurance and Industrial Injuries Acts.

The fourth category, Funeral benefit, maintains its importance despite the fact that a small Death benefit is now included in the State scheme. The Unions with low contributions, as well as those with higher contributions, usually provide it. The individual payments are in most cases small ; but they add up to a substantial total.

The fifth category, Superannuation benefit to retired members, is paid only by a small group of Unions of skilled workers, and in some cases only to a special category of members paying contributions at the highest rate. It is a costly benefit, which can usually be borne only where there is a steady inflow of young members to help meet the cost. Where a Union which pays this benefit loses members—as may happen either in a declining trade or where a particular Union has mismanaged its affairs, as well as in periods of depression—Superannuation benefit is apt to become a severe drain on the funds: it can sometimes be maintained only by special levies on the members over and above the regular rates of contribution. It is, however, for those Unions which can afford it, a highly valued benefit ; and one of its effects is to induce a high stability of membership, as those who hope to receive it keep up their contributions even in bad times.

Outside these five main categories the most important benefit is Legal Aid benefit ; but there are also, in the skilled trades, such special benefits as payments for loss of tools. Many Unions have in addition to their regular benefits Benevolent Funds, out of which grants can be made to meet special cases of distress. These funds are usually administered by the branches at their discretion, small sums being allowed them for this purpose out of the contributions paid.

On the average of the years 1946 to 1951 Dispute benefit cost 1.1 per cent of total Trade Union expenditure, or roughly 4d. a member. During the five years from 1935 to 1939 the average cost was rather under 1s. a member. During the eight years from 1927 to 1934 it was about 1s. 3d. In 1926, the year of the General Strike, it reached £1 7s. 1d. For the three years before 1926 it was about 3s. 4d. For the four years from 1919 to 1922—the years of unrest after the first World War—it was about 8s. 8d. The exceedingly sharp decline since 1926 is of course due mainly to the great decline in the extent of strike action ; but it has been accentuated by the fact that the majority of strikes in recent years have been 'unofficial', and have not entitled the participants to receive Trade Union benefits—though in a few cases 'unofficial' strikes have been subsequently legitimised on appeal to a Union Conference or Appeal Court, and benefit has then been paid. Most 'unofficial' strikes are short—partly because Dispute benefit is usually withheld from the strikers. Official strikes are apt to last longer, but have become rarities now that most disputes go to arbitration when they cannot be settled by direct egotiation between the parties.

Unemployment benefit accounted on the average of 1946-1951 or 1.7 per cent of total Trade Union expenditure recorded by the Registrar-General, as compared with 13.7 per cent in 1926, over 13 per cent during the severe depression of 1932 and 1933, and 10.6 per cent in 1935.* The fall is due mainly to the much lower level of unemployment, but is also affected by the abandonment of this particular benefit by some Unions which had found it unduly expensive before the war. During the five years 1934-1938, the average cost per member was about 3s. 5d. : since the war it has been about 8d.

On the average of the post-war years Sickness and Accident benefit amounted to rather more than 8 per cent of total expenditure, as against from 9 to 10 per cent before the war. This is a relatively stable benefit : it is subject to some fluctuations in

*These proportions exclude payments recoverable from the State Insurance scheme.

times of bad weather or epidemics, but varies much less than the benefits so far described.

Funeral benefit accounted for rather more than 5 per cent of total expenditure before the war, but now accounts for only about 3½ per cent. This is because, though the benefit remains popular, the rates have not been much increased, a basic grant being now payable from State insurance funds.

Superannuation benefit, which cost between 16 and 17 per cent of total outgoings before the war, has averaged only 13 per cent since 1945. This leaves it still the most costly of all Trade Union benefits, though it exists only in a few Unions of skilled workers.

I have set out in Appendix 3, in summary form, some specimen benefit scales of the Amalgamated Engineering Union and of the Transport and General Workers' Union, in order to illustrate the wide differences within Trade Unions which cater for diverse memberships. It will be seen that, whereas the A.E.U. pays only 20s. weekly dispute benefit to its highest grade of members, and descends to 15s. for its main 'industrial section', which consists chiefly of semi-skilled workers, the T. and G.W.U has a general scale of 20s. for male members, with supplementary payments of 6s. for a wife and 2s. 6d. for each child under 15. Women get only 10s. from the A.E.U., as against 12s. from the T. and G.W.U., though the A.E.U.'s contribution is 6d. and the T. and G.W.U.'s only 5d. (4d. till 1953). The A.E.U., however, pays the higher Accident benefit, but for a shorter period; and the A.E.U. also pays a small Unemployment benefit, for six weeks, whereas the T. and G.W.U. does not provide this benefit for members on its women's scale. Superannuation, Disablement and Tool Benefit are provided only for the highest sections of A.E.U. members: the T. and G.W.U. does not provide them at all.

It would be possible to give a much wider illustrative selection of the benefits provided by various Unions for their various grades of members; but the catalogue would soon become tedious. Although each Union has its own scales, most of the differences either arise out of special occupational conditions or are sufficiently brought out by the examples cited in Appendix 3.

It is, however, worth while to glance at the income and expenditure accounts of one or two Unions in order to get a clear idea of how the money is spent. Take, for example, the accounts of the

National Union of General and Municipal Workers for the year 1951. Total income amounted to £942,764 (excluding contributions of £47,226 to the Union's Political Fund). Of this £862,000 came from members' contributions, £72,000 from interest and dividends on investments, and the rest from various sources. Total expenditure was £798,000, showing a surplus of £145,000. Benefits cost only £72,000, of which Funeral benefit accounted for £68,000. Dispute benefit cost less than £2,000; Disablement benefit about the same. Under the various headings of Working Expenses, the biggest items were these :

	£
Salaries—Officials	105,685
Clerical, etc.	68,706
Officials' Travelling Expenses	21,575
Insurance Stamps	9,637
Cost of Annual Congress	14,707
Delegates' Fees to Congresses and Negotiations	9,295
Council and Executive Meetings	2,967
District Council and Committee Meetings	4,572
Organising, Demonstrations, etc.	1,310
Branch Management Expenses	258,765
Legal Expenses	15,070
Superannuation Fund	40.000
Auditors and Scrutineers	1,512
Rent, Rates and Office Upkeep	16,319
Repairs to Premises and Equipment	4,658
Printing, Reports and Stationery	42,016
Postages and Telephones	11,612
Cars—Tax and Insurance	11,550
Depreciation	10,000
Total	£659,956

Thus, the running of the Union cost about £660,000, out of £798,000—more than four-fifths of the total. This excludes payments to outside bodies, among which the following were the more important :

	£
Trades Union Congress	19,242
Trades Union Congress (Irish)	50
Trades Councils	2,396
Industrial Federations	4,124
National Union of Mineworkers	2,873
International Federations	1,245
Joint Industrial Councils	22,019
Others	98
	£52,048

Finally, 'Educational Grants and Expenses' came to £7,848, and 'Other Grants' to £6,282. There was an optional Sick, Accident and Funeral Fund, of which the accounts were not included in the main account. Out of this £10,675 was paid in Sick and Funeral benefits, and administrative costs of £2,479 were charged against it. The entirely separate Political Fund, with income at £47,668 and expenditure at £51,863, showed a deficit of £4,195 on the year. Out of this fund £10,000 went to the Labour Party by way of ordinary contribution, and another £10,000 as a special contribution to General Election costs. £8,374 went in grants to the Union's parliamentary candidates, and £11,945 in local affiliation fees. Administrative costs of £7,084 were debited to the fund : the rest went in a variety of small expenses.

Let us now set beside this account of the N.U.G.M.W., but in more summary form, the General Account of the Amalgamated Engineering Union for the same year. Only a few key items need be shown. The details are given in Appendix 5.

	A.E.U.	*N.U.G.M.W.*
	£	£
Total Income	2,462,789	942,764
Total Outgoings	2,251,291	798,000
Expenditure on :		
Dispute Benefits	44,685	1,923
Unemployment Benefits	21,585	—
Friendly Benefits and Grants (except Superannuation)	300,123	82,245*
Superannuation	832,293	—
Benefits, Total	£1,199,186	£84,168
Working Expenses	873,185	651,859
Affiliation Fees, Grants, etc.	137,654	66,178
Other Expenses	41,266	6,470
Out of Political Fund	£48,512	£51,863

*Including £10,675 from Optional Fund, not included in Total Outgoings.

I do not pretend that these two sets of figures are at all strictly comparable ; for each Trade Union draws up its accounts in its own way, and there are considerable differences in the methods of allocating the items. But these do not prevent the two accounts from giving a reasonably correct picture of the difference between a Union which makes considerable provision for friendly benefits and one in which benefits of all kinds play a relatively minor part and the Union's main service is that of a negotiating and bargaining body on its members' behalf. A Trade Union of the second type will naturally spend a much higher proportion of its income on covering its overhead expenses ; but the sum so spent will not necessarily be higher for each member, and may easily be smaller. In the present case, the A.E.U.s working expenses come out at 18s. 9d. a member and those of the N.U.G.M.W. at 16s. 2d.

CHAPTER VII

TRADE UNIONS AND THE LAW

TRADE Unions, in every country in which they have grown up, have been compelled to fight a hard battle for the right even to exist, and have won any reasonable recognition at law only by stages and at the cost of severe struggles that have called for high courage. Trade Unionism developed in the countries which first went through the Industrial Revolution, at a period when the doctrine of economic individualism was very strong in the rising capitalist classes, and when the older governing classes, terrified by the French Revolution and the assertion of the 'Rights of Man', were disposed to look on every working-class combination as a conspiracy against the aristocratic order. Thus, the old governing class of aristocrats and the new, rising class of capitalist entrepreneurs, though engaged in a struggle for power, were apt to join forces to repress working-class combinations, which appeared to threaten both alike. Sometimes, indeed, political alliances were formed between the capitalists and the workers against aristocratic government and aristocratic privilege ; but such alliances were always uneasy and were apt to fall apart whenever industrial issues came to the front. In Great Britain, John Bright, a leader in Radical politics and an advocate of a wide franchise, was also a bitter opponent of Trade Union demands for industrial legislation ; and the same situation existed in other countries, wherever Radical advocates of *laisser-faire* wooed the support of the workers for political reform, but at the same time fought hard against every proposal for state intervention to regulate working conditions or to introduce social legislation for the improvement of the living standards of the poor. Often, indeed, the social reformers found more sympathy among political reactionaries than among Radicals ; for some of the reactionaries held by a patriarchal conception of the duty of the upper classes towards their social inferiors, or regarded social legislation as a bulwark against revolution. Even in Great Britain, up to the latter end of the nineteenth century, Tories were responsible for as much social legislation as Whigs or Liberals ; and the major changes proceeded rather from groups that cut across parties, or from individuals, than from either of the great parties.

Trade Unionism raised the issue of 'liberty' in a particularly acute form. The more extreme advocates of *laisser-faire* denounced it as an altogether illegitimate attempt to interfere with the individual's freedom of contract, and thus found themselves in alliance with reactionaries who wished merely to suppress all insubordination on the part of the 'lower classes'. The lawyers, sharing the upper-class view that the lower classes should be industrious but never a nuisance, and at the same time taking their stand on the notion of 'free contract' between a willing buyer and a willing seller, were disposed to regard every attempt to fix wages or conditions by combined bargaining or collusion as a 'conspiracy' to 'restrain trade', and therefore as a criminal offence. It is hardly possible to say when this idea of Trade Unions as unlawful under the criminal law became fully established; but it certainly was so well before the end of the eighteenth century. The judges could have, but did not, resort to an ancient statute of Edward VI, dealing with 'conspiracies of victuallers and craftsmen', which laid down a general prohibition of conspiracies by either masters or journeymen to raise prices. This evidently referred mainly to the food trades. They did, when occasion arose, make use of certain statutes which specifically forbade combinations to raise wages in particular trades. But for the most part they relied not on statute but on common law—that is, on the traditional rules of English justice as interpreted by generations of judges in the courts. The legal notion of 'conspiracy' was very wide ; and if it was held that trade ought not to be 'restrained', or at least not unreasonably so, it was easy to go on to the conclusion that combination to restrain trade by collective wage-fixing was 'unreasonable', and as such constituted a 'conspiracy' on the part of those in the combination.

As an outcome of this doctrine, the law courts in the later years of the eighteenth century were usually ready, in any case that was brought before them, to treat combination among workers to improve wages or conditions as a punishable offence. There was one exception. Under the Elizabethan Statute of Artificers, the county magistrates were still entitled both to fix wage-rates and to disallow the employment of unapprenticed men in skilled trades. They seldom did either ; but as long as the old law remained nominally in force it was difficult for the judges to treat as criminal conspiracy a combination formed for no other purpose than a concerted attempt to get it enforced. Accordingly, combinations having this object only were usually let alone.

Against other combinations, legal penalties could be invoked. But the procedure was costly, slow and inconvenient. Charges of conspiracy at common law could be heard only in the higher courts, not by local magistrates ; and only in cases where passions had been seriously roused was it as a rule thought worth while either by employers or by anyone else to invoke the law. What the employer usually wanted was a quick way of breaking up a Trade Union that was demanding better terms or resisting a wage-reduction, or standing pat on some rule of the trade. He wanted a sharp lesson and a quick settlement, not a prosecution that would drag on for months before the case was decided and would mean his attendance at court away at the county town, or even perhaps in London. Consequently, despite the attitude of the judges, not very many prosecutions were brought. This did not much concern the Government or the upper classes until the French Revolution made them regard all workers' combinations as potentially revolutionary conspiracies ; but after 1789 the attitude changed. When one particular group of employers—master millwrights—asked Parliament for a law to put down millwrights' combinations by allowing the magistrates to deal with them by summary jurisdiction in the local courts, Parliament, urged on by Pitt and Wilberforce, turned the Bill into a general Act dealing with combinations among any kind of workers, and thus provided an easy means for the local magistrates to nip any attempt at Trade Union action in the bud.

This Act of 1799, amended in 1800, remained in force until 1824. Workers' combinations were thus doubly criminal. Trade Unionists could be prosecuted either before a magistrates' court for combination contrary to the statute, or before a high court for conspiracy at common law or for conspiracy to violate the statute. The high court could award much greater penalties than the magistrates, who could imprison only up to six months ; but the magistrates could act much more swiftly and easily.

This was the situation until 1824, when Joseph Hume, the Radical M.P. who was always a good friend to the Trade Unions, and Francis Place, the master tailor who had been a Trade Unionist himself, contrived to get through Parliament an Act not only repealing the statutes against combination, but also declaring the lawfulness of combination and thus making it impossible for judges to maintain its illegality at common law. This Act was rushed through before those who objected had had time to muster the opposition: it was part of a general liberalisation when the fears aroused by the French Revolution had died down after Napoleon's defeat. The opponents of Trade Unions got it amended the following year, so as to restrict greatly the legally permissible range of combination. But the prohibition was not reinstated. From 1825 it was lawful for workers to combine to affect rates of wages or conditions of employment ; but the Act also laid down heavy penalties against 'intimidation, molestation, or obstruction' of any worker who was prepared to work on the terms to which the workers' combination was opposed. Thus, it was barely possible after 1825 to conduct a lawful strike ; but it was difficult to do so in practice without running the risk of being judged to have broken the law, It was, however, no longer unlawful for Trade Unions to exist ; and after 1825 most of them came out into the open and tried to persuade employers to negotiate with them and agree to standard wages and conditions of labour. Nor were they without success. In many of the old skilled crafts some collective bargaining had continued even when Trade Unions were altogether forbidden : after 1825 this happened much oftener and quite openly. Moreover, some employers were ready to bargain, even in factory trades—particularly in the cotton industry, whereas in the woollen industry and in coal-mining and in the iron trades the employers mostly refused to have anything to do with Trade Unions until much later.

Trade Unions remained at law in this barely tolerated position until 1871. In 1834 the case of the Tolpuddle Martyrs showed how precarious their status was. These unfortunate agricultural labourers were prosecuted at Dorchester, not for belonging to a Trade Union, but for 'administering unlawful oaths'. It had been a common practice when Trade Unions were forbidden for members on joining to take an oath to keep the proceedings secret, and this practice had continued after 1825. The statute under which the labourers were sentenced to transportation was one of those passed during the scare after the French Revolution : it had no specific reference to Trade Unions, and was directed against revolutionary political societies. But it was now held to apply to oaths administered to Trade Unionists. The Trade Unions mostly met this decision by abolishing their oaths and ceremonies of initiation ; but this did not save the

Tolpuddle Martyrs, who were not pardoned till some years later, when the great Trade Union movement of 1834, against which the prosecution had been really directed, had collapsed.

Not till 1858 did the Unions win any further legal ground. In that year a short Act was passed making it lawful for workers engaged in a trade dispute 'peacefully to persuade' others not to work under the conditions against which they were protesting—i.e. the courts were not to regard 'peaceful persuasion' as constituting 'molestation' or 'obstruction' under the Act of 1825.

Before this, in 1855, Parliament had passed an Act dealing with Friendly Societies, designed to give such bodies means of proceeding against defaulting officers for the recovery of money belonging to them ; and the Trade Unions, which were beginning in some cases to build up substantial funds, made considerable use of this Act. Only twelve years later, in the case of *Hornby v. Close* (1867), was it decided that Trade Unions, as being despite their *statutory* legality still bodies unlawful at *common* law, because they acted in restraint of trade, could not make use of the Friendly Societies Act for any purpose. This put the Unions' funds in serious jeopardy ; for there was no means of recovering money from defaulting officers. The following year part of the difficulty was removed by the Larceny Act, under which it became possible for a Trade Union to *prosecute* a defaulter, but not to bring a civil action for the recovery of the sum owing. The year after that, a temporary Act—the Trade Union (Protection of Funds) Act—gave this further right, pending the report on the entire status of Trade Unions that was to be made by a Royal Commission which had been appointed in 1867.

The occasion of setting up this Commission had been a great attack launched on the Trade Unions by the employers and by the newspapers following on two events. One of these was the setting up of a new central body for common defence—the United Kingdom Alliance of Organised Trades, founded at Sheffield in 1866. The other, and much the more sensational, was the explosion of a can of gunpowder thrown down the chimney of a 'blackleg' employed in the Sheffield cutlery trade. This was the culmination of a series of acts of violence committed by members of certain small Trade Unions in Sheffield, and commonly known as the 'Sheffield Outrages'. There had also been some less spectacular events among the brickmakers in Manchester. Faced with the outcry caused by these affairs, the leaders of the principal

Amalgamated Societies, protesting their entire innocence of such practices, demanded a full investigation into Trade Unions and their affairs, including, when the decision had been given in the *Hornby v. Close* case, the question of protection of Trade Union funds.

The Royal Commission finally reported in 1871. It found that the outrages in no way implicated more than a very few small societies ; and it reported against the demands of those employers who wanted the Unions to be either suppressed or at least subjected to severe legal restrictions. Its report, on which the Trade Union Act of 1871 was based, indeed gave the Trade Unions their charter, and the Act still forms the main foundation of current Trade Union law. This, however, was mainly the doing of a minority of the Commissioners, the positivist lawyer, Frederic Harrison, the Christian Socialist, Thomas Hughes, and the Earl of Lichfield. The majority limited itself to rejecting the proposals for anti-Union legislation and to proposing a system of legal recognition that was to be open only to 'good' Trade Unions which gave up all restrictive practices, such as limitation of apprentices, refusal to work with non-Unionists or to allow certain machines to be operated only by qualified craftsmen, or rejection of piecework or sub-contract systems. The minority, objecting to these provisions, proposed an outright legalisation of Trade Unions, with protection for their funds, without any such conditions ; and the Liberal Government took in this matter the minority's advice.

There was, however, a fly in the ointment. When the Government Bill was produced, it was found to include, besides the clauses giving the Trade Unions their charter, a number of others, based partly on the Act of 1825 but going beyond it. These clauses laid down a series of severe penalties against persons guilty of 'intimidation', with the words 'molestation' and 'obstruction' again repeatedly invoked. The wording was very wide, and it looked as if the effect would be to make the law relating to strikes a good deal stiffer than it had been even in 1825. Moreover, the Act authorising 'peaceful persuasion' was to be repealed.

This put the Trade Unions in a dilemma. They very much wanted one half of the Bill, and equally did not at all want the other half. After much argument they got the Bill divided into two ; but they could not prevent both from being passed. They were, however, able thereafter to agitate for the repeal of the one—the Criminal Law Amendment Act, 1871—without thereby endangering the other—the Trade Union Act of the same year. This they did; and four years later a Conservative Government under Disraeli repealed the obnoxious measure and replaced it by the Conspiracy and Protection of Property Act, 1875, which went a long way towards meeting the Unions' claims. These two Acts, together with a short Trade Union Act (Amendment) Act of 1876, form the foundation of all subsequent Trade Union law.

Briefly, the position established by the Trade Union Act of 1871 was that Trade Unions were fully recognised as lawful bodies, with a right to sue and be sued in the courts, so that they could proceed against defaulting officers for the recovery of funds. They could not be treated by the courts as criminal conspiracies or as bodies unworthy of the protection of the courts because they acted 'in restraint of trade'. But at the same time they were protected against certain types of action arising out of their legality that might have had dangerous consequences. In the case of a friendly society, a member can sue the society if it fails to pay him the benefits it has promised. This would not have been practicable in the case of a Trade Union unless its friendly benefits had been entirely separated from its other activities; for benefits paid for periods of unemployment or trade dispute cannot be actuarially calculated like sickness benefits. Some critics of the Unions demanded this separation; but the Unions successfully argued that their friendly and their industrial activities were so bound up together as to make separation impracticable, and further that it would have the opposite effect to what was desired because the dependence of both kinds of benefit on a single fund made the Unions cautious in embarking on strikes—which was in fact true. Secondly, the Act of 1871 stopped short of making enforceable at law collective agreements entered into by the Trade Unions on behalf of their members, leaving the contract of employment legally a contract between the employer and each individual employee. But for this, the Union might have been held fully responsible for all damage caused to an employer by any breach of a collective agreement into which it had entered, whether it had in any way authorised the breach or not.

Trade Unions thus became a quite peculiar kind of legally

recognised association, different from friendly societies, from co-operative societies, and from joint stock companies. The Act also created a special category of 'registered' Trade Unions, which registered their rules with the Chief Registrar of Friendly Societies and received in return a few, not very important privileges connected with the holding of property and the payment of income tax. Most of the advantages conferred by the Act, however, applied equally to registered and to unregistered Trade Unions; and, though most Unions have in fact been registered, a number have not, and have suffered no serious disadvantage thereby. Indeed, one of the main advantages of registration disappeared almost by accident in 1913, when it became possible under an Act of that year for an unregistered Union to apply to the Chief Registrar for a certificate stating it to be a Trade Union and therefore to come under the Trade Union Acts. Previously, in order to secure the protection of the Acts, it had been necessary for unregistered Unions to prove in court that they were actually Trade Unions to which the Act applied.

The Trade Union Act of 1871, as amended at a few points by that of 1876, seemed for a long time to have settled satisfactorily the legal status of the Unions. Then came, in 1901, the Taff Vale case, which blew the first great hole in their supposed position of security. The question at issue in this case was whether a Trade Union could be sued in any circumstances for damages caused by it, or by its agents, to an employer in the course of a trade dispute. A strike had occurred on the Taff Vale Railway, and the railway company had tried to defeat the strikers by introducing blackleg workers under contract. The strikers, and subsequently officers of the Amalgamated Society of Railway Servants, tried to induce these blacklegs not to work—i.e. to break their contracts of employment—and some scenes of violence occurred. The company then sued the Union for the damages caused to it by these inducements to breach of contract. The case went up on appeal to the House of Lords, where the company, much to most people's surprise, won the day, and the A.S.R.S. was ordered to pay £23,000 in damages.

This legal decision caused widespread dismay; for it put all Trade Union funds in jeopardy in connection with strike action. No one knew what the full implications might be; for incitement to breach of contract was almost certain to occur wherever employers tried to use blackleg labour, or any workers remained at work during a strike or lock-out. The entire Trade Union movement therefore demanded legislation to undo the effects of the Taff Vale Judgment. The affair was the making of the then newly founded Labour Representation Committee, which became the Labour Party; for it brought the Trade Unions into politics in order to get the law altered.

Altered it was, by the Trade Disputes Act of 1906, based on a Bill put forward by the Unions as an alternative to the measure first offered by the new Liberal Government. The Trade Disputes Act gave the Trade Unions complete immunity against actions for damages caused by 'tortious' acts done by them or their members (a breach of contract is not a 'tort', but an 'incitement to breach of contract' is). Thus, after 1906, though an individual Trade Unionist could be sued for damages if he broke his contract, a Trade Union could not be sued for inciting him to do so. Moreover, no individual could henceforth be sued for damages for anything done by him in combination with others in connection with a trade dispute unless he could have been sued for the same thing done without any combination with others. The Trade Disputes Act also explicitly legalised 'peaceful persuasion' by pickets in connection with disputes, and thus put back the law in this respect to where it had been before it was worsened in 1871.

The Trade Disputes Act was a resounding Trade Union victory, won partly because the Labour Party had just become a power in Parliament, but more because the Unions had exacted firm pledges from most Liberal candidates during the election campaign. But hardly had the law of disputes been put right when a further blow fell, involving the same Trade Union as before. In the case of *Osborne v. the Amalgamated Society of Railway Servants* the House of Lords decided on appeal that it was unlawful for Trade Unions to spend any money on promoting the return of their members, or indeed of any person, to Parliament. Indeed, the implications of the Osborne Judgment went much further; for the decision meant in effect that Trade Unions could lawfully spend money only on objects that were explicitly named in the Trade Union Acts, and this ruled out such objects as education, or conducting a newspaper, and every form of propaganda that could not be brought directly within the function of regulating the conditions of employment.

The legal consequences of the Osborne Judgment of 1907 were

not undone until 1913. In the meantime the Labour Party was left almost without funds and was seriously crippled in the two General Elections of 1910. Its position would have become quite impossible had not the payment of salaries to M.P.s been introduced in 1911. In 1913, however, a new Trade Union Act authorised Trade Unions to spend their money on any object, not in itself unlawful, which their rules allowed, subject to certain special conditions attaching to expenditure for political purposes. Any Union wishing to spend money for political purposes, which were widely defined, had first to take a ballot of its members and secure a majority of those voting, and then to draw up and get approved by the Chief Registrar a set of Political Rules. These had to provide for a separate Political Fund, out of which alone all political expenditure had to be met; and provision had to be made for exempting from all payment to this Fund any member who signed a form claiming exemption.

This Act remained in force until 1927. The numbers formally claiming exemption in Unions which adopted Political Rules (some did not) were never large; but in practice a good many Trade Unionists failed to pay the 'political levy', though they did not formally claim exemption. In 1927, after the General Strike, the Conservatives, hoping to cripple the Labour Party, amended the Act of 1913 by substituting 'contracting-in' for 'contracting-out'—that is, laying down that the levy could not be collected from anyone who had not actually signed a form agreeing to pay it. This did nearly halve the paying Trade Union membership of the Labour Party; and the change lasted until the Labour Government, in 1946, repealed the entire Act of 1927. The Act of 1913 then came back into force; and the position still remains as it was then prescribed. The Act of 1927 also excluded certain Unions in the public services from belonging to either the Labour Party or the Trades Union Congress; and this too was undone in 1946.

We must now go back to the second of the basic Acts passed in the 1870s—the Conspiracy and Protection of Property Act of 1875, which dealt, not with Trade Unions as such, but with trade disputes. Under this Act, the offences of 'intimidation, molestation and obstruction' were much more narrowly defined: peaceful picketing 'for the purpose of obtaining or communicating information'—but not for 'peaceful persuasion'—was made lawful; and certain other provisions which will be explained later were made in connection with strikes in the essential public services. The Act did not wholly meet the Unions' claims; but it went a long way, and it entirely repealed the dangerous Criminal Law Amendment Act of 1871.

Closely connected with the law of trade disputes was the general law relating to contracts of employment. The Trade Unions, as we saw in a previous chapter,* had begun in 1864 a national campaign for the reform of the Law of Master and Servant, which, as it then stood, was based on the conception of 'masters' and 'servants' as essentially unequal parties. It was a criminal offence for a workman either to break a 'contract of service' or to depart from his employment 'leaving work unfinished'; whereas an employer who broke his side of the contract was committing only a 'civil offence', for which he could be made to pay damages, but not fined or imprisoned. A workman on the other hand could be fined or imprisoned, and could also be arrested and kept in prison on charge before he was tried. As, under the general rules of criminal law, a person accused of a crime could not in those days give evidence in his own defence, even if he wished to, it followed that in a case of alleged breach of contract an employer could, but a workman could not, give evidence on his own behalf.

The demand of the Trade Unions was that employers and workmen should be made equal parties to a civil contract, breach of which could lead only to the assessment of damages, and not to fine or imprisonment. In 1867 they secured a partial amendment of the law. Workmen were allowed to give evidence on their own behalf; arrest before trial was made very exceptional (only when absconding was feared); and damages became the normal, but not the only allowable, penalty. These concessions did not satisfy the Unions, which went on with their agitation side by side with the struggle over the Trade Union Acts. In 1875 the Conservative Government, angling for working-class votes, met most of their demands. The Master and Servant Acts were replaced by an Employers and Workmen Act which made both equal parties to a purely civil contract of employment—in normal cases, arrest, fine and imprisonment disappeared. But at the same time the Government introduced into the Conspiracy and Protection of Property Act sections which restored the criminal provisions in the case of workers striking in the main public utility services, and also where breach of contract might lead to loss of life or injury or

*See page 122.

serious damage to property. These sections remain in force to-day: they were stiffened up and extended by the Act of 1927, but the changes vanished when that Act was repealed.

The Trade Union (Amalgamation) Act of 1917 has been described in a previous chapter*; and no more need be said about it here. It remains only to deal with the principal provisions of the now repealed Trade Unions and Trade Disputes Act of 1927, as far as they have not been dealt with already. This Act, as we saw, was an immediate sequel to the General Strike of 1926; and its first purpose was to make strikes of a similar sort illegal. This it did by creating a new category of 'illegal strikes', to which the protection given by the Trade Disputes Act of 1906 was not to apply. Trade Unions were further prohibited from promoting or spending money on such strikes. To be declared illegal, a strike (or a lock-out) had to meet two conditions: it had to have some object beyond a trade dispute in a single 'trade or industry', in which the strikers were engaged, and it had to be designed or calculated to 'coerce the Government' either directly or by 'inflicting hardship on the community'. The procedure for getting a particular strike declared illegal was an appeal to the High Court for an injunction restraining anyone from promoting or supporting it in any way.

It was never quite clear what these provisions meant; for the words 'trade or industry' were left undefined. But clearly the Act made illegal any general or sympathetic strike designed to paralyse important public services, and also any strike involving more than one 'trade or industry' that was designed to bring pressure on the Government to take any particular action. It would have ruled out legally the threatened strike against war with the Soviet Union in 1920 as well as the General Strike of 1926; and it might have been held to rule out, say, a strike in which dockers came out in support of seamen, and thus held up work at the ports. The matter was never cleared up; for this particular part of the Act was never in fact invoked.

The 1927 Act included a number of further provisions. It made all picketing at a worker's home illegal, and seriously restricted picketing even at a works where a dispute was in progress. It forbade all picketing in numbers; and it brought back in new forms the old offences of 'intimidation' which had been done away with in 1875. It forbade Unions in the public services to federate with

*See page 89.

other Unions, and local authorities to give preference in employment to Trade Unionists. And, as we have seen, it tried to hamstring the Labour Party by altering the terms of the Trade Union Act of 1913.

Now that the 1927 Act has been repealed, the Trade Unions are back under the law as it stood before 1927. This leaves it uncertain whether general strikes are lawful or not—probably not, for probably the House of Lords would take that view, and it would have the last word; but one cannot be sure. Short of general strikes, sympathetic strike action is undoubtedly lawful; and in all lawful strikes the Trade Unions can again rely on the protection given to their funds by the Trade Disputes Act. Picketing, including picketing a worker's home, is again lawful, though of course the individual pickets can be charged with any act of violence they may be alleged to have committed. Breach of contract is entirely a civil matter, except in cases of danger to life, limb or property or in the essential public utility services. Trade Unions are fully protected from actions for damages arising out of incitement to breach of contract, or any other 'tort', and enjoy further immunities in connection with actions arising out of a trade dispute. Trade Unions have an assured legal status, and a right to use their money for any lawful purpose, subject to their rules authorising the expenditure and to their observing the provisions of the Act of 1913 in respect of political expenditure.

It has been necessary to give an account of Trade Union law in this historical framework because it can hardly be made intelligible in any other way. Trade Unions, with collective bargaining as their first object, do not fit into the structure of any legal system that takes its stand on the conception of individual 'free' contract. It is of their essence to run counter to this principle, by acting 'in restraint of trade'. Accordingly, the legal mind treats them as *prima facie* unlawful, if not positively criminal, and, even when not prosecuting them, refuses them its help, beyond the extent to which it is compelled to recognise their claims by statute law. Statutes conferring rights on Trade Unions the legal mind tends to construe as narrowly as possible. Thus, in the Osborne case, the lawyers asked themselves, not whether political action was a fully legitimate form of activity, but whether Trade Unions could produce statutory authority for engaging in it. The Trade Union Acts nowhere laid down categorically what Trade Unions could or could not do; but they did contain a section (in the Act of 1876) defining what a Trade Union was. The lawyers treated this defining section, which had clearly never been meant for any such purpose, as an enumeration of the kinds of action a Trade Union was entitled to undertake. As it contained no mention of political action, they declared that Trade Unions had no right to engage in it—though they had been doing so unchecked for more than forty years. Other lawyers declared that it was contrary to public policy to allow Trade Unions to take political action, at any rate in support of a party which imposed a discipline on its members, and that such action needed specific authorisation by statute, though other kinds of association were allowed to take political action without any special authority. The discrimination arose out of the lawyers' initial view that Trade Unions were, by the very nature of their activities, unlawful at common law.

This same attitude has affected the law's attitude towards other aspects of Trade Union activity. Powers given by statute have always been construed narrowly : the taint of unlawfulness has spread over everything not specifically authorised by statute. If, in spite of this, Trade Unions have managed to attain to a satisfactory legal status, that is not the lawyers' doing. They have only accepted facts when they have been forced upon them.

It is not possible, in this short volume, to give any account of the legal struggles in which Trade Unionism has been involved in other countries. In France, it had to fight its way against the proscription of private corporations laid down in the *Loi le Chapelier* of 1791, and got no clear legal recognition until 1884. In Germany, it had an easier passage, because the main structure of German law was less individualistic. In the United States, it is still fighting a hard struggle to secure the repeal of the Taft-Hartley Act of 1947, passed to restrict its powers after it had secured a broad legal charter under President Roosevelt's New Deal. Before that, it had been constantly battling against the use of the procedure of legal injunction to limit its organising efforts, as well as against the use of private police forces, often backed by State Troopers, to break strikes. But the legal story of these and other Trade Union movements would carry us much too far afield. It is enough to say that Trade Unionism now has an assured, though not everywhere a satisfactory, status of sorts in all advanced Western countries—unless Spain and Portugal be counted as advanced. In many colonial areas it is still hedged round with restrictions, and subject to some government tutelage; but these have grown much less onerous in recent years, at any rate in most of the British colonies. In some of the backward countries—for example, in the Middle East—the movement still barely exists, and has still to win legal recognition. In Argentina and some other States of Latin America it has been turned into a subordinate agency of the ruling party, as it was in Italy under Mussolini and in Germany under Hitler. In the Soviet Union, in China, and in the satellite States, it is in a rather different way a part of the machine of government, dominated by the Communist Party.

Thus, in totalitarian societies, Trade Unionism is recognised but firmly controlled by the State. In countries dominated by the notion of individual contract, on the other hand, it is apt to find the law against it—as it has done especially in the United States. In feudal countries, it is often repressed as politically dangerous. It enjoys both recognition and independence chiefly in advanced societies which lie between the extremes of totalitarianism and *laisser-faire*, such as Great Britain. But whenever a country moves far from a 'free market' economy to a planned economy—as most have been moving in recent years—the Trade Unions have to play their part in planning if the economy is to work ; and this means that the contacts with government become closer and more numerous. These matters can, however, be considered better when we come to discuss the wider problems of Trade Union policy. They go far beyond what is ordinarily meant by the 'legal position' of the movement.

CHAPTER VIII

TRADE UNIONS IN POLITICS

WE saw in the preceding chapter the legal conditions which in Great Britain regulate Trade Union participation in politics. Every Trade Union that wishes to engage in 'political action' as defined by the Trade Union Act of 1913 has to take a ballot vote of its members, get a majority among those voting, draw up a set of Political Rules, and get them approved by the Chief Registrar of Friendly Societies as conforming with the Act. 'Political purposes', as defined by the Act and by decisions in the courts, include all forms of electoral activity, payment of allowances to M.P.s or members of local authorities, publication of political literature, and subscription of funds for the production of a political newspaper.

There is nothing in the Act to lay down that a Trade Union undertaking political activity shall associate itself with any particular party. There is nothing to stop a Trade Union from supporting any party its members please, or acting without party connections. But in practice in recent times political action has meant almost solely action through the Labour Party, though a few candidates in local elections have stood simply as Trade Unionists, without a party label. In Great Britain, the Communists have never even attempted to persuade a Trade Union to devote its Political Fund to their support. For the purposes of this chapter, as far as recent times are concerned, Trade Union political action means action through the Labour Party.

Naturally, this was not always so. The Labour Party did not exist before 1900; and its predecessor, the I.L.P., did not rest on Trade Union support. British Trade Unions first began to take an active part in electoral politics* after the Reform Act of 1867, which first gave any considerable number of working men the vote. The London Working Men's Association took the lead in trying to persuade working-class bodies to put up candidates at the general election of 1868. The Labour Representation League took over in 1869; and the first workmen-M.P.s were elected in 1874. The Liberal Party was then still taking shape; and the two miners who secured election both sat as 'Radicals' associated

*For some earlier political activities, see pages 19ff.

with the more advanced wing of the Liberals. These two—Alexander Macdonald and Thomas Burt—were re-elected in 1880, with one additional Trade Unionist—the stonemason Henry Broadhurst, then secretary of the Trades Union Congress. Then came the third Reform Act, in 1884; and the following year no fewer than eleven Trade Union M.P.s—six of them miners—found their way to the House of Commons, all without Liberal opponents and all virtually as members of the Liberal Party. From that time until the Miners' Federation joined the Labour Party in 1909, there was always a group of Trade Union M.P.s sitting as Liberals, and the miners provided the main nucleus. Of the first Independent Labour M.P.s elected in 1892, John Burns, Keir Hardie, and the Seamen's leader, Havelock Wilson, only the last had Trade Union support, and he soon joined the Liberals. In 1900 the newly formed Labour Representation Committee could get only two men elected—Keir Hardie and Richard Bell, of the Railway Servants' Society—and before long Bell seceded to the Liberals. Only in 1906 did a solid group of Trade Union M.P.s appear under Labour Party auspices; and, though all were nominally 'independent', every one of them was in fact elected with Liberal as well as Labour support.

In effect, right up to 1914, though most of the big Trade Unions had joined the Labour Party, and their representatives in Parliament (except a few recalcitrant miners) sat as Labour M.P.s, there was no real breakaway from Liberalism. The Labour Party of those days was not, even by profession, a Socialist party; and a large number of its members had been Liberals most of their lives, and were too old to change. The miners now sent their new M.P.s, and such of the old as they could persuade to change, to sit as members of the Labour Party; but this meant little more than that they paid for them under the new label instead of the old. The Trade Unions did indeed from the outset in 1900 carry the main voting power at the Annual Conference of the L.R.C., and later the Labour Party; but they did not make much use of this power except to resist any leftward move that might embroil the party with the Liberals, or bring the Liberal Government down. The Labour Party itself had, until 1918, no nation-wide machinery in the constituencies. It relied in most places where it was active on Trades and Labour Councils,* and

*See page 137.

in the mining areas left the Miners' Associations to conduct the elections as they pleased. Only after the break-up of the Liberal Party during the first World War did Arthur Henderson and Sidney Webb reorganise the Labour Party with a moderate Socialist programme—*Labour and the New Social Order*—and a local Labour Party in almost every constituency.

These local Labour Parties, many of which developed out of the earlier Trades and Labour Councils*, were based on two kinds of membership—affiliated branches of Trade Unions and Socialist societies, and individual subscribers, whose numbers were small at first, but grew fairly fast during the 1920s. The local Parties sent delegates to the Annual Labour Party Conference; but their voting power counted for little beside that of the nationally affiliated Trade Unions, which had increased greatly in numbers and membership since before the War. Trade Union representatives were in a clear majority on the Executive of the Party: nothing could be carried either at the Conference or on the Executive against their combined will. But the Trade Unions did not often wish to line up against the other elements, of which the most important was the Independent Labour Party. Their representatives held varying views; and so for that matter did the I.L.P.'s, who included Ramsay MacDonald at one end and a group of Clydesiders at the other. Only when the I.L.P., having in effect shed MacDonald, appeared as the advocate of a policy of 'Socialism in Our Time', did a line-up of most of the Trade Union leaders against it become evident.

Trade Unionists were represented in the Labour Party—and are still to-day—in three ways—nationally, through the affiliated Trade Unions, locally through the affiliation of their branches to local Labour Parties, and individually, through individual membership of a local Labour Party or of a Socialist society. Nationally, this meant representation through groups of delegates, chosen in various ways, at the Party Conference, and through the Trade Union members (almost always full-time officials) on the Party Executive. Locally, it meant representation of such branches as chose to send delegates to the local Parties, and on the local Party Executive by Trade Unionists chosen from among these delegates or among individual party members. The resulting contacts of the ordinary Trade Unionist with the party were not, and are not, very close. The national representation is very

*See page 138.

remote from him, and in most Unions he has only an indirect part, if any, in choosing it. His contact with the local Party, unless he is a delegate or an active individual member, depends first on his branch choosing to affiliate and send a representative, secondly on the delegate reporting back adequately to his branch, and thirdly on his own presence at the branch meetings when the reports are made. For only a small minority are all three conditions satisfied. Any Trade Unionist who chooses can be active in his local Party as an individual member ; but this does not establish any organic relation between his personal activity and the Trade Union movement.

In practice, the majority of Trade Unionists who pay the Union's Political Levy and thus become affiliated members of the Labour Party do nothing more about it, except perhaps vote for its candidates in national and sometimes in local elections. Some branch delegates to local Parties are active, and there are often quite hot contests within the local Party when nominations for a parliamentary candidate are being made. This is sometimes true of municipal elections also ; but in the less important district elections and even in the counties the difficulty is often that of finding candidates willing and able to stand. The Trade Unionist who is keen on politics usually joins his local Party as an individual, in addition to paying his Trade Union Political Levy, and often acts in a dual capacity, as representing his branch and as an individual.

Above the local Parties in the Labour Party structure stand Federations of Labour Parties, usually on a county basis (and also sometimes Central Labour Parties for towns including a number of parliamentary constituencies). Above the Federations stand certain Regional Councils, which are of special importance for Scotland and for Wales. Delegates, who may be Trade Union representatives or individual party members or both, go up to these higher-level bodies ; but there is practically no organic connection between most of them and the Trade Unions. At the national level, relations between the Trade Unions and the Party are mainly in the hands of full-time officers and Executive members. As the leading officials of most of the big Trade Unions sit on the T.U.C. General Council and there is a tradition against anyone sitting both on this body and on the Labour Party Executive, the latter tends to include a good many seconds-in-command. Of the twelve Trade Union representatives on the Party

Executive in 1952-3, only one was the General Secretary of his Trade Union, a small one, too small to get a seat on the T.U.C. Council. The rest were all prominent in their Unions, mostly if not all high officials ; but they were the Trade Unions' second eleven. It should be added that three of them were also Members of Parliament.

What has been said so far refers to the Labour Party's organisation outside Parliament. In the House of Commons the Labour Party, after its narrow electoral defeat in 1951, had 295 M.P.s. Of these, 105 sat on the nomination of various Trade Unions, which bore the financial responsibility for their candidatures, and 17 were nominees of Co-operative organisations : the remaining 173 were put forward on the responsibility of local Constituency Parties. Of course, a large number of these were Trade Unionists ; but they did not sit in Parliament as representatives of the Trade Unions to which they belonged. If defeated as well as victorious candidates are included, the direct Trade Union nominees numbered 139 out of 613. Only 34 Trade Union nominees were beaten, as against 284 others. Clearly, in general, the Trade Unions were able to pick the safe seats, partly because they had the money, but also because so many of their candidates stood in mining areas.

As the Labour Party's representation in Parliament increases, the proportion of direct Trade Union members tends to fall. When the Party does badly in an election, more of the Trade Union members than of the others hold their seats : when more marginal seats are won, the successful candidates are mostly candidates put forward by the local Parties. But it is also the case that, as the Party has grown, the Trade Unions' proportion of the candidates has tended to fall. In 1945 the Trade Unions sponsored 126 candidates out of 604, a not very different proportion from that of 1951. They got elected 121 out of 393. In 1935 the Trade Unions had 79 members out of 154, a far higher proportion—and in the débâcle of 1931 they had 34 out of 52 (including the I.L.P.) In 1918, their share was 49 out of a total of 57.

Thus, the Labour Party has come to be much less than in earlier days a party in the House of Commons of official Trade Union representatives. This is not only because the proportion of 'intellectuals' has grown ; it is also because many more Trade Unionists now sit as the nominees of local Parties. The change does, however, mean that the Parliamentary Party is much less under Trade Union control, as indeed it was bound to become as its members and influence increased, and above all when it became a government party commanding a clear majority.

There is, however, yet a further way, besides those already described, in which the Trade Unions are linked with the Labour Party. This is through the National Council of Labour, which also includes representatives of the Co-operative movement. The National Council of Labour is a highest-level consultative body made up of representatives of the Trades Union Congress General Council, the Labour Party Executive, the Parliamentary Labour Party, and the Central Executive of the Co-operative Union. It makes from time to time official pronouncements on behalf of the entire Labour movement; but it does little else except in an emergency, when it meets to ensure concerted action on the part of all the bodies concerned. Actually, consultations take place much oftener between the bodies separately—for example, between the Party Executive and the Committee of the Parliamentary Party, or between the Party Executive and the T.U.C. General Council or the Co-operative Union.

We saw earlier* that in recent years the T.U.C. General Council has concerned itself increasingly with matters of wider economic and social policy, as well as with more specifically Trade Union affairs. This necessarily brings it into the same fields as are covered by the policy discussions of the Labour Party Executive, when it is drafting or re-drafting the Party Programme. The General Council has sometimes sent representatives to sit on Labour Party drafting committees dealing with particular matters, such as a nationalisation plan or a proposed piece of social legislation. On other occasions it has preferred to stand aside, reserving its freedom to criticise the drafts made by the Party or even to make its own separate proposals—though usually an effort is made to reach agreement before a policy is finally adopted. Quite often, the same questions are debated first at the Trades Union Congress, which meets in September, and then at the Labour Party Conference the following month. In the early 1930s agreement between the two bodies on the form of administration to be applied to nationalised industries was reached only after considerable difficulty, as the Trade Unions wished for firmer assurances than the Party was at first willing to give that an adequate number of Trade Unionists would be given

*See page 133.

seats on the proposed National Boards or Commissions. We shall come back to the point when we discuss the problems of 'workers' control'.*

The National Council of Labour has developed out of an earlier body, the Joint Board, first formed in 1905, just before the general election at which the Labour Party first appeared in force. It originally represented the Trades Union Congress General Council, the Labour Party Executive, and the Management Committee of the General Federation of Trade Unions.† But the G.F.T.U. was excluded after the first war. The Co-operators for a long time refused to join. They came in as 'observers' at the beginning of the second World War, and became full members in 1942.

Each Trade Union that belongs to the Labour Party has its own Political Fund, raised by contributions to its Political Levy in accordance with its rules. Out of the proceeds of this levy it pays a fixed annual contribution to the Labour Party at the rate (1953) of 6d. a member. This sum has increased steadily over the years. In 1914 it was only a 1d., and in 1918 2d. a member. During the 1930s it reached 4½d. The sums paid are based, not on the full membership of the Union, but on the number contributing to its Political Levy; and there is in many cases a big difference between the numbers on which contributions are paid to the Trades Union Congress and to the Labour Party—not mainly because large numbers of Trade Unionists sign forms objecting to pay, but rather because the numbers not paying greatly exceed the formal objectors. Floating members, for example, often fail to pay the levy; and a good deal depends on the keenness shown by local secretaries in gathering it in. The Table in Appendix 6‡ shows, for a select list of Unions, the memberships returned to the Trades Union Congress and to the Labour Party respectively for the latest available year. Appendix 1|| shows the extent of the change in the proportion of Labour Party affiliated membership made by the repeal of the Trade Unions Act of 1927. There were great variations at both dates in the proportions of members paying the Political Levy in the different Unions. In 1952 the Mineworkers were actually paying on a larger membership to the Labour Party than to the Trades Union Congress; but no other Union was paying on more than 95 per cent of its T.U.C. membership, and the Printing, Book-

*See page 226ff. †See page 126. ‡See page 301. ||See page 289.

binding and Paper Workers and the Furniture Trade Workers were paying on only one in five. The Public Employees' proportion was one in four. The big General and Municipal Workers' Union paid on half its T.U.C. membership, and the Transport and General Workers and the Woodworkers and the Building Trade Workers, among others, on two-thirds. The Engineers, the Tailors, the Dyers, and the United Textile Workers paid on about three-quarters, and the Railwaymen and the Iron and Steel Trades on four-fifths. The Transport Salaried Staffs Association reached 85 per cent, and the Shop, Distributive and Allied Workers 91 per cent. The proportions were in all cases higher than before the repeal of the Act of 1927, but the difference made varied greatly from case to case. For example, the proportion paying to the Labour Party doubled in the cases of the Engineers and the Iron and Steel Trades, and increased threefold among the Woodworkers, and fourfold in the Electrical Trades Union, whereas it hardly changed in the Transport Salaried Staffs Association and rose relatively little among the Boot and Shoe Operatives.

No doubt, the change between 1946 and 1952 was partly due to other factors besides the return to 'contracting-out' in place of 'contracting-in'. It took a little time for things to settle down after the war, and for the prestige of the Labour Government to be translated into Trade Union political contributions. But, just as the Act had made a big difference in 1927, when the Labour Party's affiliated Trade Union membership sank in one year from 3,239,000 to 2,025,000, so the change-back made a big difference.

In the House of Commons the Trade Union Members of Parliament have a group of their own, which meets to discuss matters of special Trade Union concern. Some of these M.P.s are also carrying on their Trade Union jobs, including a few who are General Secretaries of not very large Unions. But the majority are either on leave or retired, or have been given special jobs of not too exacting a sort to be worked in with their parliamentary duties. Many, who are Trade Unionists but not parliamentary representatives of their Unions, hold no Union office and depend entirely on their salaries as M.P.s—which is none too easy, when they have to pay for secretarial assistance and in many cases to live away from their homes when Parliament is in session.

Trade Unions interest themselves in local as well as in national government. As far as electoral organisation goes, this is done through the local Labour Parties, and nothing need be added to what has been said already. Labour groups on municipal and other local government Councils—especially the larger—depend considerably on local Trade Union officials for men able to attend at the required times and to give the necessary leadership. The Trades Councils also interest themselves in municipal affairs. In some of the mining areas the local administration is practically controlled by nominees of the Mineworkers.

At one time, one of the main tasks of the Trade Unions locally was to secure the observance of the 'Fair Wages Clause' in municipal contracts and the payment of fair wages to Council employees. Nowadays, improved Trade Union organisation and the practically general acceptance of Joint Industrial Council decisions have made this a much less exacting task. Some Councils on which Labour is in control have made Trade Union membership practically compulsory for their manual employees—a practice forbidden while the Act of 1927 was in force ; and in 1951-2 the Durham County Council got into hot water by attempting to enforce membership on professional as well as other employees—especially teachers and doctors—and was compelled to give way in face of the objections of the professional associations themselves. Non-manual employees, other than professional specialists, are strongly organised in the National Association of Local Government Officers, which extends downwards from Town Clerks. It refuses to join the Trades Union Congress, but has a joint committee with the T.U.C. Unions which enrol local government workers.

In general, Trade Union participation in politics is the work of an active minority that is largely the same as the minority interested in other Union affairs, but smaller. The Trade Union branches do not for the most part give any considerable part of their time to Labour Party matters, or get regular reports from their delegates to the local Parties—nor, if they did, would most of the members be present to hear what was said. Of course, some branches of Trade Unions and some Trades Councils are centres of lively political discussion—where the branch or Council contains a group—often well to the left, or Communist—that is determined to bring such matters up. But, as we have seen, branch meetings are not usually well attended, save in a few

Unions.* At higher levels, district or regional, the Union agencies have in most cases very little to do with politics, except where frequent delegate conferences are held, as among the Mine-workers. Only at the national level do political affairs receive a rather larger share of attention ; and even nationally Trade Union Executives have usually too much business of their own to spend much time on politics, except when their own trade or industry is receiving political attention. Although the Labour Party organisation is controlled in the last resort by the Trade Union vote, and though the Trade Unions, if they act together, have a veto over the Party's decisions, the Trade Union movement is not organised in such a way as to bring its rank-and-file members into democratic participation in political discussion. In the main, it looks to the Labour Party to do this job, with the participation of Trade Unionists at every level ; but the results of this division of labour are not wholly satisfactory. At Labour Party Conferences the vast majority of resolutions on the agenda come from the local Labour Parties, which have, when it comes to the point, little voting power. The big Unions especially send in few resolutions of their own, and have been always, save under very exceptional circumstances, inclined to back the platform, or to exert a negative influence. This is partly because Trade Union Executives do not for the most part regard it as their business to play an active part in the formulation of Labour Party policy, except in direct relation to their more special concerns. They prefer as a rule to accept or reject what is put forward by others, rather than make proposals of their own. This throws the task of policy-making very much into the hands of the Labour Party Executive, which has to consider what the Trade Union delegations will stand for, even more than what the local Parties' representatives would like.

*See pages 35ff.

CHAPTER IX

TRADE UNIONS AND EDUCATION

I. APPRENTICESHIP AND LEARNING A TRADE

TRADE Unions are concerned with education at a large number of separate points. Their interest of longest standing is with the learning of a skilled trade, which used to be a matter of learning in the workshop or place of work under the direct supervision of one or more skilled craftsmen. In many occupations the method was that of formal apprenticeship, by which the apprentice was bound to a master who was then under an obligation to teach him his trade and might do this either personally or through the journeymen in his employment. Often, in the eighteenth and early nineteenth centuries, the apprentice lived in the master's house, as a member of the household ; but this practice gradually gave way as the scale of employment grew larger and the relations between master and workmen less personal. The craftsmen's Trade Clubs concerned themselves both with limiting the number of apprentices a master was allowed to employ and with securing that those taken on were taught their trades properly, in order to maintain the standards of the craft.

Where work was carried on in the workers' homes, the relation between craftsman and apprentice was more direct, the boy becoming apprentice to the individual journeyman, without the intervention of a master. Such apprenticeships were often carried through without written indentures, such as were usually drawn up in most trades. In these 'domestic' industries the distinction between apprentices and mere 'learners' was often difficult to draw, especially outside the corporate towns. In rough work, such as coal-mining and ironworking, formal apprenticeship hardly existed ; but it was common for children to learn by working under their fathers or other relatives from an early age, and to graduate as skilled hewers or smelters, or whatever the trade might be, by moving away from the family group to a job elsewhere. When factories developed, at first mainly for textiles, the old system of domestic apprenticeship was not transferred to them, and the juvenile workers, except where they were 'pauper apprentices' bound by the parish authorities, were mostly taken on without any indentures or even informal understanding that they should be taught a skilled trade. Even in cotton spinning, which became a highly skilled trade after the introduction of the power-driven mule, no formal system of apprenticeship developed. In engineering, on the other hand, and in a number of other industries calling for skilled machine-workers, the workshop system of apprenticeship in effect persisted under the factory system, but with the difference that, apart from small numbers of 'premium apprentices' who were qualifying for managerial positions, apprenticeship without any written agreement became more and more common. Written indentures persisted much longer in the building trades ; but there too the numbers of boys taken on as apprentices without written agreement steadily increased, and many other boys were engaged simply as labourers without any promise of training for skilled work.

The task of training apprentices, whether under written agreements or not, necessarily fell on the skilled craftsmen. But the craft Unions had little to do with their conditions of employment, beyond attempting to limit their numbers. Some Unions enrolled apprentices ; but employers usually refused to allow collective bargaining on their behalf, even when it had been accepted for the skilled journeymen. It was indeed easier for the Unions to negotiate on behalf of juvenile workers in the textile trades, where there was no apprenticeship save in a few specialist occupations, than in the industries in which some sort of apprenticeship remained normal.

During the second half of the nineteenth century, as publicly provided or assisted technical education began to develop, craft training in the workshops was in more and more cases supplemented by training in trade schools or by attendance at evening technical courses. These facilities developed by stages into the Technical Schools and Technical Colleges of the present day, with the arrangements for National Certificates in professional subjects instituted in 1921, and with a vast number of professional associations and institutes conducting qualifying examinations and making all manner of special awards.

Trade Unions, as distinct from professional institutes, have for the most part taken no great share in these developments. In the lesser professions, some bodies are at one and the same time Trade Unions and professional associations concerning themselves with training and with examinations ; and, as we saw, some associations in the higher professions, such as the British Medical Association, act in effect as Trade Unions. But in the main technical education at all levels has grown up under the auspices either of the Local Education Authorities or of such private, but subsidised, agencies as the City and Guilds Institute, the London Polytechnics and the Technical Institutes in the other big cities, or under the aegis of professional institutes of a non-Trade Union type. There are, indeed, usually committees attached to the local Technical Colleges conducted by the Education Authorities or privately controlled ; and the Trade Unions, together with the employers, are represented on these committees, and thus play some part in shaping the provision made for the types of workers they enrol. They have also usually nowadays persons to represent their views on Local Education Authorities ; and employers no longer have the exclusive control over technical education they used in most cases to be able to arrogate to themselves. In some industries too—for example, in building—there are national agreements between employers' associations and Trade Unions for the regulation of apprenticeship. Indeed, in the building industry such agreements are supplemented by an official Building Training and Apprenticeship Council, formed during the second World War. Nevertheless it remains true that, save exceptionally, the Trade Unions have not been for the most part active in providing for or in seeking to control the arrangements made for the technical education of their members or potential members for their daily jobs.

The situation is somewhat different in the nationalised industries, old and new. The postal workers' Unions have long been much interested in the training given by the Post Office and in helping their members to study for qualifying examinations ; and in the more recently nationalised industries training is a definite part of the functions of the National Boards or Executives set up to do the management. The National Coal Board has produced an laborate 'Ladder Plan' of technical education, designed to help miners to qualify themselves for the higher posts in the industry ; and the scheme of joint consultation set up under statute in this and other nationalised industries brings the Trade Unions into consideration in the framing and operation of such schemes. But in this case, as in others, the function of the Trade Unions has been advisory ; and they have in the main regarded technical education at all levels as a matter for the public authorities, or for agencies working closely in connection with them, such as professional institutes and Polytechnics and, at the higher levels, Universities as well. Nor have the Teachers' Unions played any part in the provision of teachers' training. The National Association of Local Government Officers is the outstanding example of a body which combines Trade Union with vocational educational functions ; and it is perhaps significant that it has remained outside the Trades Union Congress, preferring to regard itself as primarily a professional body.

Trade Unions are, however, inevitably concerned with training that takes place in the factory or establishment, whether under apprenticeship schemes, formal or informal, or not. But their activity in relation to such schemes occurs chiefly at the establishment level, either through shop stewards or in connection with works committees or works councils of various kinds, including Joint Consultative Committees where they exist. The Union organisation, at the higher district and national levels, is often not involved, except where it is a question of negotiating a general apprenticeship agreement or of laying down conditions of employment for learners in schemes of statutory wage regulation through Wages Councils or similar bodies. There is, however, a growing tendency for Trade Unions to concern themselves with the conditions of young workers' employment and training, not only in relation to the wages to be paid or the proportion of juveniles to be employed, but also in order to prevent blind alley employment and to ensure that the young worker gets a proper training. In recent years there has been some discussion, especially in the building industry, of plans for introducing into apprenticeships a 'third party' besides the apprentice and his guarantors and the employer, by making some body representing the industry as a whole a signatory to apprenticeship agreements and responsible for ensuring their fulfilment should the employer default. It has even been suggested that all apprenticeship should be to the trade or industry—that is, to a central or local organisation representing it—rather than to an individual employer ; but such a plan would probably be resisted by some of the best as well as by the worst employers. Many big firms have apprenticeship schemes of which they are reasonably proud, though many more quite fail to do their duty by the juveniles they engage. There is certainly reason for much more active Trade Union participation in regulating the conditions of juvenile training and employment; but in some cases conservatism, and in others sheer apathy, stand in the way.

II. TRADE UNIONS AND WORKING-CLASS EDUCATION

Movements for working-class education go back into the eighteenth century. Members of Trade Clubs of skilled workers are found taking part in the debates and discussions held in London at various taverns and coffee-houses, or, in the case of the best-known, at Coachmakers' Hall, well before 1789. The London Corresponding Society, formed soon after the French Revolution, engaged actively in the political education of its members; and so did similar societies in many provincial towns. But it does not appear that the Trade Unions played any part in these movements as organised bodies. In the 1820s began the movement to found Mechanics' Institutes for the teaching mainly of applied science, but also of a wide range of other subjects, including history and political economy. This development gave rise at the very outset to a controversy about the content and purposes of working-class education—a controversy which is by no means at an end to-day. The original founders of the London *Mechanics' Magazine* (1823)—Thomas Hodgskin, the labour economist, and J. C. Robertson, a Scottish civil engineer—set out, inspired by some earlier work in Glasgow, to found a Mechanics' Institute that was meant to become a centre of anti-capitalist economics as well as of technical teaching. But the middle-class supporters who helped to establish the Institute had different ideas. They wanted it to become a centre where technical and scientific education would be combined with the teaching of the orthodox economics in which they believed; and they hoped to wean the working men from their misguided notions and to demonstrate the identity of the interests of *Capital and Labour* and the beneficial *Results of Machinery* for all classes. (The italicised words are the titles of two popular works produced later in connection with the movement under the auspices of Lord Brougham). In the ensuing struggle for control, both in London and elsewhere, the orthodox group got the best of it; for they had the money. In the 1830s the Society for the Diffusion of Useful Knowledge, headed by Lord Brougham, published or helped the publication of a large number of manuals dealing both with scientific and technical subjects and with economics and politics; and Mechanics' Institutes flourished in many towns. Hodgskin was allowed to deliver in the London Institute his *Lectures on Popular Political Economy*, published in 1827, and a few other unorthodox lecturers were suffered to be heard; but in the main the working-class bodies turned their backs on the Institutes, though many craftsmen attended their courses. Workers' education of an unorthodox kind was carried on during this period mainly by the Owenites, in their 'Social Institutions', or from the later 'thirties by the Chartists. The more moderate Chartists, especially William Lovett, laid great stress on education, to which Lovett, through his National Association, devoted his whole attention after his withdrawal from activity in the Chartist movement. During the period of Trade Union activity in the late 'twenties and early 'thirties the Owenites had established many connections with the Trade Unions and had done their best to persuade them to take up educational work; and these effects continued on a smaller scale after the Trade Union defeat of 1834. Indeed the next considerable educational impetus came, largely under Owenite inspiration, from the Co-operative movement, which grew fast after the foundation of the Rochdale Pioneers' Society in 1844 and the Leeds Co-operative Society in 1847. Rochdale and Leeds both became great centres of educational activity; and in both cases the emphasis was on a mixture of scientific and cultural education rather than on the technical side—though there were also active Mechanics' Institute movements in both Lancashire and Yorkshire. In Leeds the Trade Unions as well as the Co-operators played a part in the educational movements; and there were struggles which in some degree recall the dispute in London more than twenty years before.

In the years after 1848 the Christian Socialists gave a high place to workers' education in their plans for social regeneration, and tried to interest the Trade Unions. They founded, with F. D. Maurice as first President, the London Working Men's College; and E. V. Neale, through his Co-operative League, tried to interest both Co-operative Societies and Trade Unions in educational work. There was not, however, much response from the Trade Unions, whereas the Co-operatives displayed much activity up to the early 'seventies, when their enthusiasm seemed suddenly to wane. Many Co-operative Societies cut, or even eliminated, their grants for education during the depression which set in after 1874.

At almost the same time a new development began, originating with the Universities—Cambridge, Oxford, and London. This was the University Extension movement, which had close connections with the movement for the higher education of women. Requests were received from certain groups of working men for similar courses to those provided chiefly for middle-class audiences ; and for a time it looked as if a considerable movement for workers' education would grow up under University auspices. But before long the University Extension movement developed mainly as a middle-class affair, though there were always some worker students. This situation lasted until 1903, when a Co-operative clerk, Albert Mansbridge, founded the Workers' Educational Association and began a campaign for direct collaboration between the Universities and the working-class movement in the provision of types of classes deliberately designed to meet working-class demands for higher education. The new movement took definite shape in a report on *Oxford and Working-class Education*, published in 1908 by a joint committee of university teachers and working-class representatives. This report led to the establishment of a Joint Tutorial Classes Committee of similar composition at Oxford ; and the movement spread rapidly to other Universities.

The Workers' Educational Association started with quite a distinctive programme. Mansbridge and his fellow-workers were insistent on high educational standards and highly qualified teachers, and pitched their demands high by putting most of the emphasis on classes 'of university standard' to be held weekly in the evenings through two or three consecutive winter sessions. They also insisted that the education should be such as would increase the mastery of the students over their social and economic environments and make them better qualified as citizens as well as culturally. The subjects on which the main emphasis was laid at the outset were political philosophy, economics and history, but any non-vocational subject was welcomed, subject to the teaching being done at a high level. The W.E.A. also insisted from the first on the need to distinguish between education and propaganda, and to keep party-political and religious propaganda outside the classes, while not restricting the free discussion of controversial issues. In other words, they believed in the possibility of objective teaching, combined with unfettered discussion, and held that this type of education would best serve working-class interests. Almost from the beginning the W.E.A. and the Tutorial Class movement based on its collaboration with the Universities secured a large amount of Trade Union as well as Co-operative support, including that of the Trades Union Congress Parliamentary Committee (and later of the General Council) and of the Co-operative Union. Among early tutors in Tutorial Classes R. H. Tawney was an outstanding figure ; and he played throughout an important part in the W.E.A., of which he became President.

This type of education did not, however, meet with general acceptance in the working-class movement. In 1899 two Americans, with some English helpers, had managed to found in Oxford a new College for full-time workers' education. Ruskin College began with no very clear conception of teaching methods ; but within a few years a sharp controversy developed. One group asserted that the students were being poisoned by anti-Socialist economics, while others said that the Principal, Dennis Hird, was filling them with Marxist propaganda. The outcome was a split. A majority of the students, headed by the Principal, seceded and formed a rival Labour College (later called the Central Labour College), which presently received the support of two Trade Unions—the South Wales Miners and the Railwaymen—then in the forefront of the more militant section of the Trade Union movement. A minority of the students remained at Ruskin College, which was reconstructed under the exclusive control of the Trade Unions and Co-operative bodies which continued to give it support. But this was not the end of the matter. The seceders continued to denounce Ruskin College as a home of reaction ; and they also, through an auxiliary agency which they had formed—the Plebs League—vigorously denounced the W.E.A. and began, with the Central Labour College, to build up a rival movement for conducting evening classes, and to demand Trade Union support. The Plebs League attacked the entire conception on which the W.E.A. was based. It denounced the Universities as capitalist institutions, and also attacked the W.E.A. for its readiness to receive financial help from the State and from the Local Education Authorities, which also it regarded as tainted with capitalist control. By this time the W.E.A. was conducting, in addition to Tutorial Classes and Summer Schools in conjunction with the Universities, many evening classes of its own ; and the two movements were soon in keen conflict all over the country. Presently the Central Labour College had to close down ; but there remained in being a number of regional 'Labour Colleges' which were in fact not colleges but organising centres for classes like the Districts of the W.E.A. The central body came to be known as the National Council of Labour Colleges, and it won a substantial amount of Trade Union support, both from national Trade Unions and from local branches and districts. The W.E.A., on its side, started a special Trade Union auxiliary —the Workers' Educational Trade Union Committee—under exclusive Trade Union control, open to Unions which were prepared to finance special educational schemes for their members under its auspices. Thus the Trade Union activity in the educational field came to be divided between two rival bodies, the one collaborating with the Universities and receiving grant aid from public bodies, and the other denouncing all such collaboration as a betrayal of working-class interests.

At this stage the N.C.L.C. was definitely Marxist, and not only Marxist but also aggressively 'left-wing'. When Communism came into existence in Great Britain after the first World War, the Communists for a time played a substantial part in it. But then two things happened. As the N.C.L.C. won more official Trade Union support, it had to curb its more extreme tendencies ; and its leaders before long fell out violently with the Communists, who were trying to subordinate it to their own purposes. It became definitely anti-Communist, without ceasing to be Marxist ; and, despite its rupture with the extreme left, it remained as violent as ever in its denunciation of the W.E.A., which was indeed a great asset to it in appealing for left-wing Trade Union support. Ever since this situation developed in the 1920s, the conflict has continued, with some Trade Unions on the one side, some on the other, and yet others dividing their support between the contestants. The charge against the W.E.A. of being a 'capitalist conspiracy' has been throughout, of course, plain nonsense, as the support given to it by a great many prominent Socialists and Trade Unionists and the large part it has played in the education of men and women who have become Labour M.P.s, local councillors, and officers and leaders in the working-class movement plainly show. But a good deal of the mud has stuck ; and what is true is that the W.E.A. type of class has not appealed to those workers who prefer their education to be given from a propagandist standpoint, and to whom the idea of 'objectivity' in education means nothing at all, when it is not rejected as a *bourgeois* prejudice.

Indeed, the W.E.A. has been much better at conducting relatively advanced and systematic class work and at conducting less advanced classes in cultural subjects than at meeting the demand for relatively elementary classes more closely related to the mental habits of active Trade Unionists whose interest in education is *entirely* political or economic; and its classes, because of their 'literary' approach, have tended to attract a high proportion of the better educated workers (in terms of school education), especially black-coats, and to appeal relatively little to the less skilled or to the doctrinaire. The N.C.L.C., working without University or government help, has not been in a position to carry on sustained, high-level teaching of the same standard as the W.E.A.; and it concentrated for a long time mainly on shorter, simpler and less exacting courses with a direct propagandist appeal—which its supporters undoubtedly preferred. The situation, however, began to change when, after the second World War, the Trade Unions began to take more interest in the education of their members for direct service in Trade Union work, as shop stewards, committee-men and officials regularly engaged in growingly complex tasks of collective bargaining and joint consultation, and as they began accordingly to require from the educational bodies they supported a growing amount of work of this kind. We shall see in the next section how this development has proceeded, and what its effects on the general position of workers' education have been.

In 1953 the W.E.A. celebrated its jubilee, with a bigger contingent of classes and students than ever before. Ruskin College also continued in being under Trade Union and Co-operative control, and, the old quarrels ended if not forgotten, drew students from both the W.E.A. and the N.C.L.C., while receiving substantial help from public bodies. Its students—men and women—spent at least one, and commonly two years in residence; and most of them sat for a Diploma in Economics and Political Science opened to them by Oxford University. There were in 1953 several other residential Colleges designed mainly for working-class students, but not completely controlled by working-class bodies. These mostly offered a course limited to one year. In addition, there were numerous agencies engaged in providing various forms of Adult Education, not designed specifically for working-class students ; but with these the Trade Unions had no organic connection, and I do not propose to discuss them in this book. There was also a large volume of non-technical, as well as of technical, Adult Education carried on by the public Education Authorities, in Institutes and Colleges of various kinds, including both Technical, Commercial and Art Colleges and a new type of College, modelled on the Danish Folk High Schools, providing short residential courses. But the main body of non-vocational Adult Education provided specifically for 'workers' was in the hands of the W.E.A., the N.C.L.C., and Ruskin College.

The W.E.A. and the N.C.L.C. are both federal structures at national, district and local levels. Basically, they rest on their classes and on local branches, the latter made up of both individual members and affiliated local bodies, including Trade Unions. The branches are joined together in Districts or Divisions, made up of affiliated branches, affiliated district bodies, such as Trade Unions, and again individual members. The national structure is made up of representatives from the Districts or Divisions, and of nationally affiliated bodies—again largely Trade Unions and Co-operative Societies. The N.C.L.C. has a larger proportion of Trade Union affiliations to the total, because the W.E.A. also includes a considerable number of teachers' and other educational organisations. The final authority in the W.E.A. is a Delegate Conference, including their representatives of branches as well as of Districts and nationally affiliated bodies. In the N.C.L.C. it is very similar, except that the delegates from affiliated bodies come almost entirely from Trade Unions. Each body has an Executive Committee composed of representatives of its Districts or Divisions and of its nationally affiliated Societies ; but in the case of the N.C.L.C. the representation of affiliated Societies is confined to Trade Unions which have educational schemes in connection with it.

Although most Trade Unions now spend some money on education, the total, even including their expenditure on the activities to be dealt with in the next section, is not yet very large. The N.C.L.C. works chiefly by means of contributions from its affiliated national Trade Unions in proportion to their membership. The W.E.A. has a more elastic arrangement under which, after payment of a small affiliation fee, each Union draws up its own scheme and budget as it pleases. In addition, a number of Unions provide one or more scholarships for members, usually tenable at Ruskin College, but sometimes at other workers' Colleges or at a University, and a number also contribute to the scholarship funds of Ruskin or of other Colleges. The Trades Union Congress General Council, in addition to collaborating with the workers' educational bodies, has a special arrangement with the London School of Economics for a course specially provided by it for Trade Union students ; and a few other Universities also conduct special Trade Union courses. Oxford and Cambridge and a few other Universities provide special scholarships for students from extra-mural university classes—mainly W.E.A. Tutorial Classes—and most of the Universities run considerable Summer Schools for class students in conjunction with the W.E.A.

This is not the place for any attempt to resolve the conflict between the rival conceptions of workers' education held by the W.E.A. and the N.C.L.C. It would be as absurd to deny that there is any proper place for educational propaganda as to deny the possibility of objective teaching such as the W.E.A. sets out to provide. A propagandist movement has a clear right to attempt to educate its members not only to do its own work more efficiently but also to act as missionaries on its behalf ; and a worker who wants this sort of education is fully entitled to demand it. But a worker who wants something different and more closely analogous to the further education of those who stay longer at school and perhaps go on to a University is, surely, no less entitled to demand what he wants ; and a working-class movement that has always stood for a 'broad highway' of access to higher education can hardly, with any logic, denounce as illegitimate the provision of higher education for workers with public and university aid. Logic, however, is seldom the determining factor in what men or associations stand for ; and logic has been of no avail in ending the denunciations of the W.E.A. by its critics. As for the Trade Unions, most of their delegates understand very little what the dispute is about ; and some Trade Union Conferences go one way and some another. Both movements are therefore able to carry on ; and in practice there is rather little competition between them for students, because they are in the main doing different things and appealing to different types.

This, however, does not prevent them from being in keen competition for Trade Union support.

III. TRAINING FOR TRADE UNION SERVICE

When British and American leaders meet and their talk turns on 'workers' education', they usually discover that they attach widely different meanings to the words. Whereas in Great Britain Trade Union educational activity has been carried on mainly through either the Workers' Educational Association or the National Council of Labour Colleges, and until quite recently the Trade Unions have done but little directly for the education of their members, in the United States 'workers' education' has meant mainly the training of Union members for Union service or for forms of service closely related to the Union's work. There are indeed in the United States separate labour educational bodies, and the American Federation of Labor maintains an attached Workers' Education Bureau ; but these bodies are relatively unimportant, and by far the greater part of the educational work is done by the individual Unions among their own members. The high degree of concentration on this type of work is due partly to the great rapidity with which American Trade Unionism has grown and has needed to build up a large body of officers and active members, but also partly to the 'business' character of the movement, with its concentration on getting the most out of collective bargaining and its comparative absence of ideological foundations—or at any rate of desire to challenge the assumptions of a capitalistic system. The British Trade Unions, ever since the advent of the New Unionism at the end of the 1880s, have been considerably influenced by Socialist ideas ; and their ideas of education have been shaped by the desire to prepare their members for the tasks of making and living in a new kind of society. Moreover, those among the leaders who have been least affected by Socialism have been influenced by Liberalism instead, and have been believers in a broadening out of the traditional culture to embrace the whole society. Working with middle-class idealists and educational enthusiasts, both groups have been disposed to favour a wide notion of workers' education as a preparation for democratic citizenship; and most of the Socialists, not being doctrinaire Marxists, have also thought of the culture of the new society as needing to be built upon that of the past, rather than on its ruins.

This preoccupation with 'liberal' education has caused the British Trade Unions, until quite recently, to neglect the aspect of 'workers' education' with which the American Trade Unions have been almost exclusively preoccupied. They have done remarkably little either to train their officials or to equip their local representatives and shop stewards with any special preparation for facing the tasks of collective bargaining and workshop consultation. Nor was this work seriously attempted, until very recently, by either the W.E.A. or the N.C.L.C. The N.C.L.C. was concerned mainly with teaching its students to be Socialists, preferably on a Marxist foundation. The W.E.A. was concerned with giving them the means of making up their minds on a foundation of sound knowledge whether they were Socialists or not, or what sort of Socialists they were. Neither, except quite incidentally, was setting out to teach the techniques of collective bargaining or of Trade Union organisation and administration. Even Ruskin College taught such things very little : the general assumption was that they could be left to be picked up by actually doing the job.

In recent years these attitudes have been changing. The growth of workshop bargaining and of joint consultation, the development of time and motion study, job evaluation, and other techniques of 'labour management', the greater strength of the Unions under full employment, and the new responsibilities falling on them, first in wartime and then in connection with post-war economic planning and campaigns for higher productivity, have all contributed to make the work of collective bargaining, from the workshop level upwards, a good deal more technical than it used to be, and to call for greater economic as well as greater technological knowledge. This holds good for shop stewards as well as for full-time officials, and also for local spare-time officers and for members of national and district executives. Moreover, the very tasks of organisation and office administration are getting more rationalised; and there is much more business to be done with government departments and official agencies as well as with more highly organised business managements and employers' associations. Contacts with American Trade Unionists, moreover, and the work of the Anglo-American Productivity Council, and also the numerous visits paid by Trade

Union representatives from various industries to the United States for the study of American methods of raising productivity, have undoubtedly influenced the outlook of many British Trade Union leaders.

The most evident sign of the change has been the great development of Trade Union Summer Schools. The Trades Union Congress has for a long time conducted its own Summer School for Trade Unionists, usually held at Ruskin College ; and more recently a considerable number of Trade Unions have conducted their own Summer Schools, largely for the education of their branch officials, shop stewards, and local and district committee members. The W.E.A. was the pioneer in Summer School work, and some of the Unions have invited it to undertake the educational arrangements on their behalf, while others have called in the N.C.L.C. The teaching has usually been done partly by W.E.A. or N.C.L.C. tutors, and partly by Trade Union officials, lecturing on the branches of Trade Union work in which they are expert. The W.E.A. was also a pioneer in the holding of Week-end Schools and Saturday Schools for Trade Unionists ; and here again the N.C.L.C. has been an active rival. The Trade Unions have increasingly entered into this field with special Schools on Trade Union work, industrial relations, time and motion study, and other matters of importance to their local and works representatives. The most recent development, again pioneered by the W.E.A., takes the form of a series of consecutive Week-end Schools, attended by the same group of students, at which a subject can be studied more thoroughly than in a single week-end, and reading and other preparation can be arranged between the sessions. This has been a considerable success where it has been possible to find suitable accommodation.

At Oxford in particular, experiments have been made with short courses designed mainly for full-time officials, executive members, and other relatively important Trade Union representatives, for work on such matters as wage-policy, the economic aspects of collective bargaining, and problems of industrial management and consultation. But it is difficult to secure the attendance of busy officials, and this type of work is still at an early stage.

Another development has been an attempt by a few Unions—particularly the Transport and General Workers—to induce new members to study the organisation and history of the Union.

This has been done with considerable success by certain Unions in the United States. The method is that of a prepared correspondence course, to be used preferably by groups but available for individuals also, explaining how the Union works and giving some account of its achievements, in order to encourage more members to become active participants in its affairs. Unfortunately, in the Transport Workers' Union, though the course is well designed, the number of members taking it has remained small. At least one or two American Unions have succeeded in persuading a much larger proportion of new members to make use of their courses. In connection with such courses, there are great advantages in the use of film or film-strip. In the United States, these devices are being widely used. (They are also beginning to be used in carrying the gospel of Trade Unionism to some of the less developed countries). In Great Britain, I have myself prepared series of film-strips dealing in general with the history and problems of Trade Unionism and of the Co-operative movement.*

I have spoken already of the longer courses at Ruskin College and at the London School of Economics. Certain Unions, notably the General and Municipal Workers, have recently been arranging for some of their full-time officials to attend special courses at local Technical Colleges on such subjects as Industrial Management, Time and Motion Study, and Production Engineering, in order to equip them better for handling problems of negotiation with firms that make use of modern 'scientific management' techniques. But there is no practice here as yet of sending young potential officials away for longer full-time courses as part of their training. This is partly because, in most British Unions, almost all the full-time officials are directly elected by the members, whereas some of the American Unions have a practice of taking on young men and women without election or permanent appointment, trying them out and giving special training to those who are thought most promising, and then encouraging them to become candidates for elective offices. Something like this could be, but seldom is, done by those British Trade Unions, such as the Transport and General Workers, most of whose officials are not elected but appointed by the Executive Council.

There is of course always the danger that the official, if he is

*Published by Common Ground, Ltd.

selected for his qualities as an expert and given special training in managerial techniques, may get out of touch with the attitudes of the members he is supposed to represent, and may fail in the quality of personal leadership. Fear of this, as well as conservatism, is at the back of the opposition that undoubtedly exists to the development of training schemes for Trade Union officials. But it is hardly disputable that the tasks which both full-time officials and other Union representatives, including shop stewards, are being called on to perform in collective bargaining are getting more and more complex and technical as methods of production get more scientific and as the production engineer and the industrial consultant take larger shares in organising the labour process. The situation calls for some sort of training, above all for workshop representatives and for district officials who are required to negotiate concerning the conditions of particular establishments.

It is a moot point how much of the new types of training for Trade Union service can best be undertaken by individual Trade Unions for their own members, how much by the Trades Union Congress General Council, and how much through the bodies which are active in the wider fields of workers' education discussed in the preceding section. There can be no one answer to this problem; but there is much to be said for conducting a good deal of the work—except elementary courses for new members and specialised courses for officers of a particular Union, which are clearly best done by each Union for itself—in such a way as to bring members of different Unions together for exchange of experiences and to relate the study to the wider problems of the working-class movement as a whole.

It has of course to be borne in mind that Trade Unions will necessarily approach the problems discussed in this section from the standpoint of getting practical advantages in the furtherance of their own ends and policies, and that there can be no question of studying 'impartially', in the sense of questioning the Unions' aims, as distinct from their methods. But there remains within the fields we have been considering a large area for objective study. For example, what a Trade Union representative wants to know about time and motion study is not essentially different from what a manager or supervisory technician wants to know, though they may need to apply their knowledge from different points of view. Still, the element of instruction in accepted

Union policy that is involved in courses of training for Union work involves that the Unions will need, either individually or through the Education Department of the Trades Union Congress, to keep the ultimate control of this type of activity in their own hands. They certainly cannot afford to hand it over to Technical Colleges or Universities, though they can and should make use of both. Nor can they afford to delegate it entirely to the workers' educational bodies, though they need to invoke their help, especially in finding suitable teachers and collaborating in the arrangement of suitable courses of study.

CHAPTER X

TRADE UNION POLICY

I. UNOFFICIAL STRIKES

TRADE Unions have developed in a hostile environment. They have had to fight for every step in their advance—over a long period even for the right to exist. The bare right of existence conceded in Great Britain in 1824 did not carry with it any obligation, or even any encouragement, to employers to concede the right of collective bargaining. On the contrary, for long afterwards Governments looked on Trade Unions with the utmost suspicion, and again and again sided with employers who refused to recognise them ; and the law courts interpreted as narrowly as they could the statutes which allowed them to exist at all. Even after the fuller legal recognition given to Trade Unions in 1871, a stiff battle had to be fought to secure the conditions needed to make strike action possible without conflict with the law ; and the advantages won in 1871 and 1875 were upset in the new century, first by the Taff Vale and then by the Osborne Judgment. Only under the Trade Disputes Act of 1906 and the Trade Union Act of 1913 did Trade Unionism seem finally to have thrown off most of its legal shackles ; and it was put in fetters again by the Trade Unions and Trade Disputes Act of 1927, which was not repealed until 1946.

This is only the legal aspect. Recognition of the rights of collective bargaining by employers had to be fought for steadily, industry by industry, right through the nineteenth century into the twentieth. The cotton operatives began to build up firm arrangements for collective bargaining in the 1850s : the mineworkers, after advancing some way in the 1840s, were flung back, and had to rebuild first in the 1860s, and then again from 1889. The engineers were defeated in the 1850s, and had to win their way back gradually, district by district. The builders, locked out in 1859 and presented with the 'document' requiring them to renounce their Unions—as the engineers had been in 1852—barely survived, and had, again like the engineers, to win recognition in a long series of local struggles. The agricultural workers fought a great struggle in the 1870s, only to lose almost all they had won in the ensuing depression : they remained prostrate until well on into the present century. The dockers and gas-workers, pioneers of Unionism among the less skilled industrial workers, won their great victories in 1889, but had still to face many attempts to withdraw the recognition they had won : even in 1912 the Port of London Authority refused to recognise the Transport Workers' Federation. The shipowners fought against recognising the Seamen's Union and organised special corps of blacklegs to defeat it, right up to the explosion of 1911. The railway companies, except the North-Eastern, held out against recognising Trade Unionism right through the struggles of 1907 and 1911, and finally gave way only at the end of the first World War. Postal workers and later other Civil Servants had to fight the Government for the right of organisation and collective bargaining well into the twentieth century. Such groups as shop assistants, commercial clerks, bank clerks (whose struggle was not quite over even in 1953), foremen and other supervisory workers won their rights step by step in a long series of guerrilla battles which have continued right up to the present day.

Trade Unionism was not merely born in struggle—an un-welcomed bastard of the Industrial Revolution : it has been fighting against the taint of illegitimacy ever since. It bears the stigmata of its history upon it : its members have never expected to be fairly treated, and, when the unexpected happens, can hardly recognise it for what it is. Trade Unions have not been used to easy victories, or to the enjoyment of any power they might not be called on to fight for at any time with all their strength. Their instinct has been to oppose : they have never, until quite recently, had any choice in the matter. No wonder they are finding it difficult to adapt themselves to a situation in which the Government itself is sometimes on their side.

As we saw in a previous chapter, this persistent hostility to Trade Unionism has rested on a combination of political and economic motives and attitudes. There has been throughout the class motive—the will of the superior classes to maintain their superiority, and to keep their inferiors down ; and there has been also the desire for cheap and docile labour, and with it the belief that there is an 'economic law', as cogent as the laws of nature, that settles the workers' rightful share in the product of industry —so that Trade Unionism is an illegitimate and foolish flying in the face of nature. Reinforcing these two grounds of hostility has been a third—an individualism which takes its stand on the sanctity of the freedom of individual contract, regardless of the plain fact that the employer is in himself a combination in relation to the employees, and even of the growth of joint stock companies and of huge combines and financial agglomerations. The privileged classes have always been ready to chatter with righteous indignation about the 'tyranny of Trade Unions': they are doing it still; and they are reinforced by a kind of entrepreneur or technician who wishes to regard 'his' workers as adjuncts to 'his' machinery, who ought to be made to behave without question as his plans of mechanised production require.

Trade Unions, then, have been pariahs ; and, if they have nowadays often to be courted because of their power, they are still for the most part courted without love. Their duty, many employers and high administrators and managers feel, is, since they cannot be dispensed with, to act as disciplinary agents for keeping the workers in order, and reinforcing the authority which the employer can no longer exert sufficiently without their help. If we must bargain collectively, argues the director of an industrial enterprise, let us at any rate get our *quid pro quo* in immunity from strikes caused by human recalcitrance. If we must make agreements, let us make sure the workers keep them. Of course, up to a point this attitude is natural and even legitimate. Agreements are made to be kept ; and if terms in an industry are fairly settled by equal bargaining, has the employer no grievance if some group, dissatisfied with the settlement, breaks away and upsets his production plan ? Clearly he has a grievance, if this is the whole story ; but what is to be done if the settlement does inflict real and unnecessary hardship on some particular group ? Can it really be taken as final that a few men sitting round a table, with inevitably deficient knowledge of all the variations in local conditions, agree to something on behalf of perhaps hundreds of thousands of individuals whom they are supposed to represent ?

The truth is that, to some extent, unofficial strikes are the unavoidable concomitant of national bargaining which embraces great numbers of workers employed under widely varying conditions within a single collective agreement containing provisions which bind all their workers not to go out on strike until certain complicated procedures have been gone through. It can be argued that, no matter how long these proceedings may take, the workers affected by a particular grievance ought to wait until they have been complied with before even considering strike action. But it is not always in human nature for them to do so, when their grievance is one that involves what they feel to be a matter of principle. For if they wait, they will be compelled to obey the employer's orders in the meantime ; and if the trouble arises out of an attempt to introduce some novel practice to which they object, they may feel very strongly about giving way for a period of unknown duration while the question is being explored. Moreover, they may have a shrewd suspicion that unless they resist at once they will never have a chance, because the question will be settled over their heads by some remote authority knowing little of their affairs. Thus, unofficial stoppages will occur, no matter what may be laid down in national agreements ; and some of these stoppages will be legitimised later—perhaps by the Final Appeal Court to which such matters have under some Unions' rules to be referred for judgment.

This is not meant as a defence of unofficial strikes, save under exceptional conditions. It is true that unofficial strikes are often the outcome of deliberate trouble-making—in these days chiefly, though not exclusively, by Communists who are out to fight the official leadership and to make all the difficulties they can. Trade Unions must, if they are to make collective agreements at all, deal with such trouble-makers, even to the extent of suspending the persons concerned and shutting down branches which refuse to comply with the rules. But it is necessary to recognise that not all unofficial stoppages can be dismissed in this way, and that, the more remote from the actual workplaces the negotiators of agreements are and the more agreements have to applied by further negotiations to the conditions of each particular establishment, the more will occasions be likely to arise when the men on the spot simply will not wait, and obey orders they resent, until the prolonged processes of official negotiation have been gone through. Where employers are sensible, such occasions will rarely arise ; but not all employers, or managements, are sensible—any more than all workmen are.

It needs to be borne in mind that the type of strike of which I am speaking, though it is now necessarily 'unofficial' because of national agreements, would not so long ago have been normally an official strike, called by a District Committee of a Trade Union with the consent of a national Executive not bound down by an elaborate procedure agreement. It is not at all that workers strike more than they used to : in fact they strike a great deal less. It is that the conditions of official bargaining and of strike action have been changed. There are more strikes than there used to be ; but they are smaller and last less long. The change is illustrated by the following figures :

TRADE DISPUTES, *Numbers, Numbers Involved, Duration* 1909–1951

Years	*Total Number of Strikes : Annual Average*	*Average Numbers Directly involved* (*in thousands*)	*Average Working Days Lost* (*in thousands*)
1909–1914	846	675	16,394
1915–1921 (7 years) ..	974	1,185	24,092
1922–1927	521	1,473	63,219
1922–1927 (omitting 1926)	565	605	13,263
1928–1933	387	747	12,306
1934–1939	798	299	2,161
1940–1945	1,521	272	1,298
1946–1951	1,528	233	1,235

Of course, in the above Table the year 1926 includes the General Strike. I have therefore given alternative figures omitting that year. The general trend is unmistakeable. Strikes have been getting more numerous, though not in proportion to the number of workers enrolled in Trade Unions. But they have also been getting smaller. Between 1946 and 1941 the average strike was hardly more than a third as big as the average strike of the years before the first World War, and cost only one-fourteenth of the number of working days. This is no doubt a tribute to the success of collective bargaining in eliminating long and extensive strikes. It is also a sign that some penalty has to be paid for this achievement in an increased number of little strikes which mostly last only a very short time. It is a very light penalty.

II. WAGES POLICY

In the past it has always been the task of the Trade Unions except in wartime, to get as much as possible out of their members' employers, without taking account of the probable effects on the economy as a whole. They have been expected to ask for more in good times, and to make as few concessions as possible when times have been bad. The great majority of employers have always paid as little as they could and have improved conditions or reduced working hours only under pressure. Here and there, from the days of Robert Owen onwards, employers have been found offering on their own account to pay more or grant better conditions than others, either out of philanthropy or because they wished to attract and hold the best workers and believed that it was profitable to pay out more for better work from contented and unrestless employees. But such employers have always been exceptional; and even where they have done well out of their behaviour it has never been provable that they were doing more than skimming the cream of labour by being better employers than their rivals—not that all employers would have made more profits (or as good profits) if they had all conceded better conditions. True, it has been demonstrated again and again that vaticinations about the impending ruin of industry when wages were raised or hours reduced were without foundation, and even that to cut wages in the hope of restoring production during a slump is calculated in most cases to make the situation a great deal worse. But this is by no means to say that the better conditions the average employer grants, the more prosperous he is likely to be: it is the fall in wages from one level to another, not their absolute level, that intensifies a slump; and even this does not hold good except in the home market.

Trade Unions, in the past, did not need to concern themselves with such debated questions. There was never any doubt that their right course was to stand out for as much as they could get, to yield only when they could not help yielding, and to be as quick off the mark as possible in demanding better conditions on a rising market. It was the employers' business to attend to the rest—to meet rising labour costs by substituting machinery for labour, to expand or contract production as demand went up and down, and to make concessions or to resist according to their judgment of economic conditions and prospects.

All through the nineteenth century and on into the twentieth trade alternately boomed and slumped—of course, with a powerful long-term tendency towards higher production and higher productivity as techniques improved. The workers earned more when trade was good, at any rate in terms of money, not only because wage-rates rose but also because they got more regular employment, and often worked overtime. Workers who had strong Trade Unions—that is, through all the earlier period, mainly skilled workers—did better than others, both in getting more and in resisting cuts in bad times; but even strong Trade Unions had only limited powers to accentuate upward and to limit downward movements. In good times they could go only as far as employers would yield rather than fight to the end when profits were good : in bad times they could resist only to the point at which their resistance was broken by the pressure of unemployment or they were sheerly starved into submission. Nevertheless, they achieved amply enough to demonstrate what nonsense it was to argue that combinations were powerless to affect wages, as so many economists argued during the first half of the nineteenth century. What they could do was to ensure that as productivity increased wages and conditions improved with it and were not held down to an immutable 'subsistence level' or to a total inexorably determined by the size of the 'wages fund'.

Under the conditions of bargaining that prevailed up to the time of the first World War, it could always be safely assumed that, even if wages could sometimes be too low, and hours of labour too long, in relation to what the economy could bear, there was no real risk of their rising beyond what could well be afforded. The employers and the gold standard, as administered by the bankers, would see to that. The balance of payments could never go seriously wrong because, if it threatened to, deflation would automatically put it right and, while this corrective was operating, any temporary difficulty could be met by reducing overseas investment, or even, if necessary, recalling overseas loans. The workers did not need, and were not encouraged, to trouble their heads about such matters. When the bankers restricted credit, the employers had to discharge workers and to force wages down ; and when these unpleasant operations were over, things improved again, and the chance came for the Unions, first to get back what they had been forced to give up, and then to demand more—and get it if they were tough enough and if the good times held. To be sure, during the last quarter of the nineteenth century the situation was complicated by a persistent tendency of prices to fall as production rose faster than the means of paying for it. This meant that a stationary, or even a falling, money wage might be a rising real wage for those in regular work, and that it was accordingly much harder to win actual advances in money wages. The Trade Unions came in for a good deal of undeserved blame during this period because the success of their efforts in resisting, or checking, wage-reductions went unrecognised. It is much more spectacular, and better appreciated, to win a wage-advance than to evade a reduction.

This is not to say that the workers did not suffer in what was called the 'Great Depression' of the 1870s and 1880s. They did, but from unemployment and underemployment rather than from reductions in wage-rates, except in a few industries, such as coal-mining and woollen manufacture, in which special circumstances made the fall in wages much greater than the average. In the organised trades, real wages for full-time employment actually rose during the period of falling prices ; whereas, when prices began to rise again after 1896, real wages fell. This complication, however, does not affect the general validity of what I have been saying. Trade Unions, up to 1914, had to take the conditions of trade and monetary supply as 'acts of God' and to make the best of their bargaining power under these conditions, without considering the effects of their own actions upon them.

To-day, though Trade Unions sometimes try to behave as if this were still the environment in which they need to act, every Trade Union leader, and indeed every intelligent Trade Unionist, really knows better. The old epoch ended with the first World War : the period between the wars was one of transition, during which the governing classes, the bankers, and the major part of the employers continued to behave as if the old rules still held good, but the Trade Unions, instead of accepting the rules, kicked against them—and were beaten. The struggles of 1921 and 1926, with the Mineworkers on both occasions in the centre of the battle, were in effect a challenge to the view that Trade Unions must bow to 'economic laws' as believed in and acted upon by their betters. On both these occasions the miners went on strike, not so much against the mine-owners as against deflation, or rather against its consequences. They were staking out a claim that it was somebody's duty—in effect the Government's—to see to it that living wages should be paid and employment maintained at a satisfactory level ; and J. M. Keynes, challenging the prevalent economic orthodoxy, reinforced their claim with arguments which set a whole generation of economists, and even bankers, by the ears.

Keynes could not save the miners, or prevent the old notions being acted on when the slump hit Great Britain in 1931. But even under the 'National' Government it was no longer possible for deflation to be carried to the extreme. Wages were prevented from dropping nearly as far as they dropped in most other countries—including the United States. Social services, though sliced as far as orthodoxy dared, could not be so reduced as to cease to afford a fair amount of protection. It was not admitted that the Government had any responsibility for maintaining either wages or employment ; but up to a point they were maintained, because no one in authority dared to push the attack on them to the extremes to which it would have been pushed before Trade Unions had become a power and before the 'New Economics' had at any rate shaken a great many persons' confidence in the 'Old'. The 'New Deal' in the United States went a long way towards acceptance of the view that fair wages and the maintenance of employment were public responsibilities, which Governments could no longer evade.

The second World War brought with it both planned employment and a great reinforcement of Trade Union strength. The Labour Party's victory of 1945 confirmed the obligation on the Government to accept the responsibility for full employment, with the assurance that, given full employment, the Trade Unions would be well able to look after their members' interests. It looked as if the road were clear for the Unions to exact from industry every penny that it was able to afford in wages, or to spend on improved conditions of work. But, in the event, things did not work out quite like that. During the years after 1945 the Trade Union movement found itself under the necessity of practising 'wage-restraint' in face of high and rising profits and of explaining to its members that they would only defeat their own ends if they attempted to use their increased strength in the traditional ways. Why was this?

At bottom, it was because, ever since the first World War, the British economy had been losing ground. This deterioration was partly concealed in the 1930s, because the world slump brought down the prices of agricultural produce and of many imported materials to levels which made them dirt-cheap in terms of export prices. This, of course, reduced the volume of exports that could be sold, and led to unemployment in the export trades ; but for the consuming public as a whole cheap imports meant that the slump did not cause the standard of living to fall, especially as Great Britain stopped exporting capital and even used some of its overseas investments to pay for current consumption. Investment at home was also allowed to fall, at the cost of a failure to keep methods of production up to date ; but the deterioration had not gone far enough to react on standards of living when the second World War broke out.

The second war led to further deterioration in many industries not essential to the war effort, partly compensated by improvements in others. But it also put an end to the period of low import prices—by leading to a world shortage of food—and caused a further heavy fall in British overseas capital holdings. It left the United States immensely more productive than before, and other countries mostly much less productive : it left Great Britain dependent, until it could restore and advance its productive power, on American loans or bounty for the means of buying imports that could be had only for dollars and were indispensable for maintaining the standard of life. True, within a few years Great Britain had so far recovered as to be again barely paying its own way in terms of current production and consumption, but not so as to be able to afford out of its own resources the sums needed for investment either at home or for the development of colonial areas or the stimulation of the demand for British exports. These could be maintained—and even so inadequately—only with aid from America ; and the British economy depended accordingly on such aid. It was recognised that this could not go on for long ; but just as the effort to climb out of the dependence seemed to be meeting with some partial success, the outbreak of the Korean War brought on a new crisis. Intensive war preparation set in ; and largely under the stimulus of American buying, the prices of raw materials, and of many foodstuffs, soared to fantastic heights, utterly ruining the precariously improved British balance of payments. Crisis measures had to be taken ; and they were taken at the cost of slowing down the rate of investment in British industry and thus postponing the prospects of stable economic recovery to an indefinite future.

These were the conditions under which the British Trade Unions, with all the strength given to them by large membership and full employment, had to act after 1945. Every rise in wages, not at once counteracted by an equal rise in the cost of living, meant a demand, direct or indirect, for more imports ; for most of the things on which more money would be spent were either imported, or made of imported materials, or were just the things that could most easily be sold abroad to pay for imports urgently required. The possible level of real wages, it became clear, depended, not on what employers could afford to pay, but on the quantities of consumable goods that could be made available for the workers to buy—unless indeed any wages above this could be compulsorily diverted into forced savings by taxation or by some other device.

As for profits, they were high because employment was full and because even obsolescent plant was needed to meet the current demand. But the high profits could not be used as a source for higher wages because, if they had been, the increased consumers' demand, pressing on limited supplies of goods, would have raised prices, and with them profits, higher still. So the workers were puzzled to discover that under a Labour Government profits rose at a great rate, and they were told to exercise 'wage restraint' as the alternative to causing an inflation that would do them more harm than good. For if the cost of exports rose, the volume of exports would fall so much that fewer imports than ever could be afforded, and supplies of consumable goods, instead of increasing, would actually fall.

Moreover, this was mostly true, at any rate within the limitations of the type of mixed economy to which the Labour Government was committed. Indeed, even if it had been possible to distribute among the workers the whole surplus income accruing after taxation to the wealthy, the position would have remained much the same. The British economy, in the condition in which it was in the early 'fifties, simply could not afford any wage-increases that would involve increased imports of consumable goods—or perhaps even enough to maintain the existing supply.

Consequently, although money wages rose in 1951 and 1952, prices rose at least as fast, even after the temporary price boom of 1951 had come to an end. Formal 'wage-restraint' had been given up; but instead higher wages that were conceded were promptly cancelled by the rising cost of living.

What, in these post-war circumstances—for in effect the dilemma has existed ever since 1945—should the policy of the Trade Unions have been, and what should it be now? Hitherto, each Trade Union—or each Federation, where several Unions work together within a single industry—has framed its own wage policy and has negotiated with the appropriate body of employers, without any consultation with the Trades Union Congress or the General Council. The only attempt to co-ordinate demands over several industries was that of the Triple Alliance; and even in this case, as we saw, there was no effective submission of the programme of any of the three partners to the judgment of the others. The only co-ordination has come from the arbitration tribunals to which matters have been referred after the parties to negotiation have failed to agree ; and even in these cases the arbitrators have been supposed to deal with each demand on its merits, and the use of panels of arbitrators has meant that there has been no one group of persons judging all the claims. Each Union has been jealous of its right to control its own programme and to conduct its own bargaining ; and in most cases programmes have been drawn up by some sort of delegate conference and proposed settlements referred back to such conferences for acceptance or rejection. The democratic nature of this procedure makes it difficult to alter : we have seen how the Miners argued both in 1921 and in 1926 that only their Delegate Meeting could instruct them what terms to accept. Of course, while compulsory arbitration was in force, and also when it had been agreed to refer a particular dispute to arbitration voluntarily, the final decision was taken out of the delegates' hands. But even in these cases the decision what to demand continued as a rule to be made by a delegate conference, except when the delegates handed the power to frame a demand over to some other body, such as the Executive of a Federation.

When the Labour Government approached the Trades Union Congress and the Trade Unions generally with its post-war request for 'wage-restraint', the General Council, in giving its broad support to the request, had to make clear that it had no authority to bind its affiliated Unions. All it could do was to recommend the Government's policy, subject to certain safeguards, and to lay it before the next full meeting of Congress for general approval. This approval, which was given in face of some opposition, no more bound the individual Unions than the General Council's own recommendation had done. The policy of 'wage-restraint', while it lasted, was no more than a 'gentlemen's understanding', which any Union was free to disregard. The real sanction behind it was the existence of compulsory arbitration, the unlikelihood of arbitrators failing to take note of the Government's advice and of its general acceptance by the Trade Union movement, and the further unlikelihood of any Union defying the law by resorting to an official strike in support of a rejected claim. These, taken together, were powerful safeguards ; and some argued that they were too powerful, because they were liable to provoke unofficial strike action. This was part of the Labour Government's reason for giving up compulsory arbitration in 1951. The Trades Union Congress, for its part, had gradually become more restive, and in 1950 had decided, against the General Council's wish, to end its support of wage-restraint. But neither of these events greatly altered the actual situation. No Trade Union embarked on a national wages strike. References to arbitration continued to be accepted in practice. The only difference was that Unions bargained rather harder, especially in the nationalised industries, and perhaps that arbitration courts awarded rather more than they would have done had compulsory arbitration and 'wage-restraint' remained in force.

Throughout the years after 1945 there was constant discussion of the idea that this system of unco-ordinated Union bargaining was obsolete and that some sort of 'national wages policy' ought to be introduced. A very few Trade Unionists of some influence favoured this notion; but it was strongly opposed by the General Council and rejected by large majorities whenever it was brought up at the Trades Union Congress. Its principal advocates came largely from the Trade Unions in the Civil Service, which felt they had done badly out of the existing arrangements, and that these favoured the industries most important in the productive drive. The 'general' Unions, as well as the big industrial and craft Unions, were almost solidly opposed.

The proposal that there should be a 'national wages policy' could mean any of a number of things. It could mean that the Unions themselves should establish some common body to pass judgment upon, or at least to advise upon, the claims put forward by the separate Unions. To this, for the reasons already given, it was most unlikely that the Unions would agree. It would have been regarded as undemocratic, and as in effect transferring the control of Union affairs from the members to a junta of leading officials. The officials themselves would have none of it, because they feared that it would cost them the support of their own members, and would never work. A second form of the proposal was that the Chancellor of the Exchequer, in drawing up his annual Economic Survey, should include, after consultation with employers' and Trade Union representatives, an estimate of the total amount the country could afford to have paid out in wages during the coming year, and that this figure should be communicated to Unions and employers' associations, and also to arbitration tribunals, as a guide to their action in making agreements or awards. This would have amounted to a development of the 'gentlemen's understanding' about 'wage-restraint' into something much more formal, and embodying a definite figure, but would have left each Union to formulate its own claim and each claim to be decided by separate negotiation or arbitration as before. The Union leaders did not like this proposal any better than the other. They saw themselves being tied down in advance to an acceptance of conditions which would compel them to oppose their own members' wishes when claims were being drawn up. A third form of the proposal for a 'national wages policy' was that there should be set up a Central Wages Council representing employers, Trade Unions, and the Government and also including a few economic experts, to replace the various arbitration tribunals and to serve as a final court of reference in all wage disputes. This too most of the Trade Union leaders rejected : they preferred not to share in the responsibility for arbitration awards, and they also felt that the existence of such a central body would undermine the traditional forms of collective bargaining.

It is hardly surprising that the Trade Union leaders took this view. The case for a 'national wages policy' is really part of the case for a 'planned economy', in which it would be evidently out of the question to plan the other factors of production and distribution while leaving wages unplanned. Great Britain after 1945 was not a 'planned economy': its annual Economic Surveys were, and are, not plans, but estimates of what is likely to happen : its so-called 'Planning Board' had only narrow functions : a good deal of its production was 'controlled', but not fully planned—and the 'controls' were being relaxed, not tightened. It had practically no control over the distribution of incomes, though it had large powers to re-distribute them through taxation. A planned allocation for wages would not have worked without a parallel allocation to profits and to other forms of income ; and this the Government was by no means ready to undertake. At some stage, if Great Britain continues to advance towards a socialist economy, wages will have to be planned ; but to plan them as was suggested, in the 1940s would have meant putting the Trade Unions into a strait-jacket while profits continued to be uncontrolled.

If a 'national wages policy' was for the time being impracticable it does not appear that the Trade Unions, in handling the wages problem, could have done anything much different from what they actually did. The 'restraint' which they in fact used, and for some years officially recommended through the Trades Union Congress, was undoubtedly necessary in face of the economic situation. No one can say what would have happened if each Trade Union, under conditions of shortage of labour, had gone out to get all it could. In the past, except in time of war, there has always been unemployment—sometimes more and sometimes less, but always enough, actual or at least potential, to set limits to Trade Union power. But when employment is really full, and will remain so even if wages rise considerably, the terms of the wage-bargain become economically quite indeterminate. Trade Unions *can* stand out for any wages they please; and employers can give way or decide to resist. If a strike ensues, the determining factor will be not the ability of the employer to pay but the pressure the Government or public opinion is able to exert on the disputants. Wages will then be settled by political rather than by economic considerations; and the structure of prices and production will respond to whatever wages are so fixed. These responses will determine the amount of the real, as distinct from the money, wage; and whether wage increases leave the workers better or worse off, or as they were, will depend on their effects on the whole economy, and especially on their effects on the national ability to purchase the imported supplies on which the standard of living so largely depends. This will depend largely on the effects of the higher wages on export prices, which in turn will depend on the exchange value of the national currency. This in its turn will affect the prices of imports. Indeed, it all comes back to the point that, under any given economic system, the height of real wages depends on the size of the available supplies of consumers' goods.

The Trade Unions, then, could in the post-war situation do nothing else than press for better terms as far as they felt they could do so without unduly upsetting the rest of the economy. This was by no means a satisfactory situation; but there was no practicable alternative. It was unsatisfactory, in particular, because it necessarily presented the appearance of wages being held down while profits were allowed to soar. Consideration was given on this ground to the idea of imposing a statutory limit on dividend distributions ; but the Government contented itself with a 'gentlemen's agreement' on this matter parallel to the agreement with the Trade Unions, but not backed by any sanction such as compulsory arbitration provided in the case of wages. The Government also taxed profits, including undistributed profits, much to the annoyance of the business interests, which argued that all their high reserved profits were needed to pay for capital maintenance and development. But the existence of very high profits, even if they were subject to high taxation, made it very difficult to persuade Trade Unions that the restraints on wages (which were also taxed) were not an employer's dodge to swindle them out of their share in rising production. It would have been easier to persuade them if the whole of the excess profits had gone to the Exchequer ; but this would have been inconsistent with the maintenance of capitalist industry—and the Labour Government was in no wise ready to dispense with it.

III. PRODUCTIVITY

Until Joint Production Committees—now transformed into Joint Consultative Committees—were introduced during the second World War, British Trade Unions had a tradition against associating themselves with joint bodies formed to stimulate higher output. Trade Union leaders had taken part during the first World War in campaigns for higher production ; but save in a few exceptional firms no joint machinery for the purpose was set up. The Joint Industrial Councils formed under the Whitley scheme after 1918 were intended to concern themselves with such matters, as part of the general improvement in industrial relations they were designed to bring about. But only a very few ever did : most of them soon turned into negotiating bodies of the ordinary kind. In Trade Union nostrils, the word 'productivity' smelt of 'speeding up' and breaking down cherished craft customs : it suggested Scientific Management, efficiency experts, and industrial consultant firms such as Bedaux. Most Trade Unionists were hostile to these methods when any attempt was made to apply them. Nevertheless they made headway, especially in mass-production factories where a high proportion of less skilled labour was employed ; and Trade Unionists learnt during the bad times in the 1920s and 1930s to adapt themselves to them, but not to like them. During the second

World War, when almost all the workers were on the side of the war effort, 'efficiency' methods made great progress in the war industries with very little opposition; and on the whole the Joint Production Committees worked well where managements gave them a chance. After 1945, it was manifestly necessary to continue production at a high level in the converted war trades, which were called on to supply a high proportion of the larger volume of exports needed to pay for essential imports; and there was little attempt to revert to old practices that had been suspended during the war. It was realised that mass-production techniques were indispensable, in face of their enormously successful application in the United States, if British industry was to hold its own; and as they offered a fuller pay-packet, in which the skilled men got their share under various bonus arrangements, not much resistance was offered. In the later 1940s, no one needed to feel that by producing more he was doing anyone else out of a job; and that made all the difference.

If, however, many Trade Unions ceased to regard the word 'productivity' with the same suspicion as before, it became necessary to take up a more positive attitude towards this problem. High output was seen as benefiting not only the capitalist, but the whole country; and it was what the Labour Government wanted. Moreover, the British Trade Union leaders, in the process of reconstructing the world Trade Union movement, came into much closer contact with the American Trade Union leaders, and especially with the Congress of Industrial Organisations, the principal organiser of the workers in the mass-production industries of the United States. They found the attitude of these leaders to be different from their own. The Americans argued that, given strong Trade Unions, the more industries produced the more the workers would be able to get out of them, and that, accordingly, the Unions should not merely back employers' efforts to increase productivity, but should compel backward firms to introduce better methods. The British leaders found the Americans 'production-minded'; and the teams sent to the United States to study American methods mostly came back impressed, and in a mood to borrow at least something from American Trade Union practices. Their views met with criticism, especially among the older craftsmen on the one hand and from 'leftists' who hated 'class-collaboration' on the other. But, with many more employers seeking, under conditions of full employment, to substitute some form of consultation for the old works discipline that had broken down, a good many Trade Unionists in the workshops were also changing their attitudes ; and on the whole the new precepts of the leaders were not ill received.

We saw in a previous chapter how certain Trade Unions began to give attention to the training of some of their officers and shop stewards in such techniques as time and motion study, in order to improve their quality as negotiators and in the work of joint consultation. This tended to encourage participation in projects for increasing output and a more elastic attitude towards old rules about demarcation of trades. In many factories, a good deal of hostility remained to new methods which destroyed traditional craft practices ; but this hostility was less solid than of old ; and in a number of factories, where the pay and conditions were good, it largely disappeared.

Indeed, nearly all thinking Trade Unionists, unless they have firmly closed their minds to such dangerous thoughts, are by now well aware that they cannot afford any longer to adopt a merely negative attitude towards plans for increasing output. They know that Britain's industrial future and their own standard of living depend on keeping pace with the rapidly rising production standards set by the United States and now being rapidly developed in such countries as Germany and Japan, as well as in the Soviet Union. They are aware of these things ; but many of them are still suspicious—especially among those who remember the long period of heavy unemployment between the wars. There may have been little risk of doing anyone out of a job by producing more in the 1940s ; but even a moderate recession in 1952 (it was more than that in the textile industries) brought the old terrors back.

There is, moreover, the fear that the Trade Union official or representative, if he becomes more of a technician and takes to collaboration with employers over productivity, will forget how to fight—or has forgotten already. The more active Trade Unionists are not sure that they may not soon be called on again to fight hard for their rights. No doubt, American Trade Unions fight hard, despite their co-operative attitude over production. Indeed, they have had to fight very hard indeed, not so long ago, to establish their present position ; and they have to face much more militant anti-Unionism than now shows itself in Great

Britain. But there is the big difference that the American Unions, though they fight hard for 'recognition' of bargaining rights and for better wages and conditions, are not fighting against capitalism as a system and are thus not challenging the foundations of American society. It may be said that, in practice, the British Unions are not doing this either ; but the fact remains that most of them, by their affiliation to the Labour Party, are committed to a moderate, evolutionary sort of Socialism, and that most of their active leaders, local as well as national, are broadly Socialists. This makes them much more suspicious than the Americans of any policies which involve collaboration, or any kind of joint responsibility, with private employers in ensuring the successful conduct of industry. The main body of Trade Union members probably do not clearly know whether they are Socialists or not, though most (not by any means all) of them steadily vote Labour. But the movement, in its spirit as well as in its collective action, is definitely anti-capitalist ; and this attitude is too deeply embedded in its traditions to be easily changed.

That is why, despite recognition of the need for high productivity in the workers' own interests, formal joint organisation to promote it finds powerful obstacles in its way, and why even leaders who have come to wish for it have to walk warily if they are not to lose their members' confidence and support. There is also, of course, the fact that many employers and managers still hanker after a return to the old discipline, which depended on the fear of unemployment, and are quite incapable of putting their hearts into making joint consultation work. There are many factories in which Joint Production Committees and after them Joint Consultative Committees have failed to work because neither side has really wished them to succeed.

There are, however, many more firms than there were which are trying to make joint consultation work and serve as a means to the introduction of new methods of production by mutual consent. In some of these firms, a real attempt is being made to study the processes of production not merely from the standpoint of the mechanical engineer or the cost accountant but also with regard for their human consequences. Such studies may be self-interested, in that they are started in the belief that happiness, or at least content, in work is nowadays the best way of getting higher production ; but they have the virtue that, whatever the motive, they are made with a view to reducing the unpleasantness and irksomeness of daily toil and that, where they succeed, the sheerly human gain is great. Such bodies as the Institute of Industrial Psychology, founded at the end of the first World War, and the more recent Tavistock Institute of Human Relations, have done valuable work in studying the psychological conditions of the labour-process ; and it is to be regretted that Trade Unions have not taken more interest in them. For example, the recent Tavistock study* of the human conditions of longwall coal-mining, as practised to-day in certain mines regarded as highly up-to-date, throws a flood of light on the mistakes the mechanical engineer can make when he is not made to study the effects of his work-arrangements on the human structure and relations of the working team. Some good work has also been done in the field of vocational selection and guidance ; but the Trade Unions have mostly taken too little notice of it.

IV. NATIONALISATION AND CONTROL

Trades Union Congress resolutions in favour of nationalisation go back to the 1890s, when the influence of the 'New Unionists' first made itself felt. From 1900 an increasing number of Unions were connected with the Labour Party ; and there too resolutions in favour of nationalisation were repeatedly carried, though the Party did not fully commit itself to Socialism until it endorsed the programme embodied in *Labour and the New Social Order* towards the end of the first World War. Thereafter, though the Trades Union Congress made no formal profession of Socialism, it was working in double harness with a political party which did ; and most of the important Trade Unions were affiliated to both. It was therefore more or less assumed that the Trade Unions stood for nationalisation ; but as far as most industries were concerned the assumption remained of little practical importance, for no one expected them to pass under public operation in the near future. In practice, the Trade Union advocacy of nationalisation was limited to those industries and services in which the Trade Unions directly concerned were pressing for it ; and this meant in practice mainly the mines and the railways. In the already nationalised Post Office the policy of the Postal and

******Some Social and Psychological Consequences of the Longwall Method of Coal-getting*. By E. L. Trist and K. W. Bamforth. In *Human Relations*, Vol. IV, **No. 1,** 1951.

Telegraph Clerks, taken over by the Union of Post Office Workers on its formation by amalgamation of the P. and T.C.A. with the Postmen's Federation and certain smaller Unions, was to press for the conversion of the Post Office into a self-governing service by the establishment of a 'Guild'.

Only among the Miners and the Railwaymen was there a really strong movement in favour of nationalisation ; and in both these cases the demand by 1918 was for public ownership combined with a large measure of 'workers' control'. The Miners' Federation demanded that the conduct of the mining industry should be entrusted to a Mining Council, of which it should nominate half the members, the other half being chosen by the Government mainly to represent the managerial and administrative elements. The National Union of Railwaymen too demanded half the seats on the managing board that was to take over the conduct of the railways.

In 1919, the question of nationalising the mines was argued out, on the Miners' demand, before the Sankey Coal Commission; and a majority of the Commission, including the chairman, pronounced in favour, and also asserted the desirability of associating the workers in some way with the management. When the Government refused to act on these parts of the report, the Miners' Federation appealed to the Trades Union Congress for help, urging concerted industrial action to force the Government's hand. The T.U.C., however, would not do more than inaugurate a propagandist campaign—The Mines for the Nation Campaign—in favour of public ownership ; and this campaign, the first large-scale effort to influence public opinion in favour of nationalisation—fell flat. In the case of the railways, the Government launched as an alternative to nationalisation the Geddes plan for the amalgamation of the numerous separate concerns into four great main-line companies ; and the Railwaymen, under the influence of J. H. Thomas, in effect bartered national ownership for full Trade Union recognition, coupled with a plan of joint consultation through a system of District and Sectional Councils. With the onset of the post-war depression the entire question receded into the background. The Labour Government of 1924, dependent on Liberal support, could do nothing about it ; and the Trade Unions, then and during the ensuing years, were too preoccupied with immediate matters of wages and conditions to bring the matter to the front. Nationalisation remained on record as an aspiration, both of the Labour Party and of the Trades Union Congress ; but it did not receive a high priority until the second Labour Government took office in 1929. Even then, the Government, again dependent on the Liberals, did not attempt to transfer either the mines or the main-line railways to public ownership. It limited itself to a Bill for taking over London passenger transport—a Bill that was left to be finally enacted, in a mutilated form, by the 'National' Government that succeeded it. Before that, the B.B.C. had been taken over, and the electricity 'grid' set up under public ownership by the Conservatives.

Only in 1931, after the fall of the second Labour Government, did nationalisation proposals for a number of industries and services come to take a leading place in the planning of the new Labour programme, and also to occupy seriously the attention of the Trades Union Congress General Council. Working on earlier plans for a co-ordinated socialisation scheme for the fuel and power industries, the Party Executive drew up and successive Party Conferences approved a series of plans for public ownership and operation of coal, railways, electricity, water supply, and the Bank of England, while the Trades Union Congress, dividing the work, produced similar socialisation plans for the steel and cotton industries, besides collaborating in the issue of the plan for coal. It was in connection with this spate of socialisation projects that the Party and the Unions first seriously faced the question of the form to be taken by the agencies to be set up to administer the nationalised services. The Labour Party, under Herbert Morrison's influence, was hostile to any representation of 'interests', and wished for Boards or Commissions nominated entirely by the appropriate Minister, after consultation with the Trade Unions and other interested groups, but without any element of representation. The members, on this view, were to be chosen entirely for their personal capacity to serve the whole public under the general directions of the Government. Many of the Trade Unions concerned, on the other hand, wanted to make sure of having their own men on the Boards, though their actual demands differed, and were by no means always clear. Some held by the old demand for half the seats to be given to representatives of the Trade Unions organising the workers : others demanded only some such representatives. What was often left unclear was the position to be occupied by the representatives. If, as the

Labour Party's schemes involved, they were to be mainly full-time employees of the National Boards, were they to sever connections with their Unions on appointment, or to be recallable by their Unions and in a status of dual responsibility to their Unions and to the Ministers at the head of the departments which would relate the nationalised services to Parliament and one to another? Or, if they were to be part-timers, keeping up their Union connections, could they in fact manage the huge services of which they would be in charge? It appeared in the course of the discussions that the Trade Unions, apart from a minority that agreed with Herbert Morrison's attitude, were divided into those which wanted representatives over whom they would have some sort of control (e.g. the Railwaymen), and those which were insistent only on having an adequate number of Trade Unionists on the proposed Boards and on being given a real voice in the appointments. Finally, the Labour Party Executive and the T.U.C. General Council, after the matter had been argued at the conferences of both bodies, patched up a somewhat ambiguous compromise, which laid down the need for adequate Trade Unionist membership of the Boards, but left it quite vague how the persons in question were to be chosen or what their subsequent status was to be. In effect, Herbert Morrison won, by making concessions to Trade Union opinion that were hardly more than verbal.

Thus, with no early return of the Labour Party to office in prospect, the question slept through the rest of the 1930s, to come up again as an urgent matter when the Labour Party set about re-drafting its plans with a view to the election of 1945. On this occasion the Morrisonians had a much easier victory; the Trades Union Congress General Council, in a report approved by Congress in 1944, declared in favour of Boards to be appointed by the Ministers concerned, without any representative element—though not of course without Trade Unionist members; and the actual nationalisation measures which became law under the third Labour Government were all on the Morrisonian pattern. Trade Unionists were included in every case on the National Commissions, Boards and Executives to which the socialised services were handed over. But they became, in nearly all cases, full-time public servants, and had to renounce all Union connections when they took office. A good many more Trade Unionists became district or local officials in the service of the new public bodies, on the same terms. A sop was thrown to the advocates of workers' control by the institution under statute of compulsory joint consultation at every level, the Unions providing the workers' side of the consultative bodies at all levels above the establishment, and in effect at the establishment level also, even where every employee was given the right to vote for members of the Joint Consultative Committees. Thus, a considerable number of former Trade Union officials found themselves transmuted, usually at much increased salaries, into Board members or Board officials, most often in charge of the Labour and Welfare aspects of the Boards' activities. But there was no 'workers' control' and no representation of the Trade Unions as such on any body responsible for managing a socialised service or any part of one.

Before long this situation began to provoke protests. But the Trade Unions were by no means at one in the attitudes they took up. The National Union of Mineworkers, once among the fervent advocates of 'workers' control', made clear that it did not wish to be represented, at the price of having to share responsibility for the conduct of the industry. It preferred to remain outside, assured of being consulted and of having former officials of its own to consult with, and to be free to criticise and make demands upon the National Coal Board, as it had done formerly upon the colliery owners. The National Union of Railwaymen, on the other hand, soon became deeply discontented with the working of nationalisation, when it found that the new management was very like the old ; and it began again to press for direct representation. The Union of Post Office Workers joined the debate, renewing its demand for the conversion of the Post Office into a 'Guild' enterprise, under the management of a Council representing the various grades of employees, with the Postmaster-General as Chairman. This claim, opposed by the smaller Post Office Engineering Union, was rejected by a large majority at the 1948 Trades Union Congress : neither the Trades Union Congress nor the Labour Party has been prepared to go beyond pressing for the appointment of more Trade Unionists to Boards and to official positions in the nationalised industries. The General Council, in its most recent pronouncements, has deliberately sidestepped the problem, saying that there is no need to pronounce upon it with a Conservative Government in power. It is, however, bound to come up in connection with the plans for further measures of nationalisation which the Trades

Union Congress of 1952 instructed the General Council to prepare, and with the new programme which the Labour Party has drawn up for submission to its Conference in 1953.

On the question of nationalisation itself, there have been evident hesitations in recent years. The Labour Party Programmes of 1950 and 1951 contained only very modest projects for the transference of additional industries to public ownership. A section of the Party, headed by Herbert Morrison, then favoured a period of 'consolidation' of what had been already done before further large-scale measures were attempted; and for the time being this view prevailed. The Morecambe Conference of 1952, however, showed itself unmistakeably in favour of including a considerable further instalment of nationalisation in the new Party Programme; and in the early months of 1953 the Labour Party Executive was considering what industries to include. It approached the General Council and invited it to participate in the committees to which the preparation of this part of the programme had been entrusted; but the General Council preferred to go on with its own plans separately, leaving itself free to criticise whatever the Party Executive proposed. In taking up this position the General Council was certainly influenced by the dispute that had arisen within the Party between the supporters of Aneurin Bevan and the right-wing advocates of 'consolidation'—a dispute which, as far as it concerned the extent of nationalisation, seemed in a fair way to being brought to a harmonious end. The majority of the General Council, in 1953, seemed to be hesitant about backing further nationalisation plans; but this majority was made up of different elements—some wishing to go slow with further nationalisation, while others were pressing for more 'industrial democracy' as a condition of further schemes.

There is indeed a very real difficulty about workers' participation in the management of industries, whether socialised or not. In the case of socialised industries, it is simply impracticable for some of the members of a managing Board, but not others, to be at one and the same time full-time salaried servants of the State, responsible to a Minister, and representatives of the workers, responsible to a Trade Union. The two responsibilities cannot be harmonised; for if persons in such a position are outvoted on the Board, or given ministerial directives of which their Trade Union disapproves, what are they to do, and what is to happen ? Are they to resign ? That is no solution ; for the Union will presumably choose successors who will take the same view. It would be practicable, if it were thought desirable, to hand over the entire administration of an industry to persons nominated by the workers engaged in it, as the Union of Post Office Workers has in effect demanded. It would be possible, under such a system, to reserve to the Minister, with the approval of Parliament, the power to issue to the Board certain directives on general policy to which it would have to conform ; for the Unions would presumably accept the necessity of doing what Parliament told it to do. But it is quite a different matter to have a Board composed partly of ministerial and partly of Trade Union representatives, with the latter in a minority ; for this would mean that the Union representatives would have to accept, not only ministerial directions, but also the view of a majority of their Board colleagues, or else resign.

Guild Socialists have always advocated, as a long-run objective, the management of publicly owned industries by Boards either entirely composed of nominees of the workers in the industry—including all grades—or containing a majority of such representative members. But they have never suggested that such a system should be introduced at once, or without a considerable period of preparation. They have, moreover, argued that this preparation must begin at the bottom rather than at the top, with the granting of an increasing amount of 'workers' control' at the workplace level—for example, through participation in the appointment of supervisors, the arrangement of group work, promotions, training of learners, and so on. They have insisted that the appointment of a few Trade Union officers to national or regional Boards, or to official positions under them, is not 'workers' control' at all, and that real workers' control must be built up from the workplaces to the higher levels, so as to rest on the knowledge and experience of the workers in relation to their actual jobs. Guild Socialists have therefore stood somewhat aloof from the demand that more Trade Unionists shall be appointed to positions in the nationalised industries at the higher levels, and have preferred to stress the need for an advance from joint consultation in the workplaces to a gradual transfer of workplace control as a necessary preparation for the introduction of industrial democracy at the higher levels, This conception, however, makes no appeal to most Trade Union leaders ; for, having made the centralisation of collective bargaining on a national scale their principal objective, they are disposed to insist on the need for a corresponding centralisation in the control and management of nationalised industries. They are moreover, as we have seen, suspicious of workplace autonomy, and inclined to fear that any building up of workers' control inside industry from the workplaces to the higher levels would create a new focusing point for the workers' loyalty apart from the Trade Unions, and would thus undermine Trade Union power.

This explains why, on the whole, most national Trade Union leaders are opposed to Guild Socialist conceptions of workers' control based on the free co-operation of small working groups, and why there has been a certain unreality about the renewed debates concerning 'industrial democracy' since 1945.

There are, of course, still greater difficulties in the way of applying 'workers' control' to industries which remain in private hands. Joint control, in such cases, implies a community of objective between employers and workers which neither most Trade Union leaders nor most active Trade Unionists would be at all prepared to accept. It may be possible, when there is a willingness on both sides to make joint consultation work well and to accept the raising of output as a shared objective, to advance beyond mere consultation to the transfer of certain forms of control in the workplace into the workers' hands. In France, for example, there are factories where, under the system known as *le contrat collectif du travail* (collective labour contract), the workers in a workshop make a collective bargain to produce the goods required at a collective price, which they divide among themselves in agreed proportions, taking the entire supervision into their own hands and dispensing altogether with foremen and workshop superintendents chosen by the firm. Such a plan does not involve any representation of the workers on the board of directors, or any profit-sharing or acceptance by the workers of the profit system ; but it does transfer a real element in industrial control into the workers' hands*. There has, however, been little sign that the workers in Great Britain are interested in this approach, though a few experiments akin to it have been made among the dockers at Liverpool and Grimsby in recent years.

*See, for this system, the writings of Hyacinth Dubreuil over many years. The latest is a pamphlet, *Les Trois Bases de toute de la Vie : clé de toute organisation sociale,* 1951.

CHAPTER XI

STRENGTH AND WEAKNESS

I. INTRODUCTORY

AT the end of 1951 there were 704 Trade Unions known to the Ministry of Labour, with a total membership of 9,480,000. Of these, 17 had more than 100,000 members, and accounted for 6,305,000 members, about two-thirds of the total; 322 of the Unions had fewer than 500 members, and 398 fewer than 1,000. Only 32 had more than 50,000, and 50 more than 25,000. The two big general Unions between them had over two million members, and the six largest Unions over four millions. More than three-quarters of the total membership were in Unions with more than 50,000 members, hardly more than 1 per cent in Unions with fewer than 1,000. Unions with from 1,000 to 10,000 members accounted for about 7½ per cent of the total.

Thus, Trade Union membership was highly concentrated in a few big Unions. Largest of all were the two great general Unions —the Transport and General Workers and the General and Municipal Workers. Next to them came the Amalgamated Engineering Union and the National Union of Mineworkers, and then, after a long gap, the National Union of Railwaymen and the Union of Shop, Distributive and Allied Workers. Another gap separated these from the Electrical Trades Union, the Amalgamated Society of Woodworkers, and the National Union of Public Employees. In the next group were the National Association of Local Government Officers, the National Union of Teachers, the Union of Post Office Workers, and the Civil Service Clerical Association; the only other Unions with more than 100,000 members were the National Union of Agricultural Workers, the National Union of Tailors and Garment Workers, the National Union of Printing, Bookbinding and Paper Workers, and the Iron and Steel Trades Confederation—unless one counts the United Textile Factory Workers—a federation of Unions in the cotton trades.

The total membership of 9,480,000 was made up of 7,705,000 males and 1,775,000 females. Of the female members, 310,000 were in general labour Unions, 254,000 in the textile trades, and

149,000 in the boot and clothing industries; 148,000 were in the distributive trades, 183,000 in teaching, and 244,000 in the national and local government services. The rest were widely scattered—71,000 in the engineering and metal Trade Unions; but this figure is not significant, because many women in these trades were in the general Unions. The number of women in Trade Unions compared badly with the number of women in gainful employment. At the end of 1951 the total number of persons in employment in Great Britain, excluding those in the armed forces, was 22,500,000—made up of over 15 million males and over 7¼ million females. Thus, about half the males and less than one quarter of the females belonged to Trade Unions, despite the high proportions of organised females in the teaching profession, in the public services, and in the cotton industry. This difference was partly accounted for by the fact that, although many married women remain in employment, a good many drop out on marriage, and the female labour force includes a high proportion of girls and young women who do not expect to remain in gainful employment all their lives and are not deeply interested in Trade Unions, or so much influenced as men by notions of class-solidarity.

It is unfortunately impossible to present from the available statistics any picture of the strength of Trade Unionism industry by industry or occupation by occupation. The general Unions cut right across any classification of this kind; and some Unions organised on a craft basis have members in many industries, while industrial Unions include members of many crafts. Accordingly, the Table opposite, which shows the number of Trade Unionists in the principal groups under which Unions are classified in the official returns, cannot be related to the numbers employed in the various industries without considerable misleading consequences, especially in the groups marked with an asterisk in the Table.

In the Table, I have given the comparative figures, as far as they are available, for 1922 and for 1939. It will be seen that between 1922 and 1951 the numbers in the general Unions much more than doubled, and those in the metal trades and in agriculture nearly doubled. On the other hand, the number of Trade Unionists in the cotton industry was almost halved, and there was a less catastrophic fall in the other textile industries. In coal-mining, well organised at both dates, there was hardly any change.

TRADE UNION MEMBERSHIP BY INDUSTRIAL OR OCCUPATIONAL GROUPS, 1951

Membership in Thousands

Group	1951			1939			1922		
	Males	*Females*	*Total*	*Males*	*Females*	*Total*	*Males*	*Females*	*Total*
øGeneral Unions	1,837	310	2,147	1,135	84	1,219	764	50	814
*Agriculture, Forestry and Fishing ..	165	8	172	49	1	50	91	2	93
Coal Mining	791	16	807	705	2	707	809	5	813
*Other Mining and Quarrying ..	7	1	8	—	—	—§	37	—	37
*Treatment of Mine Products ..	17	19	36	—	—	—§	—	—	—§
*Chemicals, etc.	14	6	20	—	—	—§	—	—	—§
*Metal Industries and Trades ..	1,632	71	1,703	928	9	936	860	7	868
Cotton	77	162	239	87	162	249	145	255	400
Other Textiles and Textile Finishing	91	92	183	94	77	171	136	122	257
Leather and Fur	14	4	18	—	—	—§	—	—	—§
Clothing (except Boots)	34	109	143	36	87	122	35	46	81
Boots and Shoes	58	40	98	66	35	101	60	24	84
Wood and Cork	112	16	128	—	—	—‖	60	4	64
Paper and Printing	224	73	297	171	53	224	138	49	186
*Food, Drink and Tobacco ..	48	21	69	—	—	—§	34	4	29
*Other Manufactures	10	3	13	—	—	—§	46	24	69
*Building and Contracting	486	—	486	413	7	420†	389	—	389
*Gas, Electricity and Water ..	34	4	38	—	—	—§	—	—	—§
Railways	532	31	563	461	9	470	438	5	443
Other Transport and Communication	393	60	453	73	1	74‡	102	—	102
Distribution	250	148	398	199	86	245	94	40	134
Insurance, Banking and Finance ..	78	19	97	81	11	92	77	6	83
*National Government	225	130	355	340	87	428	307	69	375
†Local Government	291	114	405	184	50	234			
Education	134	183	317	89	161	249	64	145	210
Other Professional Work	88	108	196	—	—	—§	—	—	—§
*Entertainment and Sports ..	61	26	87	28	9	37	28	7	36
Other Services	2	—	2	—	—	—§	—	—	—§
*Others	—	—	—	121	44	165	48	7	55
Totals	7,705	1,774	9,480						

*Partly in General Unions. †Including Woodworking. ‡Water Transport only, other Transport included with General Labour.
§Not shown separately. ‖Included with Building. øIncluding other Transport, except Water Transport.

Sharp rises occurred in clothing, in the printing and paper trades, and, still more, in distribution, government services, and teaching. Clearly, the proportion of non-manual workers and of less skilled workers in the total increased ; and so did that of women. There were 872,000 women in Trade Unions in 1922, out of a total membership of 5,625,000 : in 1939 there were 976,000, out of 6,234,000 : by 1951 there were 1,775,000, out of 9,480,000. The percentages are 15.5 for 1922, 18.6 for 1939, and 18.7 for 1951. Thus, the change took place before 1939 : the great employment of women during the war has not had any lasting effect on the proportion of women to men organised in Trade Unions. It was substantially higher at the end of 1944—22½ per cent.

The above figures cover all Trade Unions, not only those which belong to the Trades Union Congress. If Congress Unions only were included, the main effect would be to remove the Teachers and most of the Local Government Officers, and also some of the Civil Servants. No other group would be greatly affected. For 1951 the totals would fall, for men, to 6,702,000 and, for women, to 1,318,000, giving a female proportion of 16½ per cent.

The strength of Trade Unionism in 1951 thus amounted to one male worker out of every two, and one female worker out of every four in civil employment. But these proportions include juveniles : the proportion of adults enrolled in Trade Unions are somewhat larger. Moreover, the state of organisation differs greatly from occupation to occupation. A high proportion of the unorganised are in scattered industries or in occupations, such as domestic service, which the Trade Unions have hardly been able to reach at all. In most of the key industries organisation is relatively strong, above all in coal-mining and in steel. The cotton industry too is well organised : the fall in membership there is due to the heavy reduction in the numbers employed. Engineering is highly organised in its main branches : non-unionism prevails chiefly in the minor metal trades and among women workers. Of the great industries, building is the worst organised, mainly because of discontinuous employment and the failure effectively to unionise the less skilled workers. Clerical workers remain poorly organised, except on the railways and in banking and some branches of insurance. The distributive workers are highly organised in the Co-operative stores and in many of the big department stores and multiples : their weakness is in one-shop businesses and most of all in the small shops. Civil Servants, local government employees and teachers are all highly organised groups. Supervisory workers and technicians, on the other hand, are well organised only in a few cases : some of them belong to special Unions, some remain in manual workers' Unions to which they belonged before promotion. Draughtsmen are a remarkably well organised group of non-manual workers. Among agricultural workers Trade Unionism is much stronger than it used to be, but still relatively weak. The printing and paper trades are a highly organised group, including the less skilled workers, men and women.

At the Trades Union Congress in 1952, the two big general Unions commanded between them 2,093,000 votes out of 8,020,000—more than a quarter. The four next largest had together 2,113,000. Thus, six Unions out of 183 were in a clear majority. The remaining nine Unions with more than 100,000 each totalled 1,375,000. Thus, 15 Unions had 5½ millions out of the total of eight millions. The system of election to the General Council—to represent the occupational groups—prevents the largest Unions from capturing all the seats ; but half the members of the Council came from these 15 Unions, and most of the rest from Unions in the size-group next below them. On the next page are the groups from which the members are elected by the whole Congress.

II. THE STATE OF ORGANISATION IN THE MAIN INDUSTRIES AND OCCUPATIONS

In this section an attempt will be made to describe very briefly the state of Trade Union organisation as it was in 1953 in the main industries and occupational groups.

Coal Mining

The coal miners are the most highly organised of all the great industrial groups. Their organisation has entirely recovered from the serious setback which it suffered after the great defeat of 1926. The separatist 'non-political' Unions then established in Nottinghamshire and in South Wales had been liquidated before 1939; and the Miners' Federation of Great Britain had already recovered most of its strength. But up to the outbreak of war the miners were still suffering from the economic effects of their inter-war defeats and of the severe depression of the early 1930s. They had

TRADES UNION CONGRESS GENERAL COUNCIL—GROUPING FOR ELECTION OF MEMBERS

	Group	*Membership* 1952	*Number of Delegates at Congress*		*Members on General Council*
I.	Mining and Quarrying	653	129	3	Mineworkers (2), North Wales Quarrymen
II.	Railways	554	48	3	Railwaymen, Locomotive Enginemen, Transport Salaried Staffs
III.	Other Transport*	1,401	96	3	Transport and General Workers (2), Seamen
IV.	Shipbuilding	118	16	1	Boilermakers
V.	Engineering, Founding and Vehicle Building	1,290	106	3	Engineering Union (2), Patternmakers
VI.	Iron and Steel and Minor Metal Trades	194	40	2	Blastfurnacemen, Iron and Steel Trades
VII.	Building, Woodworking and Furnishing	592	69	2	Woodworkers, Building Trade Workers
VIII.	Printing and Paper	289	55	1	London Compositors
IX.	Cotton	182	39	2	Card and Blowing Room Operatives, Weavers
X.	Other Textiles	107	30	1	Dyers, Bleachers and Textile Workers
XI.	Clothing	181	23	1	Tailors and Garment Workers
XII.	Leather, Boot and Shoe	111	19	1	Boot and Shoe Operatives ; Shop, Distributive and Allied Workers
XIII.	Glass, Pottery, Chemicals, Food, Drink, Tobacco and Distribution ..	485	69	2	Pottery Workers
XIV.	Agriculture	135	16	1	Agricultural Workers
XV.	Public Employees	252	24	1	Health Service Employees
XVI.	Civil Servants	428	56	2	Post Office Workers, Inland Revenue Staff
XVII.	Non-manual Workers	231	47	1	Theatrical and Kine Employees
XVIII.	General Workers	816	61	3	General and Municipal Workers (3)
XIX.	Women Workers	(1,318)	?	2	Clerical and Administrative Workers, Transport and General Workers

*Including Transport and General Workers' Union

lost their position as the best-paid large body of industrial workers ; and there had been a continuous drift out of the industry and a sharp fall in the recruitment of young entrants. For a time these tendencies were even intensified during the war. Too many miners were allowed, and even encouraged, to leave the pits for the armed forces or for other occupations when the export trade in coal was greatly reduced ; and by the latter part of the war there was a serious shortage of man-power and too high a proportion of the workers who remained were in the older age-groups. When the war ended, the miners were therefore in a very strong position, and were able to insist on considerable improvements in wages and working conditions. The industry was the first to be nationalised by the Labour Government of 1945 ; and the way for national operation had been prepared by the control which had been in force during the war.

The miners, in order to cope with the new situation, had in 1945 consolidated their Federation—founded in 1888, and made up of a large number of district Associations—into a single National Union of Mineworkers, of which the old Associations became sections. The N.U.M. also incorporated as special sections the separate Unions of Colliery Enginemen and of Coke and By-product Workers, and reached a special agreement with the General and Municipal Workers, whose members among the surface workers in Yorkshire and elsewhere became an Affiliated Section of the N.U.M. The N.U.M. was thus in effective control of almost the entire manual-working personnel, including most of the 'deputies'—who are the nearest equivalent to foremen. The higher grades of employees, in order to deal with the National Coal Board on a national scale, drew together in a National Association of Colliery Officials, independent of the N.U.M. There were difficulties in some areas—especially in Yorkshire—with the enginemen, some of whom broke away and attempted to negotiate apart ; but they were unsuccessful, and the N.U.M. was able to establish its position as the sole recognised bargaining and consultative agency, except for the higher officials. It was also able to insist that the Pit Consultative Committees, which were at first elected directly by the workers in each pit, should be chosen by, and should report to, the local Lodges (branches) of the N.U.M.

As we saw in an earlier chapter*, the policy of the N.U.M. has

*See page 229.

been to make full use of joint consultation, both in the pits and at higher levels, but to refuse any joint responsibility for the conduct of the industry under nationalisation. This has not prevented it from giving support to campaigns for higher output, or from entering into agreements with the Coal Board for the encouragement of voluntary shifts on Saturdays : nor of course has it made the N.U.M. less insistent on the need for the National Board and the Divisional Boards to include an adequate proportion of former Trade Unionists among both members and salaried staffs. What it has meant is that the Miners are, for the present, less interested in developing 'workers' control' within the industry than in consolidating their Trade Union strength and using it as a means of national bargaining.

One of the tasks of the National Coal Board was seen clearly from the first to be the devising of a national wage structure to replace the widely varying district arrangements hitherto in force. In 1953 the N.U.M. and the Board were still negotiating on this difficult issue, and were at loggerheads about the minimum standard to be taken as a basis for the higher rates and for the fixing of piecework prices. The minimum wage to be paid to day workers, both on the surface and underground, was a particularly contentious issue.

In 1952 the National Union of Mineworkers had a membership returned to the Trades Union Congress as 613,000, and to the Labour Party as 660,000. Outside it, the only Union of importance—apart from the Officials' Association—was the National Association of Colliery Overseers, Deputies and Shotfirers, with 30,000 members affiliated to the Trades Union Congress. This body had its strength mainly in Northumberland, Durham, Yorkshire, and some of the Midland coalfields.

The Railways

The railway workers, apart from some of those employed in the railway locomotive and carriage shops, were organised in 1953 in three Unions. The largest of these, the National Union of Railwaymen, is in theory an 'industrial' Union, open to all grades of railway employees. But in practice it has in its ranks only a small proportion of the engine drivers, firemen and cleaners, very few of the clerical, administrative and supervisory workers, and not very many of the skilled craftsmen employed in the railway shops. The drivers, firemen and cleaners—the 'locomotive grades'—are mostly in the Associated Society of Locomotive Engineers and Firemen. The salaried employees—except some of those who have been promoted from the manual-working grades—are in the Transport Salaried Staffs Association, which was formerly known as the Railway Clerks' Association, but changed its name and widened its appeal when other branches of transport were nationalised together with the railways. The railway shopmen are divided between the large number of separate Unions of engineering, woodworking, vehicle-building and other craftsmen—which enrol mainly the more skilled workers—the N.U.R., and the general workers' Unions. The workers on railway-owned road vehicles are partly in the N.U.R. and partly in the Transport and General Workers' Union. There are joint arrangements for negotiation covering both the shopmen and the road transport workers. The N.U.R. enrols the railway catering staffs and a number of other miscellaneous groups.

The railway workers are strongly organised, though not so strongly as the mineworkers. When the N.U.R. was founded in 1913, great hopes were entertained that it would be able to cover the entire industry ; but both the Railway Clerks and the Locomotive Engineers refused to merge their identity, and the N.U.R., which at first had a considerable section of the locomotive men in its ranks, gradually lost ground in these grades. It was more successful in enrolling the less skilled workers in the railway shops, and even some of the skilled ; but it came up against strong opposition from the craftsmen's Unions, which drew together in a special Federation to oppose its claims, and were able partly to hold their own. Negotiations still take place separately for the 'traffic grades' and for the shopmen : the N.U.R., the Locomotive Engineers and the Transport Salaried Staffs Association act rather more closely together under the special negotiating machinery set up before nationalisation.

Side by side with this bargaining structure for dealing with wages and general conditions there existed before nationalisation a system of District Councils on each of the separate railways. This was akin to the Whitley Scheme in the Post Office, and had functions which combined joint consultation with negotiations about questions affecting the employees of a particular company, or a section of them. It operated locally, as well as for each company as a unit. When the railways were nationalised, this system was taken over and adapted to the new regional units into which the railway administration was divided; but there has been a good deal of discontent with its working. The railway workers are also dissatisfied with the treatment they have received in respect of wages and general conditions under the Railway Executive; and, unlike the Mineworkers, they have been disposed to press for a change in the system of administration that would give them direct representation on the national and local controlling bodies. Or rather, this has been the N.U.R.'s attitude: the T.S.S.A. seems to be in general hostile to such projects of 'workers' control'.

Other Transport

The great amalgamation of 1922, which set up the Transport and General Workers' Union, covered the dock and other waterside workers, carters and lorry-drivers, busmen and tramwaymen, river and canal workers, and also a large number of workers in other occupations who had belonged to the old Dock, Wharf, Riverside and General Workers' Union. Subsequent amalgamations brought in many more workers from industries other than transport, and also some transport workers who had originally held aloof. But there remained outside the new Union the seafarers, organised mainly in the Sailors' and Firemen's Union (now the National Union of Seamen), and also the mercantile marine officers—then organised in several rival associations, but now mostly in the Navigating and Engineer Officers' Union. The Ships' Cooks and Stewards, who had a Union of their own, subsequently amalgamated with the Transport and General Workers. The Radio Officers maintain their small separate Union.

The amalgamation which formed the Transport and General Workers' Union was practically complete at the outset in the waterside group. But later secessions resulted in the establishment of a separate Scottish Transport and General Workers' Union, which competes with the T. and G.W.U. on the Clyde and belongs to the Scottish Trades Union Congress. There were secessions in London also; and to-day there are in the Port of London rival Unions of Lightermen and of Stevedores and Dockers—both much smaller than the corresponding sections of the T. and G.W.U. In road transport, the Scottish Horse and Motormen and the United Road Transport Workers' Association (mainly in Lancashire and Yorkshire) refused to join the amalgamation, and have maintained their separate existence : they are both affiliated to the Trades Union Congress. There was for a time a breakaway Road Passenger Transport Union in London; but it was almost extinct by 1953. Throughout the country the great majority of road transport workers, as well as of dockers and other waterside workers, are in the Transport and General Workers' Union.

The T. and G.W.U. is, indeed, reputed to be the biggest Trade Union in the world. It is certainly by far the largest of the British Unions ; but of its 1,285,000 members in 1952 well under half a million were transport workers, the rest being scattered widely over a great variety of industries and occupations. Its position outside the transport industries will be considered in a subsequent section.

The Transport and General Workers' Union was formed by the fusion of most of the Unions which had previously been federated in the Transport Workers' Federation, originally formed in 1910, under the leadership of Tom Mann and Ben Tillett. The first secretary of the amalgamated body, and its principal creator, was Ernest Bevin, previously Tillett's second-in-command in the old Dockers' Union, which arose out of the London Dock Strike of 1889. At the time of the fusion, the dockers were divided among a number of Unions, with separate Unions in Scotland and in the North-West. The road passenger transport workers—busmen, tramwaymen, and cab drivers—were in the United Vehicle Workers, and the lorrymen were partly in the National Union of Vehicle Workers, partly in the Dockers' Union, and partly in various general labour Unions. The amalgamation brought all these groups together : it was partly the outcome of Bevin's outstanding success as the 'Dockers' K.C.' in the Transport Enquiry of 1920-21, which resulted in the granting of the dockworkers' claim for a wage of 16s. a day. The amalgamation scheme, which was mainly Bevin's work, provided for a structure designed to ensure both some degree of sectional autonomy and a centralisation of financial control. Each Section—Dockers, Busmen, Tramwaymen, Commercial Road Transport Workers, and so on—was to have its own separately elected governing and negotiating committee and its own officials, but the right to declare or continue a strike was to be vested in a central Executive Committee representing the geographical regions as well as the Trade Sections, and all the officials were to be servants of the Union as a whole, and not of its separate sections. The Union's first successes were mainly in improving organisation, as well as payment, at the waterside. Later, it repeated its successes in the road transport groups, especially in securing an Act of Parliament for the fixing of minimum wages for commercial road transport employees. At the docks it was able to secure during the 1930s a system of registration which eliminated casual workers ; and during the second World War an elaborate system of control was worked out, in order both to ensure the best use of labour at each port and to facilitate transfers from port to port as need arose. Out of this wartime plan arose the post-war system under which every registered docker is entitled to a 'fall-back' wage in case of unemployment, subject to holding himself available for any work that may offer, the scheme being administered by a National Dock Labour Board jointly controlled by employers' associations and Trade Unions. This scheme has not worked altogether smoothly : there have been in recent years a number of strikes at the docks, particularly in London and Manchester, which have been attributed to Communist influence, though there have been real grievances behind them. Part of the difficulty has been that under the system which limits employment to registered workers and gives the docker a guaranteed part-wage, the Transport and General Workers' Union has necessarily become responsible to some extent for enforcing discipline among its members, who have been used to working under less orderly conditions and are apt to resent the change, especially where it involves the break-up of voluntarily formed gangs of men accustomed to working together. On the whole, however, the change for the better in dockers' conditions has undoubtedly been great—though by 1953 the register had become swollen to a size well exceeding the current demand for workers, with the result that many dockers were partially employed or were out of work altogether and had to fall back on the guaranteed wage.

The dock workers have been in recent years much the most militant section of the Transport and General Workers' Union, which has waged a vehement campaign against Communist influence among them and other sections of its transport membership—e.g. the busmen. The Union has adopted a rule excluding from all forms of office members of the Communist Party, and has on a number of occasions suspended branch officers and committees, or wound up and re-formed branches alleged to have fallen under Communist control. The rule excluding Communists from office has been subjected to a good deal of criticism, as setting a dangerous precedent ; but it has been upheld by large majorities.

The Seamen, whose Union affairs used to be marked by much turbulence, including bitter disputes between rival Unions, seem now to have settled down to stable organisation and to relatively good industrial relations, in marked contrast to those which existed up to the first World War. Till then, except in Liverpool, the shipowners still mostly refused to recognise the seamen's rights of collective bargaining, and many attempts were made to break strikes by the use of blacklegs. Standard wages and conditions were introduced under government control during the first World War, and remained in force after control was lifted. The transport industry as a whole now ranks high in respect of Trade Union organisation and comprehensive arrangements for collective bargaining.

Iron and Steel

The iron and steel workers are highly organised in two main Unions—the Iron and Steel Trades Confederation and the National Union of Blastfurnacemen. Steel works employ a fair number of engineering and other craftsmen, who belong to the Unions catering for their particular crafts, such as the Amalgamated Engineering Union, the Amalgamated Union of Foundry Workers, and the Amalgamated Union of Building Trade Workers (bricklayers). Wages for these craftsmen commonly follow those laid down for the same types of workers in the industries in which they are mainly employed. Some of the less skilled workers are in the general labour Unions—especially the Transport and General Workers' Union, which has a substantial section in the tinplate trade in South Wales. In Scotland the blastfurnacemen belong to the Iron and Steel Trades Confederation : the National Union of Blastfurnacemen organises them in England and Wales. It used to be a federation of regional Unions, but these have now amalgamated to form a single body.

The Iron and Steel Trades Confederation is the result of a fusion at the end of the first World War of a number of Unions between which acute rivalries used to exist. The Steel Smelters'

Union, the real centre of the amalgamation, was largely the creation of John Hodge, and stood for the elimination of the old 'contract' system of work under which the skilled 'contractor' used to be able to exploit at day wages the less skilled workers under him—just as the 'butty' used to do in some of the coal-fields. The Steel Smelters had largely succeeded by 1914 in getting this system abolished, and with its ending the road was clear for taking over the old Unions in which it had flourished, and for establishing an effective Union for all the workers in the industry, skilled and unskilled, except those who were eligible for membership of craft Unions primarily concerned with other industries.

The Blastfurnacemen's Federation refused to join the Confederation, and has maintained its separateness as the principal Union in the pig-iron section of the industry. The Confederation took over one of the Unions of enginemen and cranemen—the one which had most of its members in the iron and steel industry; but the rival National Union of Enginemen remains separate, with members scattered over a great number of industries. The Confederation is mainly concerned with the works at which crude steel is produced, or with such finishing branches as the production of steel plates, sheets, sections, bars, tubes, etc. The Wireworkers have two separate Unions, one in England and one in Scotland. The Amalgamated Union of Foundry Workers and certain smaller specialised Unions cater for the main bodies of workers engaged in the various kinds of ironfounding and steel-founding. In this field the frontiers between iron and steel founding and engineering are often difficult to draw; but no important Trade Union conflicts arise.

The steel industry has a very highly developed system of collective bargaining, based on regional conciliation boards established during the nineteenth century. The Steel Smelters' Union was highly centralised; and the Iron and Steel Trades Confederation retains this character. Branch organisation is based mainly on the works, or on the departments of a works, the older conciliation boards having been made up of works delegates before the Unions had achieved full recognition. In recent times, the steelworkers have been notable for the absence of strikes, despite the large fluctuations of employment up to 1939. Since that date, they have been very fully employed. Their Trade Union history has been recently written by Arthur Pugh, who succeeded John Hodge as their leader and was Chairman of the Trades Union Congress General Council during the General Strike of 1926.

Engineering

Engineering, though in a sense an 'industry', is better described as a large group of occupations concentrated mainly in certain metal-working industries but also extending into almost every industry and service. The skilled 'engineer' or 'mechanic' is a type of craftsman who can be found wherever machinery is at all extensively used; for machines need not only making but also maintaining in good order, and in many cases can be either operated only by skilled workers or by less skilled workers under skilled supervision. This double character of engineering, as a group of crafts and as a group of mainly metal-working industries, has impressed itself on the structure of Trade Unionism. It is hardly accurate to call the Amalgamated Engineering Union either an 'industrial' or a 'craft' Union, because it is both. Its origins are in community of craft skill; but it has been forced, under the pressure of technical change, to open its ranks more and more widely, and to develop into something like an industrial Union covering a number of related metal-working industries.

The A.E.U., formed in 1920 by the amalgamation of the Amalgamated Society of Engineers with the Steam Engine Makers, the Toolmakers, the United Machine Workers, and a number of lesser Unions of mechanics, is now by far the largest engineering Union. Its chief forerunner, the A.S.E., formed in 1851, was itself a similar amalgamation of craftsmen's societies, of which the most important was the Society of Journeymen Steam-Engine Makers, founded in 1825. The movement thus developed out of the new skills used in the making of steam-engines, and grew as their use increased and as other machines came to be made more and more of metal, and less of wood. In course of time it took over the older societies of Millwrights and Mechanics who had been employed in creating and maintaining the older types of machinery; and those who drew up the plans for the Amalgamated Society of Engineers in 1850 had visions of a Union wide enough to include every type of skilled metal-worker, except those engaged in the earlier processes of making iron and steel. This ambition was not realised: the Ironfounders, the Boilermakers, and a number of other groups preferred to maintain their separate Unions ; and new Unions also grew up, especially towards the end of the nineteenth century, among machine-workers whose skills the A.S.E. was not prepared to recognise as equal to those of the turners and fitters who made up the main nucleus of its membership. The A.S.E.'s ranks were made open to such workers, and later even to the unskilled, but not with equal rights ; and as semi-skilled and even barely skilled forms of machine-operating continued to develop, many of the less skilled operatives joined the general labour Unions. Thus at the time of the first World War the workers in engineering and other metal-working factories were divided among at least four types of Unions—the A.S.E., largely skilled, but including some less skilled workers ; the sectional craft Unions, such as the Iron-founders, Patternmakers, Coppersmiths, Blacksmiths, and Boilermakers—not to mention Carpenters, Painters, and other crafts employed principally in other industries ; the 'second-line' Unions of skilled machine-operators—Toolmakers, Machine Workers, and the A.S.E.'s still older rival, the Steam Engine Makers (not the *Journeymen* Steam Engine Makers, but a rival which had refused to join forces in 1851) ; and the general labour Unions, then more numerous and competing than they are to-day.

The A.E.U. brought together the first and third of these groups, both much swollen during the first World War, and also inaugurated a period of lively competition with the fourth group for the allegiance of the less skilled male workers. It did not open its ranks to women until well on into the second World War ; nor did it make any attempt to enrol ironfounders or boilermakers. It did, however, like the A.S.E. before it, compete actively with the craft Unions of patternmakers, blacksmiths, coppersmiths, brass finishers, and certain other trades. It preserved, and preserves to-day, a complicated grading of members, with varying rates of contributions and benefits, the top grades being still open only to recognised craftsmen, though the less skilled are no longer excluded, as they once were, from all share in Union government.

The 'opposite number' of the A.E.U. on the employers' side is the Engineering and National Employers' Federation, itself an amalgamation of two big federations which used to divide the field between them—one in the central machine-making sections and the other mainly in the lesser metal-working trades of Birmingham and the West Midlands. On the workers' side, the

A.E.U. is linked with the separate craft and general Unions in the Confederation of Shipbuilding and Engineering Trade Unions, which covers the other shipyard trades as well as those common to shipbuilding and engineering. This body, in an earlier form, as the Engineering and Shipbuilding Trades Federation, goes back to the 1880s; but for a number of years the A.S.E. and the A.E.U. were at loggeheads with it, because its old constitution gave equal votes to large and small Unions, and the Engineers found themselves repeatedly outvoted by much smaller societies. The breach was healed by a change of constitution; and general wage and other movements are now usually conducted through the Confederation, though the Unions belonging to it have not given up their right to launch independent movements of their own.

The A.E.U. in 1952 had 756,000 members affiliated to the Trades Union Congress, including over 45,000 women. The next largest Union in the T.U.C.'s engineering group was the Electrical Trades Union, with 198,000, including nearly 6,000 women. The E.T.U. has expanded very rapidly in recent years: it includes, besides the workers in electrical engineering factories, the electricians employed in the building and civil engineering industries and also a large body of workers in power stations and electricity distributing stations and depots. The professional grades in the electricity supply industry are mostly in a separate Electrical Power Engineers' Association, which is also affiliated to the Trades Union Congress. The E.T.U. is the principal Union concerned with the system of joint consultation set up under the British Electricity Authority since nationalisation.

Both the A.E.U. and the E.T.U. are important in the engineering sections of the motor industry. In this field, the other leading Unions include the National Union of Sheet Metal Workers and the National Union of Vehicle Builders; and of course a large number of other craft Unions are also concerned. The general labour Unions are also active in both vehicle-manufacture and the less skilled branches of electrical engineering.

The foundries, both those connected with engineering factories and the separate iron and steel foundries, are organised mainly by the Amalgamated Union of Foundry Workers, an amalgamation based mainly on two craft Unions of very long standing—the Friendly Society of Ironfounders and the Associated Iron Moulders of Scotland—but now open to less skilled workers. The patternmakers in both types of foundry are mostly in the United Patternmakers' Association, though some are in the A.E.U. There is also a separate Union, the National Union of Stove, Grate and General Metal Workers, in the light castings industry, as well as several lesser societies.

The brassworkers have their own Union, the National Society of Metal Mechanics. This has its main nucleus in the brass trades in and near Birmingham, which was its place of origin ; but it has spread to other areas and includes a good many of the brassworkers employed in engineering factories. The skilled brassfounders and brassfinishers are, however, largely in the A.E.U. or other engineering societies. The Coppersmiths have a small craft Union, in direct competition with the A.E.U. ; and there are also a number of other small specialist societies. The National Union of Operative Heating, Domestic and Ventilating Engineers belongs partly to engineering and partly to the building industry, in which there have been many disputes about demarcation between it and the Plumbing Trades Union.

In the minor metal-working trades there are a number of small Unions—the Gold, Silver and Allied Trades, the Cutlery Trades, the File Trades, the Lock and Metal Workers, the Wire Drawers, and so on. But a good many small societies of this type have disappeared in recent years by amalgamation either with the A.E.U. or some other of the metal-workers' Unions, or with one of the big general labour Unions.

Two Unions of particular interest in the engineering group are those of the Draughtsmen and of the Supervisory Staffs. The Association of Engineering and Shipbuilding Draughtsmen is a highly organised body, open to tracers as well as skilled draughtsmen. It belongs to the Trades Union Congress and is fully recognised by the employers for purposes of collective bargaining. The Association of Supervisory Staffs, Executives and Technicians is still relatively weak. It grew out of the National Foremen's Association founded during the first World War, chiefly in the railway engineering shops, as a rival to the Foremen's Mutual and other benefit societies set up and subsidised by employers in order to prevent their supervisory staffs from becoming unionised. It has had, and continues to have, a difficult passage. Its best stronghold to-day seems to be in civil aviation, where it has a recognised place in joint consultation. Another section of the technicians belongs to the Association of Scientific

Workers, which is described in the pages dealing with Trade Unionism in the Professions.*

The organisation and methods of collective bargaining in general engineering have been described in a previous chapter. There is unfortunately no room to deal with the corresponding features of the lesser metal-working industries.

Shipbuilding

The marine engineering trades are organised as part of the engineering group, by the Amalgamated Engineering Union, the Electrical Trades Union, and the other societies catering for engineering workers. Sea-going marine engineers often alternate between work on board ship and work ashore ; and many who do this belong to the A.E.U. A great many trades, from woodworkers and plumbers to upholsterers, are concerned with the fitting out of ships : most of these belong to the Unions which cater for the same occupations in other industries.

This leaves the groups principally occupied in construction of the hulls and decks of vessels. The two main Unions in this branch of the industry are the United Society of Boilermakers and Iron and Steel Shipbuilders, and the Shipconstructors' and Shipwrights' Association. The Boilermakers' Society includes such workers as rivetters, drillers, angle-iron smiths, caulkers : it has also many members employed in locomotive and other engineering workshops. The Shipwrights were originally a group of woodworkers, but have come, with changing methods of construction, to work in a variety of materials. Their main concern is with the deck and interior structure, rather than with the hull. The Associated Blacksmiths' Society is a separate Union, with its main strength in the shipyards, but with members in engineering and other industries as well. (There is also a smaller Blacksmiths' and Farriers' Society, for the workers in rural blacksmithing and similar work). The London Barge Builders still have a small, separate Union of their own.

The Unions in the shipbuilding industry belong to the Confederation of Shipbuilding and Engineering Trade Unions, and usually conduct their movements in close conjunction with the engineering Unions. They negotiate together with a separate employers' body—the Shipbuilding Employers' Federation. Between the wars they suffered from very serious unemployment

*See page 272.

and lost many members. Since 1939 they have made a great recovery ; but changing techniques have lessened the importance of the Shipwrights in comparison with the Boilermakers and other groups. The less skilled workers, here as in engineering, are organised partly in the general labour Unions.

Building and Civil Engineering

The building industry is not well organised save in a few sections, such as woodworking and plumbing. The discontinuity of jobs, except for a small minority of those employed, hampers organisation, especially among the less skilled workers, who are moreover split between rival Unions.

There is a fairly powerful federation—the National Federation of Building Trades Operatives—to which all the important Unions belong. It is made up of 18 Unions (3 of them Scottish), *plus* a 'Composite Section' of the Federation which enrols workers of all trades in places too small to maintain branches of the separate Unions. In general, each craft has its own Union—Painters, Plumbers, Plasterers, Slaters and Tilers, Asphalt Workers, Constructional Engineers, Street Masons and Paviors. The Amalgamated Union of Building Trade Workers consists mainly of bricklayers and stonemasons : the Amalgamated Society of Woodworkers includes cabinet-makers as well as carpenters and joiners. The Woodcutting Machinists have an Amalgamated Society of their own. The Painters, Plasterers and Slaters have separate Scottish Societies. The Electrical Trades Union belongs to the N.F.B.T.O. as well as to the Shipbuilding and Engineering Confederation, of which the Woodworkers and the Painters are also members. The N.F.B.T.O. also had among its affiliates the National Builders' Labourers' and Constructional Workers, now merged in the A.U.B.T.W. The big 'general' Unions enrol builders' labourers, and belong to the N.F.B.T.O. ; but a majority of the labourers are unorganised, and members are continually drifting in and out. Finally, there is a small Association of Building Technicians, largely architectural draughtsmen and other office workers attached to the industry. This association is in the N.F.B.T.O. : the Architects are well organised in their professional institutes, but these stand quite apart from the Trade Unions.

The N.F.B.T.O. acts as a negotiating body on wages and other matters of general concern, and it also takes an active part in the attempt to regularise apprenticeship.* By tradition the building Trade Unions have been strongly hostile to piecework systems, on the ground that output is too dependent on weather conditions and quality of materials to be fairly paid for at piecework rates, and also on the ground that payment by results tends to undermine craft standards. During the second World War, however, various 'incentive' payments were introduced, and these have continued to some extent since 1945 and appear to be gaining ground.

The industry is divided between firms of widely varying types and sizes. Civil engineering is mainly in the hands of big contracting firms, which also do a good deal of factory and other institutional building and have tended since the early 1930s to invade the housing field. Next come a number of big building firms, mainly in or near London, some of them long established and others set up mainly for work on large housing estates. Then come the general run of middle-sized urban builders, to be found in every town. Below these come the small firms which undertake some construction as well as repair work. Many of these are specialists, confined to a single branch of building work and often engaged as sub-contractors by the general building firms. Below these again are the host of small jobbing builders, down to one-man businesses, engaged almost exclusively on repairs and decorations ; and finally there are the building workers employed by ironmongers and other shopkeepers who do odd building jobs. Electrical wiring and fitting, asphalting, and roofing work are often sub-contracted.

The small jobbing builders are almost wholly unorganised ; and most of their employees are outside the Trade Unions, largely because they are 'handymen', who need to work at a variety of trades and cannot be held to the rules of demarcation laid down by the craft Unions. The training of apprentices for the skilled crafts is done mainly by the middle-sized firms and by a few of the better large firms ; but many men have become craftsmen without completing their apprenticeship, or even without any formal apprenticeship at all. The building industry remains the least mechanised of all the great industries ; and it has been, next to shipbuilding, that in which employment has fluctuated most widely, with disastrous results. The industry is also subject to large seasonal fluctuations in respect of outdoor

*See page 190.

work, and to serious loss of time when the weather is bad. These conditions led to a long struggle between the wars to secure some form of payment for 'wet time', or 'guaranteed week'; and since the war a 'guaranteed week' of 32 hours has been generally in force.

The building employers and the N.F.B.T.O. are both organised on a basis of large regional areas, within which there are numerous local groupings. Wage claims are nowadays usually made on a national basis, the country being graded for wage-rates into a number of zones—London, large and small towns, and country areas. Most firms keep a permanent nucleus of skilled workers; but a high proportion of the total labour force is always shifting from employer to employer, and there is a good deal of movement from place to place.

The N.F.B.T.O. has recently declared in principle for the nationalisation of the building industry, and has drawn up a plan for the introduction of public management by graded stages. After the first World War the Federation and many of the Unions gave their support to the Building Guild movement, which was an attempt to establish self-governing local Guilds for the co-operative execution of building contracts on a non-profit basis—chiefly municipal housing schemes subsidised by the State. For a short time this movement prospered—indeed, for as long as the conditions of state financing of housing schemes made it possible for the Guilds to manage with very little capital, receiving payment by instalments as each stage of the work was done and approved. When these conditions were withdrawn in the economy drive of 1921, the Guilds at once fell into financial troubles, and the whole movement collapsed. At the same time as the Guild movement was being developed, an attempt was made to convert the Whitley Joint Industrial Council which had been set up for the industry into a real joint controlling body; but this attempt caused the secession of the employers' associations, and the entire Council collapsed. Since then, the industry has been through many vicissitudes; but the attempt to convert it into a Co-operative enterprise without State ownership has not been renewed. During the second World War there arose a small 'socialised sector', in the shape of a moveable squad of workers who could be sent to different parts of the country for urgent work; and this method was continued for a time on a diminishing scale after the war, especially for the preparation of sites for new housing estates. It was under the auspices of the Ministry of Works; but by 1951 it had been allowed to die away.

Furnishing and other Woodworking

Outside the building industry the principal Union consisting largely of woodworkers is the National Union of Furniture Trade Operatives, which covers the whole country but has its main strength in London and High Wycombe. This Union has taken over a number of smaller societies; but there still remain small separate Unions of French Polishers and one or two other trades. The cabinet-makers are largely in the Amalgamated Society of Woodworkers, and the sawyers in the Amalgamated Society of Woodcutting Machinists. Some of the sawyers however are in the National Union of Packing-case Makers and Boxmakers, who work in metals as well as in wood. The Journeymen Coopers have an old-established Federation, within which the local Societies enjoy a good deal of autonomy. But in the miscellaneous woodworking and furnishing trades a high proportion of the less skilled workers are either unorganised or belong to one or other of the big general labour Unions.

Printing and Paper

The printing and paper trades are strongly organised in a number of sectional Unions which cover all types of workers and leave hardly any room for the entry of the general labour Unions into the industry. All the Unions are federated in the Printing and Kindred Trades Federation, which acts as a negotiating body on matters of general concern, but leaves each Union free to deal with the special problems of its own section. The compositors have perhaps the longest tradition of organisation of any skilled trade. Their local 'chapels'—branches composed of the members working in a particular establishment—were well established throughout the eighteenth century. They have three Unions—the London Society of Compositors, the Typographical Association, and the Scottish Typographical Association. The last of these admits some less skilled groups, including women: the L.S.C. also has a very few women members. The L.S.C. in its present form dates from 1848, when the Londoners seceded from the National Typographical Association formed in 1844. The provincial branches of the N.T.A. then formed the Typographical Association (1849); and four years later the S.T.A.

was organised as a separate body. Both the T.A. and the S.T.A. are based on earlier local societies, some of which can trace their history back well into the eighteenth century. The London Compositors, through their local society, entered into a general agreement with the master printers as early as 1826—that is, almost as soon as the Combination Acts had been repealed.

The London Compositors are very jealous of their privileges, and do not allow members of the T.A. or S.T.A. to work in London shops. They maintain their system of chapels*, which has spread from the compositors to all the other printing trades. The Union most closely allied to the compositors' societies is the small Association of Correctors of the Press, largely drawn from their ranks.

In printing proper, as distinct from composing, there are two main Unions—the fairly small Printing Machine Managers' Trade Society and the much larger National Society of Operative Printers and Assistants, known as 'NATSOPA'. This Union began by organising the printers' assistants and then spread to include a number of other grades, in addition to printers. It organises, for example, employees in the offices of printers and publishers, including workers other than journalists in newspaper offices. It built up a high reputation for efficiency under George Isaacs, who was its Secretary until he became Minister of Labour in 1945.

Largest of all the Unions in the printing and kindred trades is the National Union of Printing, Bookbinding and Paper Workers—an amalgamation of the Printers' Warehousemen and Cutters and the Paper Makers with the old-established Bookbinders' Society, which still keeps some autonomy within it. This, apart from its skilled sections, is the principal Union for the less skilled manual workers in all branches of the printing and paper trades. It accounts for almost half the entire membership of the group ; and it covers all types of paper-making, including packing and wrapping papers as well as paper for use in printing. The Wall-paper Workers, however, have a small separate Union.

There are a number of smaller specialised Trade Unions in the printing industry, catering mainly for skilled workers. These include the Lithographic Artists, the Lithographic Printers, the Electrotypers and Stereotypers, and the Monotype Casters and Typefounders. To these must be added the Press Telegraphists

*See page 46.

and the powerful National Union of Journalists, which works with the other Unions in the newspaper industry.

As a rule, the Printing and Kindred Trades Federation leaves each Union free to negotiate its own terms and conditions, including wages, but deals on a general basis with working hours and is prepared to come to the help of any trade which gets into difficulties over its own negotiations. It was formed in 1890, exclusively by the Unions of skilled workers, but a few years later admitted the Unions of less skilled workers which had been formed as part of the 'New Unionism' movement of 1889. Relations with employers are usually good ; but there is trouble with small printing works, which sometimes try to use too high a proportion of apprentice labour, and also occasionally with a big firm which attempts to stand out against the highly enforced system of Union regulations. In the newspaper industry, especially in London, the Unions are very strongly entrenched ; and they have now managed to conquer nearly all those bigger general printing firms, few but important, which stood out against them up to the second World War.

Cotton

The British cotton industry, which in 1911 employed 646,000 persons and in 1921 still 621,000, by 1951 employed only 320,000. These figures exclude the dyeing and finishing sections. This great decline in employment has naturally been accompanied by a sharp fall in the membership of the Trade Unions. The cotton group in the Trades Union Congress, which had 457,000 members in 1920, had fallen to 182,000 in 1952. The industry is, however, still well organised within its reduced compass.

There are two main sections, dealing respectively with the preparation and spinning of cotton yarn, and with weaving and finishing. The special processes of dyeing and bleaching are covered by a Trade Union which is common to the cotton and woollen industries, and will be dealt with in the next section. Apart from the dyers and bleachers, there are two main groups of employers—the Master Cotton Spinners, and the Master Cotton Spinners and Manufacturers—the latter being made up of weaving firms and of firms which both spin and weave.

The Trade Unions in the cotton industry began as local associations, which then gradually joined together to form what are known as 'Amalgamations'—the three most important being the Card, Blowing and Ring Room Operatives, the Spinners, and the Weavers. The Amalgamations are made up partly of purely local societies and partly of 'Provinces', or districts—that is, of regional Unions formed before the whole craft joined up to form an 'Amalgamation'. Both the local associations and still more the Provinces keep a considerable amount of autonomy, especially in relation to friendly benefits. Thus, within the Spinners' Amalgamation, which has a uniform *central* contribution, the Provinces and local branches have varying rates of contributions and benefits. The Amalgamations are essentially negotiating bodies, dealing with general questions of wages, hours and conditions, and leaving to the regional or local bodies both friendly benefits and to a considerable extent local industrial issues. The Weavers' local bodies are even still registered as separate Trade Unions.

The cotton Trade Unions for the most part operate only over a limited area—Lancashire, Cheshire, and parts of Yorkshire and North Derbyshire. Scattered cotton mills in other parts of England and Wales are mostly organised, if at all, by the general workers' Unions. The Scots have a number of separate Unions for textile workers of different types. But the cotton industry is so highly concentrated in and around Lancashire that the failure to organise the outlying mills has little or no effect on the bargaining power of the Unions in this area.

In the spinning section, the highly skilled mule spinners, together with their assistants—the 'piecers'—are organised in the Cotton Spinners' Amalgamation, which has high rates of contribution and benefit for its spinner members. The piecers were for a long time admitted only to an inferior grade of membership in the local associations, and had no place in the central affairs of the Amalgamation; and the Union is still run mainly by the spinner members. It consists entirely of men. Mule-spinning is being gradually superseded by ring spinning—and would be so much more rapidly but for the high cost of installing the new equipment. Ring-spinning is a relatively unskilled process, carried on mainly by women. The ring spinners are organised, together with the workers in the various preparatory processes which precede spinning of the yarn, in the Card, Blowing and Ring Room Operatives' Amalgamation, four-fifths of whose membership are female. These two Unions, together or separately, negotiate with the Master Cotton Spinners' Federation, uniting on such matters as hours, but each formulating and negotiating upon its own wage programme.

In the manufacturing section, which is the larger, the main Trade Union is the Weavers' Amalgamation. Smaller, but important, are the Beamers', Twisters' and Drawers' Amalgamation, and the General Union of Power Loom Overlookers—the latter supervisors of the machine process. There is also, at the finishing end, an Amalgamation of Textile Warehousemen. In the manufacturing branches of the cotton industry, the Unions are federated both centrally and locally—centrally in a Northern Counties Textile Trades Federation, and locally in similar local federations. These do not cover the producing and spinning sections.

All sections of the industry belong to the United Textile Factory Workers' Association, which is affiliated as a unit to the Labour Party. The U.T.F.W.A. is not a negotiating body : it is rather the successor of the Short Time Committees and Factory Reform Associations of the nineteenth century, through which the cotton operatives brought pressure to bear on Parliament for shorter hours and improved factory regulation. It is the body representing, from the Trade Union angle, the general interests of the industry on any issue that may arise ; and it has naturally taken over the political affairs of the Unions since Labour representation developed into a movement commanding general Trade Union support.

Woollens and Worsteds

Trade Unionism in the Woollen and worsted industry has had a troubled history, which goes back to the eighteenth century, when the Woolcombers had a strong Union and the Weavers made many attempts to combine. In the 1830s there was a bitter struggle between the employers and the so-called 'Leeds Trades' Union'*, which was an attempt to combine all kinds of workers in a 'General Union', but had its main strength in the woollen and worsted trades, then greatly affected by the development of power-driven machinery. The employers refused to employ any member of the 'Trades' Union', which was forced to proceed secretly, but was crushed in 1834 together with the better-known 'Grand National Consolidated Trades Union' of the Owenites.†

*For the full story of the Leeds Trades' Union see my *Attempts at General Union, 1819-1834*. †See page 19.

Trade Unionism in the woollen and worsted industry took long to revive after this blow : indeed, it has remained relatively weak in most sections ever since. A few sections, such as Woolsorters, Woolcombers, and Overlookers, had built up strong craft Unions by the 1870s ; but attempts to organise the main body of spinners and weavers met with little success until the 1880s, when the Huddersfield Weavers' Society began to develop into a wider combination, which became the General Union of Textile Workers. Even this body, however, remained weak right up to 1914. It grew during the first World War, and in 1922 joined with the National Society of Dyers to form the National Union of Textile Workers. In the 1920s, in conjunction with other Unions forming the National Association of Unions in the Textile Trade, it fought a series of engagements with the employers, and came off worst. Its membership declined, and in 1936 what was left of it amalgamated with the two principal dyers' Unions to form the National Union of Dyers, Bleachers and Textile Workers, which is now the main Union for woollen and worsted operatives as well as for dyers and bleachers of textiles generally, including cotton. This is a strong and well-organised Union ; but its main strength is in dyeing and bleaching rather than in the woollen industry as such.

There are a number of fairly strong, though small, craft Unions in various branches of the woollen and worsted industry, mostly in Yorkshire. These include two Unions of Power-Loom Overlookers and of Managers and Overlookers, the National Society of Woolsorters, and the Wool, Yarn and Warehouse Workers ; the Carpet Weavers have separate Unions in England and in Scotland ; and there is an independent local Union of Weavers and Woollen Textile Workers at Saddleworth. There are two or more similar local Unions in Scotland.

Other Textile Industries

In other textile industries, the most important body is the National Union of Hosiery Workers, formed by the amalgamation of a number of local societies, some of long standing. Its main strength is in the Midlands, but it extends to Scotland. The Dundee and District Union of Jute, Flax and Other Fibre Workers is local, or rather regional ; but the trades in question are highly localised. The Lace Operatives have two complementary Unions, both centred at Nottingham : the National Silk

Workers' Association is confined to the Cheshire area and to Scotland. The United Society of Engravers and the Trade Society of Machine Calico Printers are mainly attached to the cotton industry, but prefer to be assigned to the 'Other Textiles' group of the Trades Union Congress. In some of the lesser textile trades the general labour Unions have come in, because of the absence of other suitable Unions outside the main textile areas. There are no separate Unions in the rayon or similar new industries. The producers of rayon yarns are in the general Unions, where they are organised : rayon weaving is mostly carried on in conjunction with cotton or woollen weaving ; and rayon machine-knitting is part of the hosiery industry. Incidentally, at the Trades Union Congress, the Hosiery Workers belong not to the Textile but to the Clothing Group.

Clothing and Leather

By far the biggest Trade Union in the Trades Union Congress's Clothing Group is the National Union of Tailors and Garment Workers, which is the outcome of a fusion between the old-established Society of Tailors and Tailoresses and the United Garment Workers' Union—the latter the result of previous amalgamations chiefly among the factory workers. The N.U.T.G.W. organises all sections of the industry, skilled and unskilled, including both factory employees and those who work in small workshops or at home. Wages in the tailoring trades have the protection of a Wages Council, the successor to the Trade Board set up under the Act of 1909 ; and in practice the Wages Council is used to negotiate standard rates for all types of workers, including the more highly paid, and to regulate the conditions of learners. The Union covers Scotland as well as England and Wales ; about three out of four of its members are women. It is the only large mixed Union with a woman as General Secretary.

If the Hosiery Workers are assigned to the textile group, there is no other large Union in the clothing trades except the Boot and Shoe Operatives, who are put by the Trades Union Congress in a separate Group with other workers in leather. The remaining Unions in the Clothing Group include a small society of Waterproof Garment Makers and two closely connected Societies of Felt Hatters and of Felt Hat Trimmers, one of men and one of women, with a Secretary in common.

The boot and shoe industry is dominated by the old-established National Union of Boot and Shoe Operatives, open to both men and women, the male members being in a majority. It has long had a complete system of conciliation boards covering the older branches of the industry, which have for a long time been remarkably free from trade disputes. But it has had difficulty with the newer mass-production factories, such as Bata. Outside it are the locally powerful Rossendale Union of Boot, Shoe and Slipper Operatives and a smaller Lancashire Union, the Amalgamated Society of Boot and Shoe Makers and Repairers, centred at Preston. The leather workers have two Unions—the Amalgamated Society of Leather Workers, and the smaller National Union of Leather Workers and Allied Trades, both with women members in a minority. There is also a National Union of Glovers with headquarters at Yeovil.

Pottery and Glass

The National Society of Pottery Workers is the only Union catering for the china and earthenware trades, though some workers in outlying potteries are in the general labour Unions. Women are in a slight majority among its members. Organisation in the Potteries has had a long and chequered history, which goes back to the eighteenth century. Modern Unionism among the potters began in the early 1830s, when the Potters' Union formed part of John Doherty's National Association for the Protection of Labour, and managed to survive the collapse. After the first World War the Pottery Workers were pioneers in trying to develop the Whitley scheme of Joint Industrial Councils on constructive lines of joint consultation ; but the advances then made were largely lost in the ensuing depression. They are, however, well organised in the 'Five Towns', but much less so in the 'Outpotteries', of which Bristol and Newcastle-on-Tyne are important centres.

The glassmakers used to possess a number of local societies ; but most of these have now been merged in the general labour Unions. There remain only the once-important London Glass Bottle Makers and the Midland Glass Bevellers, both very small.

Chemicals

The majority of organised chemical workers are in the general Unions. The Transport and General Workers' Union has had since 1945 a separate Chemical Trade Group. There is, however, a growingly important Chemical Workers' Union which began chiefly in the fine chemical trades, but has spread to other branches. About one-third of its members are women. There are also two small Unions of Salt and Alkali Workers in the Cheshire area.

Food and Tobacco Trades

The workers in the food processing trades are largely organised in the general labour Unions. The Transport and General Workers' Union, for example, has a special Flour Milling Section, with over 16,000 members in 1951 ; and the National Union of General and Municipal Workers is also active. The only important special Unions are the well-organised Amalgamated Union of Bakers, Confectioners, and Allied Workers and its Scottish counterpart, the Scottish Union of Bakers, Confectioners and Bakery Workers. Both these Unions admit women ; but men are in the great majority.

The Tobacco Workers' Union is the leading body in the tobacco trade. It includes a majority of women members. On the other hand, the small Cigarette Machine Operatives' Society, centred at Bristol, consists entirely of men, the women being partly in the general Unions.

Agriculture

Agricultural workers are difficult to organise, both because they work for the most part in very small groups and are widely scattered and because until quite recently they had often to contend against strong pressure to prevent them from joining Trade Unions. This pressure still exists, but has lessened since agricultural wages have been subject to effective statutory regulation and since farmers have themselves become an outstanding example of the success of collective bargaining directed towards the Government. The only Union catering exclusively for land workers is the National Union of Agricultural Workers, which covers England and Wales. The formerly separate Scottish Farm Servants' Union is now a section of the Transport and General Workers' Union, which has also some agricultural branches in England. In all, about one in three of the male workers employed in agriculture belongs to a Trade Union : the proportion is much smaller among women.

General Workers

The two big Unions catering for General Workers, after many amalgamations, are the Transport and General Workers' Union and the National Union of General and Municipal Workers. Only about 40 per cent. of the membership of the T. and G.W.U. consists of transport workers: if these are deducted, the two Unions are about equal in size. But whereas the T. and G.W.U. is organised by Trade Groups and Sections, each enjoying a limited autonomy, the N.U.G.M.W. is organised mainly on a geographical basis, with branches usually drawn from a wide variety of occupations and industries, and with local officials who are called upon to negotiate and act for workshop groups irrespective of the industries to which they belong. The N.U.G.M.W. has, of course, more specialised officers at its headquarters; but even these are usually responsible for a considerable variety of groups. I have given, in Appendix 2, a list of trades and occupations on behalf of which the two big general Unions participated (in 1952) in some kind of national negotiating machinery, or in some cases in regional or local machinery for a number of regions. The trades listed are enough to show the enormously wide field over which these Unions operate. Originally, I intended to show which of the two Unions catered for a particular group, where they were not both involved; but I kept on finding that where one was, there the other also was to be found, until at last so many trades appeared to involve both Unions that I became distrustful of my ability to assign relative degrees of importance where both were involved, and abandoned the attempt. It is fair to say that, although the T. and G.W.U. preponderates in the transport industries and the N.U.G.M.W. in municipal employments, over the rest of the field they are active competitors in almost every instance. There are indeed many 'gentlemen's agreements' under which neither will normally enter a factory or workplace in which the other is well established; but these understandings usually apply only to particular workplaces or, occasionally, to whole trades in a particular area, and do not prevent both Unions from organising actively in the same trades or occupations.

It is natural in these circumstances to ask why the T. and G.W.U. and the N.U.G.M.W. do not complete the process of amalgamation, of which they are both the outcome, by joining forces in a single Union. Such a fusion would obviously make it both cheaper and easier to provide effective negotiating machinery in a host of smaller trades and occupations in which they are both involved. The obstacles to such an amalgamation are, no doubt, partly personal; but, apart from questions of personality, the difference in methods of organisation is a formidable obstacle. Moreover, it is likely that, if the T. and G.W.U. were to merge in an inclusive general Union, there would soon be a secessionist move to form a separate Transport Workers' Union; and the N.U.G.M.W., for its part, may fear a breakaway of its municipal members to the National Union of Public Employees and a number of other Unions catering for such groups as Local Government Officers, Hospital Workers and Clerks. I am not saying that these things would happen, but only that the fear of their happening acts as a deterrent to amalgamation.

The N.U.G.M.W., as we have seen, is organised on a geographical basis, and has no largely autonomous Trade Groups, such as exist in the T. and G.W.U. The latter body is divided into the following groups:

Group	*Membership* 1950 (*thousands*)
TRANSPORT:	
Docks	86
Waterways	10
Road Passenger Transport	216
Commercial Road Transport	162
OTHERS:	
Metal, Engineering and Chemical (Chemical Section 38)	235
Building	61
Power Workers	45
Government Workers	77
Municipal Workers	67
Agricultural Workers	28
General Workers (Flour Milling 16)	77
Administrative, Clerical and Supervisory	29

Distributive Trades

Distribution is almost the largest occupational group of employed workers, accounting in 1952 for 2,172,000, and coming second only to the engineering, shipbuilding and vehicle-building group, taken as a single unit. This total excludes the independent shopkeepers: the industrial classification of the Census of 1951 showed about 2,695,000 in all engaged in the distributive trades.

Trade Union organisation is still weak in the smaller shops ; but it is practically complete in the Co-operative stores and wholesale depots, and strong in many of the big department and multiple concerns. The main society is the Union of Shop, Distributive and Allied Workers, formed in 1946 by the amalgamation of the two big Unions which had previously divided the field between them. The larger of these was the National Union of Distributive and Allied Workers, itself the product of a fusion of the Amalgamated Union of Co-operative Employees with the Warehouse and General Workers' Union. The other—and the older—was the National Amalgamated Union of Shop Assistants, Warehousemen and Clerks, which also catered for Co-operative employees, especially in Scotland, but had its main strength among the workers in private trade. These two Unions had negotiated and balloted vainly about amalgamation for many years before they finally came together.

There are comprehensive arrangements for negotiations about wages and conditions throughout the Co-operative movement, with separate machinery for the local Stores and for the Wholesale Societies, and for distributive and productive workers. Trade Union membership is usually a condition of employment. For the distributive trades in general there are statutory Wages Councils which fix minimum wage-rates for various types of workers. Separate Councils exist for the following retail trades : Bookselling and Stationery ; Drapery, Outfitting and Footwear ; Food Trades ; Furnishing and Allied Trades ; Newsagency, Tobacco and Confectionery ; and also for Milk Distribution. In some of these cases—Food Trades, Newsagency, etc., and Milk Distribution—there are separate Councils for Scotland. In the other cases the same Council serves for Great Britain as a whole. The institution of these Councils, which fix graded minima according to the area and the character of the work, has made a great difference to shop assistants' conditions, especially in the smaller shops.

Civil Service

Civil Servants include, in one sense, all persons who are employed by government agencies. In a much narrower sense the words mean simply the administrative and clerical staffs of government departments. In an intermediate sense, they include, in addition to the latter, a varied group of persons ranging from park-keepers in the royal parks to caretakers, night-watchmen and office-cleaners. For the purpose of the present paragraph, the words can be taken as including the administrative, technical and professional workers, and the clerical staffs employed in civilian capacities by government departments, but as excluding the Post Office workers, the industrial employees of the Admiralty, the War Office, the Ministry of Supply, and other departments, and as excluding also the wage-earners employed in manual capacities in other departments.

Civil Servants, in this sense, are highly organised. Much the largest Trade Union catering for them is the Civil Service Clerical Association, about equally composed of men and women. It organises the lower and middle grades of clerical and executive employees in most of the government departments. The technicians in the Civil Service have a separate Union, which is also affiliated to the Trades Union Congress. The Professional Civil Servants and the higher administrative grades (First Division Civil Servants) also have separate associations ; but these do not belong to the T.U.C. The Ministry of Labour has a separate Staff Association, which is in the T.U.C. : so is the Inland Revenue Staff Federation. A number of special grades are organised in the Civil Service Union, another T.U.C. society. There are also a large number of small societies catering for specialised grades, which remain outside the T.U.C. The manual workers in government employment are largely in the general labour Unions or in the Unions catering for the occupations or industries to which they belong, irrespective of the distinction between public and private employment. The Civil Service Unions and the other Unions with members employed by government departments or agencies negotiate directly with the employing departments, but have recourse, in the event of disagreement, to the Civil Service Arbitration Tribunal. There are Whitley Councils in the departments and also a general Civil Service Whitley Council for the clerical and administrative grades, and much negotiation takes place in the first instance in these Councils. Under the Trade Union Act of 1927 (repealed in 1946) the Civil Service Trade Unions were forbidden to belong to either the Labour Party or the Trades Union Congress. They mostly remain outside the Labour Party despite the repeal of this Act.

Post Office

The Post Office employees are highly organised, mainly in two Unions, the Union of Post Office Workers and the Post Office Engineering Union. The P.O.E.U. is confined to the engineering department, and includes both skilled and less skilled workers. The U.P.W. caters for all other grades, except the supervisory grades and the small section belonging to the Secretary's office : these latter are in the Civil Service Unions. Both the U.P.W. and the P.O.E.U. belong to the Trades Union Congress, and the U.P.W. belongs to the Labour Party as well. There is a separate Federation of Supervisory Workers in the Post Office ; and the Sub-Postmasters also have a federation of their own. The Post Office Unions negotiate directly with the department and have a highly developed system of departmental Whitley Councils. They are also represented on the Civil Service Whitley Council ; and they use the machinery of the Civil Service Arbitration Tribunal when differences cannot be settled by direct negotiation.

The Post Office workers had a long struggle before they achieved recognition of collective bargaining rights. This was conceded by the Liberal Government of 1906 ; but up to the first World War the method of dealing with conditions was to appoint parliamentary committees to enquire into and report upon terms of employment. Up to 1918 there were separate Unions for postmen, postal and telegraph clerks, and sorters ; but these amalgamated to form the Union of Post Office Workers, the engineering section refusing to come in.

The Union of Post Office Workers was an early convert to Guild Socialism, and has always stood for the principle of 'workers' control'. In recent years, it has vainly pressed this policy on the Trades Union Congress, and has demanded control of the Post Office undertaking by a Council representing the various grades, with the Postmaster-General as Chairman. It has succeeded in establishing, through the effective use of Whitley Council machinery, a small measure of joint control—especially a voice in the selection of employees for promotion to higher grades.

Other Public Employees

In the Local Government services the manual workers are divided between the National Union of Public Employees, which has grown very rapidly from small beginnings in recent years, and the two general Unions—the National Union of General and Municipal Workers being the more important in this field. Skilled craftsmen usually belong to the Unions catering for their particular trades—e.g. the Amalgamated Engineering Union, the Amalgamated Union of Building Trade Workers, and the Amalgamated Society of Woodworkers. The clerical and administrative workers, up to the higher office-holders, are strongly organised in the National Association of Local Government Officers, which does not belong to the Trades Union Congress, but has a working arrangement with it. NALGO acts as a professional and examining body as well as a Trade Union. There are Joint Industrial Councils for the negotiation of wages, salaries and conditions both for the administrative and clerical and for the manual grades, including separate Councils for trading and non-trading services. Workers in the health and hospital services are organised partly in the craft and general Unions, partly in NALGO, and partly in the Confederation of Health Service Employees. The Women Public Health Officers have a separate association. All these bodies, except NALGO, belong to the Trades Union Congress; but there are also a number of small societies, on the borderline between Trade Unions and professional associations, which remain outside the T.U.C. The remaining important body is the Fire Brigades' Union, which is in both the T.U.C. and the Labour Party. The Health Service Employees also belong to the Labour Party as well as to the T.U.C.

Teachers

The teaching profession is highly organised; but its associations remain outside both the Labour Party and the Trades Union Congress. It has its own special machinery—the Burnham Committee—for fixing salary-rates for the various types of teachers through a number of 'panels' for primary, secondary, technical, and other teachers in public employment. The largest Union is the National Union of Teachers, which is open to all grades and kinds of teachers, but consists mainly of teachers in public elementary and modern secondary schools. The N.U.T. has much smaller rivals in the National Union of Women Teachers, which is strongly feminist and accuses the N.U.T. of lukewarmness in pressing for 'equal pay', and in the National Association of Schoolmasters, which is hostile to 'equal pay'.

There is also a separate Association of Head Teachers, halfway between a professional association and a Trade Union. Grammar School and 'public school' teachers are organised mainly in the Assistant Masters' Association and in the Association of Assistant Mistresses. Technical teachers have their own Union—the Association of Teachers in Technical Institutions. So have university teachers—the Association of University Teachers—and teachers in adult classes—the Association of Tutors in Adult Education. In Scotland school-teachers of all grades are organised in a single body—the Educational Institute of Scotland. There are also in England and Wales a number of more specialised bodies; but most of these are rather professional associations than Trade Unions. The two headmasters' bodies—the Headmasters' Conference ('public schools') and the Headmasters' Association (mainly grammar schools)—are definitely not Trade Unions. Some scientific teachers and research workers are in the Association of Scientific Workers, which goes down to such grades as laboratory assistants. The School Caretakers have an association, but many of the manual and clerical workers in the educational services are still unorganised. The clerical staffs of the Local Education Authorities belong to the National Association of Local Government Officers.

Clerical and Administrative Workers

There is a Clerical and Administrative Workers' Union, belonging to both the Trades Union Congress and the Labour Party, which enrols clerical workers of all types, except those for which recognised special Trade Unions exist. But the Union is weak, except in the clerical grades of employment in such bodies as Trade Unions and other working-class organisations and in a few industries, such as Iron and Steel, in which it co-operates closely with the manual workers' Unions. Railway clerks, and some from other branches of transport, are strongly organised in the Transport Salaried Staffs Association (see under Transport); civil service clerks in the Civil Service Clerical Association; post office clerks in the Union of Post Office Workers; local government clerks in the National Association of Local Government Officers. The Transport and General Workers' Union has a fairly strong Administrative and Clerical Group; and a number of other Unions have special sections for clerical and similar workers attached to their respective industries.

The largest remaining Union of clerical and administrative workers is the National Union of Bank Employees, which has fought a long fight for recognition by the joint stock banks, and is still not accepted by some of them as a negotiating body. The recalcitrant banks have internal Staff Associations, through which they strive to keep NUBE at bay.

Insurance

There are three main Unions in this field, which includes both administrative and clerical staffs and insurance agents. The largest of them, catering mainly for agents, is the National Federation of Insurance Workers, the smallest the National Amalgamated Union of Life Assurance Workers. The third, the Guild of Insurance Officials, is mainly clerical and administrative. They are all in the Trades Union Congress, but only the Life Assurance Workers and the Prudential Staff Union—a constituent of the main federation—belong to the Labour Party.

Amusement Trades and the Arts

The Actors are fairly well organised in the British Actors' Equity Association : the variety artists much less strongly in the Variety Artistes' Federation. There is also a small Film Artistes' Association. The Musicians' Union is very strong. The technical grades in the film world are fairly strongly organised in the Association of Cinematograph and Allied Technicians, and the manual workers in both film studios and cinemas and theatres in the National Association of Theatrical and Kine Employees. All the Unions so far mentioned belong to the Trades Union Congress : only the Cinematograph Technicians and the Musicians to the Labour Party. There are also a few highly specialised associations in other branches of the amusement trades—e.g. the Football Players' Union ; but these do not belong to the Trades Union Congress.

Outside both the T.U.C. and the Labour Party is the Society of Authors, which includes the majority of regular imaginative writers, but is weak among scientific and educational writers. It has specialised affiliates, such as the League of British Dramatists, the Screenwriters' Association, the Radiowriters' Association, and the Musical Composers' Association. It acts as a defensive and negotiating body on behalf of its members in dealing both with publishers and with such organisations as the B.B.C.

Journalists (see under Printing) have their separate Union for full-time members of the profession. Occasional, as distinct from salaried, journalists are catered for mainly by the Society of Authors.

Other Professional Workers

The only Union of any importance belonging to the Trades Union Congress that has not yet been mentioned is the Medical Practitioners' Union. This is a small body consisting of general practitioners ; but the main Trade Union of the doctors is the British Medical Association, whcih is both a professional organisation and the principal negotiating body for doctors in the National Health Service as well as for those in salaried employment. The B.M.A. first figured prominently as a Trade Union in the negotiations over the National Insurance Act of 1911 ; and it has since acted consistently in this capacity. Dentists have a number of organisations ; the most important is the British Dental Association, which consists mainly of medically qualified dentists. The leading associations acted together in the negotiations over the institution of the National Health Service. The Opticians also have a national association ; pharmaceutical chemists are organised largely in the Pharmaceutical Society ; nurses in a variety of bodies, including the British Institute of Nursing. Psychiatric Social Workers, Hospital Almoners, Physiotherapists, are other instances of specialist associations which serve to some extent as protective as well as professional bodies. But all these are on the borderline of Trade Unionism ; and none of them belongs to the Trades Union Congress.

The Association of Scientific Workers, already mentioned in passing, caters for technicians in various industries as well as for scientific research workers in Universities and research institutes. The Association of Supervisory Staffs, Executives and Technicians is connected mainly with the engineering and kindred industries, and has been mentioned in the engineering section of this chapter.

The numerous professional institutes which exist for almost all the recognised professions do in fact perform a number of protective functions on behalf of their members ; but they cannot properly be regarded as Trade Unions and are accordingly omitted from the present outline.

CHAPTER XII

TRADE UNIONS IN THE MODERN WORLD

TRADE Unionism has been, through most of its history, an opposition seeking to establish itself in face of strong reluctance by the rulers of society to admit even its bare right to exist—much less to welcome it as the legitimate exponent of the workers' claims. It has had to force its way, first to bare toleration and later to positive recognition of its place in society; and at every stage it has had to fight its way against the tendency of the law courts to treat it as a 'conspiracy' to interfere with the freedom of individual contract, as well as against the tendency of governments to regard it as politically dangerous. It has had to meet the hostility of autocrats and of aristocrats to combination among the unprivileged, as well as that of employers to a force which restricts their 'freedom' to order their employees about as they please. Compelled by the sheer necessities of its situation to seek to establish a monopoly of labour and to secure common action by all the workers concerned in any particular matter it takes up, it has been continually accused of using illegitimate methods of coercion and intimidation, of violating individual rights, and of usurping a coercive authority which should belong only to the State as the representative of the entire people. Clearly, unless it had set out to establish a common discipline among the workers, at any rate in particular trades, it would have been powerless to win standard rates or conditions of labour, or to protect its members against arbitrary or tyrannical conduct on the part of employers or business executives, down to the level of workshop foremen. It could not, however, in dealing with large bodies of men, hope to establish this collective discipline without some measure of coercion of recalcitrant or apathetic individuals, who would otherwise be made use of by employers to break down every attempt to establish common standards. Of course, the coercive power of the Trade Unions is always narrowly limited: at most it can seldom go beyond insistence on compliance with Trade Union regulations as the condition of getting or holding a job in a workplace where its organisation is already strong. Instances of more forcible coercion, such as occurred in Sheffield in the 1860s, have been rare, and have been found only where Trade

Union development is at a rudimentary stage and has been driven underground by the denial of freedom and recognition of bargaining rights. But even the unviolent forms of coercion, such as the attempt to insist on a 'closed shop' in which only members of a particular Trade Union can be employed, are still widely denounced as examples of 'Trade Union tyranny'; and not so long ago the very attempt to insist on standard rates and conditions was branded as 'tyrannical' because it interfered with the freedom of employers and individual workers to enter into such bargains as they pleased.

Having to make their way against the general hostility of employers, ruling classes, courts of law, *laisser-faire* economists—indeed of almost every social force except their own—the Trade Unions naturally and inevitably grew up opposition-minded, expecting no sympathy and no understanding of their aims, and reckoning on their strength and solidarity alone to give them any chance of success. It was, in the view of their 'betters', none of their business to help in rendering labour more productive or to take any share in the responsibility for the efficient conduct of industry. Any attempt on their part to intervene in such matters was denounced as illegitimate meddling with 'managerial functions', even when their right to bargain collectively about such matters as wages and hours of labour had been grudgingly conceded. Their attempts to impose regulations on the conditions of employment—for example in respect of apprenticeship or of the exclusive operation of particular kinds of machine by members of a particular skilled craft—were repulsed as unjustifiable restrictions on the employer's right to decide how the labour he engaged could be most efficiently used, as well as what kinds of workers he chose to engage, and in what proportions.

Doubtless, regulations of these kinds had everywhere an element of corporate self-interest, and the skilled workers who attempted to enforce them had often scant regard for the claims of the less skilled. Nevertheless, there was in them an element not merely monopolistic—the assertion of a human claim to be treated as men and not as mere commodities to be bought and sold at a market price. The craftsmen who laid down regulations for the conduct of their trade were affirming the dignity of their calling, as well as seeking to get a good price for the sale of their labour-power. To regard their rules simply as so many restrictions on the employer's right to turn their labour to such uses as he might please was to assume that the labourer could properly be treated as no more than an instrument of production devoid of human claims. Even if the rules were sometimes serious obstacles to the flexible and efficient use of labour-power, and accordingly galling to the technician intent on getting the highest production at the lowest practicable cost, it did not follow that the workers in question were doing wrong in insisting on such rules, as long as there was no other way open to them of protecting either their standards of living or the dignity of their crafts, or of holding in check the drive of employers who would not scruple to throw them on the scrapheap in bad times or when some new invention superseded their painfully acquired skill. The Trade Unions of skilled workers were often under the sheer necessity of insisting on working rules which would have been indefensible if their members had been assured of economic security or if they could have relied on the human, as well as the financial, consequences of technical changes being taken into proper account.

As matters were, the Trade Unions could rely only on their own strength to protect their members' economic interests and to uphold their human dignity. All their strength enabled them to do, even where it was greatest, was to bargain for certain minimum or standard wage-rates and for certain maximum or standard hours of work, and to impose certain conditions on the use to be made of their members' labour. As they were excluded from all share in 'managerial functions' these conditions could be only restrictive ; for the Trade Unions were accorded no right to lay down positively how the employer should carry on the business of production. Once engaged, the worker had to obey orders, with the power to strike in the background as a weapon of last resort—but a dangerous weapon, which might condemn him to unemployment if it failed to bring the employer to terms.

As long as Trade Unionism was relatively weak, employers were usually in a position to enforce the acceptance of new techniques involving changes in methods of work and in the distribution of employment among workers of different trades and degrees of skill. A particularly powerful Union organising the workers in a highly distinctive craft—e.g. compositors, or patternmakers, or plumbers—might be able to stand out for a time against a technical change which threatened its monopoly or worsened its members' conditions of work ; but its power to do this seldom went beyond delaying action which enabled it to negotiate terms on which a new process could be accepted. If it attempted to stand out completely against the proposed innovation, it was apt to find itself circumvented either by the establishment of non-union shops or by the giving way of its weaker sections, so as to enable some employers to introduce the new methods and thus subject the rest to a competition against which they could not hold out. In face of such competition, the Union had usually to make the best terms it could, and to abandon its outright opposition to any new method or process which clearly did bring down costs. Thus, technical change made its way, often in face of delaying action by the craftsmen whose livelihood or working conditions it threatened—or who disliked it for any reason, including sheer conservatism or, more often, distrust of the employers' intentions. But in the more highly mechanised trades, in which jobs previously requiring the services of fully skilled craftsmen were being continually broken up and simplified so that they could be done by less skilled workers, the power of the craftsmen's Unions to resist such changes was steadily reduced, not only because the economies achieved were often very great, but also because it was to the interest of the less skilled workers to take on the new jobs and because the skilled men did not wish to operate the new machines, but did wish to have the job of setting them up for the less skilled operators and sometimes also that of supervision. Moreover, the craftsmen's Unions in due course discovered that it was to their interest to help the less skilled workers to organise and to secure better conditions ; for the more the employers had to pay the less skilled operatives the less inducement there was to push simplification and sub-division of jobs to the limits of technical possibility. Thus, in negotiation both in the workshop and at higher levels, the Unions of skilled and less skilled workers —where the two groups were organised apart—tended increasingly to act together, though not without a good deal of friction.

Mass-production, wherever it was introduced, had two opposite effects on the position of the skilled craftsmen. It tended in most cases to destroy the old craft monopolies and to transfer much of the work previously done by craftsmen to less skilled workers. But it also tended, in most cases though not in all, to enlarge total production to such an extent that there were soon as many jobs as before for the craftsmen, though these latter came to be a smaller percentage of the total labour force. Moreover, the work still required of the craftsmen often included a good deal that called for higher skill and responsibility than most of the work transferred to the less skilled ; and the craftsmen were often able to secure special bonuses and allowances for this work, over and above the standard rates. Thus, in the rapidly expanding industries—such as vehicle-making and electrical engineering—the craftsmen, save in exceptional cases, did not suffer as a result of increasing mechanisation and readily adapted themselves to technical change. A much more difficult situation arose in those industries in which new methods did not bring with them a great increase in total output. In the textile industries, for example, the more highly mechanised methods were often such as could be readily adopted in low-wage countries, which could then produce the simpler yarns and tissues at costs with which it was impossible for relatively high-wage countries to compete. In such cases, the increase in total output occurred mainly in the low-wage areas, and the craftsmen in the high-wage areas found themselves engaged in a losing battle. If they surrendered their customs in face of the employers' pressure, there were no new skilled jobs—or not nearly enough—in which they could find employment : if they resisted, markets were lost to foreign competitors, and their field of employment shrank in consequence. The cotton industry in particular has been beset for many years by problems of this sort.

When such conditions arise, it becomes impossible to maintain the doctrine that the management of industry is a matter for the employer alone, and that the Trade Union has no positive function in relation to it. The problem of what is to be done about the cotton industry, including its methods of working, becomes clearly one of concern to employers and workers alike ; and it becomes impossible for the Trade Unions either to stand out against technical change to the utmost of their power or to leave it to the employers to do as they think fit. There have to be negotiations—for example, about converting ordinary looms to automatic or semi-automatic working, and about the number of looms a weaver is to be allowed to operate—and these negotiations have to be conducted on both sides so as to discover what is best for the industry as a whole—including the workers' interests as one of the factors, The Unions, in dealing with these questions, cannot afford to act irresponsibly, or to take up a merely negative attitude. They have, in their members' interest, to try to work out jointly with the employers an agreed way of dealing with an unpleasant situation.

Thus, the question of the Trade Unions' share in responsibility for the determination of the 'managerial' conditions under which an industry is to be carried on forces itself to the front when an industry gets into economic difficulties and needs to be rescued by a common effort. It does not arise so obviously or immediately when an industry is expanding fast ; for in that case the employers can usually offer the workers sufficient inducements to the acceptance of technical changes that are really desirable. The question does, however, arise in expanding industries as well, particularly in relation to exports. Even if an industry is expanding fast, it may not be doing so as fast as it could, or as fast as it needs to expand in order to meet the possibilities of the export as well as of the home market. It may, because of high costs, be losing foreign markets even though its sales in the home market are rising fast ; and the proceeds from higher export sales may be urgently needed as a contribution to meeting the cost of necessary imports. In such circumstances, the Trade Unions concerned have a responsibility for seeing to it that they are not, by the regulations on which they insist, keeping costs unduly high and thus damaging the national interest. I do not mean that they ought to accept any technical change that would reduce costs, regardless of their members' interests : I do mean that they have a duty to examine their regulations with care, and not without strong reason to oppose technical developments which would increase the industry's contribution to the national standard of living.

To-day, most Trade Union leaders and many other Trade Unionists will accept this doctrine as correct. But in its practical applications, it comes right up against the strong tradition that the Unions' business is to exact the best terms they can from employers, and to leave the employers to adapt their methods to these terms. This was indeed, until quite recently, the only attitude it was practicable for the Trade Unions to take up ; for employers insisted on excluding them from any share in the determination of managerial policy. But it is rapidly becoming untenable now that higher production has become not merely desirable, as it always was, but indispensable for the maintenance, and *a fortiori* for the improvement, of the standards of living of the British people. For, under the conditions of to-day, higher production evidently depends on securing the workers' positive collaboration, and not merely their acquiescence in what the management decides to do. Under conditions of, or approaching, full employment, the workers can no longer be driven to higher output by the fear of the sack : they can only be induced to it by better payment and conditions as the reward of effort, or by being given a sense of partnership in the task, not only in their own interests, but also in those of the whole people.

Doubtless, if unemployment were to become widespread, or if the power of the Trade Unions were to be broken in an embittered conflict with the employers, the old discipline might conceivably be restored and the Trade Unions might be reduced to their former role of mere opposition within the limits of their decreased power. But such a defeat would be likely, under the conditions of to-day, to be followed by strong political reactions which would sweep into office a Labour Government with a mandate to achieve by legislation a reversal of the balance of economic power. Its consequences might well be a speeding up of the advance towards Socialism that would face the Trade Unions with a much increased, instead of a lessened, responsibility for promoting industrial efficiency. It seems likely that, even if unemployment does return on a significant scale, the employers' organisations will hardly risk taking advantage of it to launch a mass offensive against the Trade Unions. They would, no doubt, under such conditions, hit back to a limited extent—for example, by selective dismissals of alleged 'troublemakers' and by trying to withdraw some of the bargaining concessions made under full employment. But for the most part it would suit them better to stop short of mass industrial warfare, and to attempt to come to terms with the Trade Unions—terms which would commit the Trade Union executives to continue disciplining their members in the observance of agreements and agreed procedures of negotiation.

It seems, indeed, fairly safe to assume that the position of outside consultants about industrial policy which the Trade Unions won during the war and have been able to maintain since will continue—though of course the attention paid to their advice will be affected by changes in the strength of their economic position. The question, then, is how this consultative status will react on the Trade Unions themselves, and what changes in their attitudes and policies, not already made, are likely to be involved in it.

Involvement in joint determination of industrial policy arouses keen hostility wherever it is felt as implying any sort of partnership with capitalist employers. Even where, as in the nationalised industries, the employer is a non-profit-making agency set up by the State and including former Trade Unionists on its governing board, the Trade Unions concerned may hesitate to accept any share in responsibility for the conduct of the enterprise. They are not *represented* on the Boards of the nationalised industries : the Trade Unionists who sit on them have been required to renounce their active Trade Union connections. The Trade Unions are only consulted : the decisions taken are those of the Boards or, in certain cases, of the Ministers responsible to Parliament or of the Government as a whole. Nevertheless, when, say, the National Union of Mineworkers makes an *agreement* with the Coal Board for Saturday working, both parties become responsible for its observance. Doubtless, such an agreement falls within the traditional scope of collective bargaining ; but where exactly is the line to be drawn between matters about which the Trade Unions can bind themselves by agreement involving responsibility, and matters about which they must leave the Boards of the nationalised industries to reach their own decisions after consultation with the workers' representatives ? In both nationalised and private industries an attempt has been made to draw a line by distinguishing between the bodies concerned with collective bargaining on the one hand and with joint consultation on the other ; but it is an unreal line. In the workshops, questions of wages and hours and conditions of work cannot be clearly separated from questions of productivity or working amenities ; and at the higher levels of district and national negotiation the separation becomes quite artificial when, for example, the effect on productivity of a particular wage-structure, of a particular arrangement of working hours, or of the conditions of apprenticeship has to be considered. It is in the nature of the case that the Trade Unions, as their power increases, will negotiate over a widening field, and will make collective agreements about matters which were previously ruled out by the employers. Joint Consultation, if it is to mean anything real, is bound to turn by stages into collective bargaining and to take shape in agreements which the Trade Unions, equally with the employers, will be responsible for carrying out.

This is the case most evidently in the nationalised industries; but it holds good for private industry as well. Power, in a democratic society, cannot be had without responsibility; and if, in such a society, private enterprise is to continue at all, both employers and workers will have to accept a measure of responsibility to the public for the efficient conduct of its affairs. I do not mean that the Trade Unions will have to go into partnership with the capitalists: nothing of the sort. I do mean that joint decisions will have to be taken, not only about such questions as wages and hours, but also about matters of industrial policy, including above all matters arising out of the development of productive techniques. The question whether, and under what conditions, new machines or methods of production are to be introduced will inevitably have to be settled jointly by employers and workers' representatives, and no longer left to the exclusive decision of the employer, subject to the possibility that an unpopular innovation may be met by a concerted refusal, leading to a strike. No other solution makes sense, as soon as Trade Unions become powerful enough to be in a position to assert the claim that whatever affects their members' working lives falls within the range of their functions as the workers' chosen representatives.

It is impossible to stop at joint consultation: it is bound to turn either into joint decision of policy by collective agreement or into actual joint management. These two, however, are by no means the same, though they both involve an acceptance of responsibility. The essential difference is that decision by collective agreement leaves the execution of the agreed policies entirely to a managerial authority of which the Trade Unions form no part, whereas joint management would mean that the Trade Unions would become participants in executive action as well as in the shaping of policy. This distinction, which is of key importance, has often gone unrecognised in discussions of the question whether the workers should demand a share in the 'control' of industry. The claim to a share in the 'control' has often been put forward as a demand for Trade Union representation on the managing Boards of the nationalised industries; and it has been pertinently objected that no man can serve two masters, and that the actions demanded of such representatives by the Trade Unions and by their duty to Parliament and to the public would be bound on some occasions to clash. It has been possible to meet this objection in part by demanding, as the Post Office Workers have done, that the Trade Unions should not merely be represented, but should constitute the whole, or at least the majority, of the Board—in effect, that the entire management should be given to the Trade Unions, on their honour to exercise it in the public interest, and subject to general policy directions from the Minister or from Parliament. But this solution, though it would save the Trade Union representatives from the risk of being outvoted and having either to fall in with the view of a majority of the Board or resign, would still leave them in the position of having to serve two masters; for the Government or Parliament might require them to follow a policy of which their direct constituents disapproved. Possibly this difficulty could be met by drawing a clear line between matters of policy on which they could be directed by Parliament or by the Minister and managerial functions which were left to their sole discretion. But the line could not be easy to draw in practice. Nor is it clear that Trade Union representatives are the best persons to *manage* industrial enterprises; for they have no special training or qualifications, save accidently, for such a task.

These objections have no force against the alternative course—joint decision embodied in collective agreement. Trade Unions are eminently suitable bodies to enter into agreements on their members' behalf, not only about wages and conditions of labour, but also about technical innovations and methods of work. No doubt, in order to deal effectively with such matters, the Trade Unions would need to enlist the aid of qualified technical experts and to take steps to train their officials for handling problems of technique. But this need confronts them already; and some of them are already taking measures to meet it. From the Trade Union standpoint, surely the right course for dealing with the immediate situation is to widen the range of collective bargaining and agreement to embrace matters now covered by joint consultation rather than to claim minority representation on the managing boards of nationalised industries—or, *a fortiori*, on the boards of private concerns.

This policy, however, must not be thought of as enabling the Trade Unions to avoid a share in responsibility for the efficient conduct of industry. That responsibility cannot be avoided: it is a direct consequence of power, and is limited only by the limitations of the power the Trade Unions are in a position to exert.

It may surprise some of my readers that I, as a Guild Socialist, should take this view. But my undiminished belief in the virtue of 'workers' control' does not lead me to the view that this control is best to be exercised by Trade Union participation in management. The Trade Unions are essentially bodies which exist to protect their members against exploitation and injustice—not to become the employers of those whom they are under an obligation to protect. If 'workers' control' is to develop, it must do so through the building up of organs specially designed and fitted for this function, and not by assigning to the Trade Unions functions which are at variance with those for which they were made. 'Workers' control', if it is to mean anything real, must mean control by the actual workers engaged in industry, not by outside bodies. It must be built up gradually from the bottom, not imposed from the top ; and it must accordingly begin, and have its foundations, in the workshop. Workers' control, at the workshop level, means that the workers, instead of labouring under the orders of foremen and supervisors appointed from above, will work as a group, appointing their own production leaders and accepting a collective responsibility for the organisation of the work and for output. At the establishment level, it means that works managers and other officers will be the nominees of delegates from each shop or department, or at least will not be appointed without such delegates' consent. At district and national levels, it means that the appointment of the higher management will become increasingly a matter for agreement between the policy-making Board and the representatives of the workers from the various establishments—not Trade Union officials, but delegates directly chosen within the industry for this purpose.

The view stated in the preceding paragraph is apt to give rise to strong objections from Trade Union stalwarts who fear that the development of a structure directly representative of the workers in industry, as producers, would weaken the Trade Unions by establishing a rival point of focus for the workers' loyalty. In capitalist industries this danger is evidently real : it would be most perilous to allow a structure of workers' representation to be created apart from the Trade Unions and emancipated from their authority. But the danger has been successfully met already at the works level in the provisions made for the creation of Joint Consultative Committees. Service on such committees can be reserved for Trade Unionists only, even when all employees are entitled to vote ; and the Trade Unions can be sure of getting enough of their key men elected to prevent the committees from being used against Trade Union interests. Special problems would arise if it were decided to build up out of representatives chosen by the various establishments district bodies to exercise the functions of 'control' which I have outlined ; but there is no good reason why these problems should not be satisfactorily solved.

At any rate, if there is to be a development of 'workers' control', as in my view there should be, this surely is the form it will need to take, leaving the Trade Unions to carry on their functions of protecting their members' interests and of negotiating agreements covering a wider and wider range, but not involving them in participation in actual management. Some will argue that the whole idea of 'workers' control' should be rejected, on the double ground that management is a professional job needing special qualities and training and that the great majority of workers have no wish to participate in it. These objections do not seem to me to be valid. Of course, managers need special training and special qualities ; but they *also* need to be leaders of men, and neither nigger-drivers nor technicians so in love with their techniques as to have no sense of the human effects of their orders. The first of these requirements makes it necessary to insist that only qualified persons shall be eligible for managerial posts : the second makes it requisite that the managed shall have the choice between the properly qualified candidates. As for the argument that most workers do not wish to participate in management, I cannot see its force. At the workshop level, there will surely be enough who do, if the conditions are made such as to give them a chance ; and at higher levels the ordinary workers are not being asked to become managers, but only to take part in choosing representatives who will represent them in the making of managerial appointments. The case for such participation, at all levels, is that industry can be carried on efficiently, save by slave-driving methods which are now ruled out, only by inducing the workers to accept responsibility for helping to make it efficient, and that they cannot be induced to do this unless they are given due recognition as human beings entitled to a say in working arrangements and policies which intimately affect their happiness and well-being.

This is a book about Trade Unionism, not about 'workers' control', which comes into it only to the extent to which it is a matter for Trade Union action. For the present, the task of the Trade Unions is mainly that of equipping themselves to widen the range of collective bargaining and to accept the enlarged responsibilities which their increased power involves. This, as we have seen in earlier chapters, calls for a thorough overhaul of Trade Union machinery, especially with a view to increasing the participation of rank and file members in Trade Union affairs and to providing better links between the workplace organisations and the higher-level organisations, local and central. It calls too for a much more vigorous educational effort, directed both to bringing about a better understanding of Trade Union purposes and structures among the general membership and to the more specialised preparation of shop stewards, works representatives, and local and district committee-members and officials—to say nothing of their national analogues—for the increasingly complex and technical tasks of collective negotiation and policy-making.

APPENDICES

THE GROWTH OF TRADE UNION MEMBERSHIP (*thousands*)

		All Trade Unions	*Trades Union Congress T.U.s only*	*Total*	*Labour Party T.U.s only*	*Labour Party Total*
1866	..	—	110	199	—	—
1873	..	—	509	735	—	—
1880	..	—	381	476	—	—
1890	..	—	1,593	1,927	—	—
1892	..	1,501	1,155	1,651	—	—
1900	..	1,972	1,205	— ‡	353	376
1910	..	2,565	1,662	—	1,394	1,431
1914	..	4,145	2,682	—	1,572	1,612
1918	..	6,533	5,284	—	2,960	3,013
1920	..	8,334	6,418	—	4,318	4,360
1925	..	5,522	4,366	—	3,338	3,374
1928	..	4,804	3,673	—	2,025*	2,292†
1930	..	4,839	3,719	—	2,011*	2,347
1933	..	4,392	3,295	—	1,899*	2,305
1939	..	6,298	4,867	—	2,214*	2,663
1940	..	6,613	5,079	—	2,227*	2,571
1945	..	7,875	6,671	—	2,510*	3,039
1946	..	8,803	7,540	—	2,635*	3,322
1947	..	9,145	7,791	—	4,386	5,040
1948	..	9,319	7,937	—	4,751	5,422
1949	..	9,273	7,883	—	4,946	5,717
1950	..	9,242	7,828	—	4,972	5,920
1951	..	9,480	8,020	—	4,937	5,849

*These figures show the effects of the Trade Unions Act of 1927, which was repealed in 1946.

†Figures of individual membership included in totals from 1928.

‡Trades Councils were excluded from the T.U.C. from this date.

Appendix 2

THE TWO GREAT GENERAL UNIONS: OCCUPATIONS FOR WHICH THEY PROVIDE (1953)

THE following list shows all the trades or groups mentioned in current Reports of the Transport and General Workers' Union and the National Union of General and Municipal Workers for which either of these Unions either negotiates collective agreements or participates with other Unions in some form of collective bargaining machinery. The list does not, of course, include all the trades in which one or the other Union has agreements covering particular factories; nor can I hope that it is complete or entirely correct within the limits of what it is intended to cover. It does, however, give a reasonably good idea both of the immense range of occupations covered by these two Trade Unions and of the extent to which they both enter into the great majority of the trades and industries concerned. The letter 'T' or 'N' against a particular trade does not necessarily mean that the Union in question is represented on the Council or Board or Committee mentioned in the preceding column, though it is so represented in the great majority of instances in which it claims to have members. Nor has it been possible to distinguish between cases in which one or the other Union holds a preponderant position. The letters used in the second column indicate the form of negotiating machinery in the trade or group concerned; for their signification see the key attached to the list. The head offices of the two Unions have kindly checked the list for me (in February, 1953): I have not attempted to revise it beyond this date.

KEY TO TABLE

A.	National Agreement
A.(L)	Local Agreements
A.I.C.	Area Industrial Council
C.B.	Conciliation Board
C.C.	Conciliation Committee
I.C.	Industrial Council
I.T.C.	Industrial and Trade Council
J.C.	Joint Council
J.Cte.	Joint Committee
J.C.C.	Joint Conciliation Committee
J.I.C.	Joint Industrial Council
J.I.C.(L)	Joint Industrial Council (Local or Regional)
J.L.C.	Joint Labour Committee
J.N.C.	Joint Negotiating Committee
J.T.C.	Joint Trade Committee
J.W.B.	Joint Wages Board
J.W.C.	Joint Wages Committee

N.C.	..	National Council
N.C.B.	..	National Coal Board
N.Cte.	..	Negotiating Committee
N.I.C.	..	National Industrial Council
N.J.C.	..	National Joint Council
N.J.S.C.	..	National Joint Standing Committee
N.J.W.C.	..	National Joint Wages Council
N.N.C.	..	National Negotiating Committee
N.S.C.	..	National Sectional Council
N.St.C.	..	National Staff Council
T.B.C.R.	..	Trade Board of Conciliation and Reference
W.B. ..	..	Wages Board
W.C. ..	..	Wages Council
W.Cte.	..	Wages Committee
Wh.C.	..	Whitley Council
Wh.Cte.	..	Whitley Committee

TRADES IN THE TWO GENERAL UNIONS FOR WHICH COLLECTIVE AGREEMENTS ARE IN FORCE

Trade	*Method of Negotiation*	*T. & G.W.*	*N.U.G.M.W.*
MINING AND QUARRYING			
Briquetting and Patent Fuel ..	N.J.C.	T.	N.
Chalk Quarrying	N.S.C.	T.	N.
China Clay Mining	Committee	T.	
Coal (Clerical Workers)	J.N.C.	T.	
Coal Mining	J.N.C.	T.	N.
Colliery Coke Ovens	J.N.C.	T.	N.
Freestone Quarrying	N.I.C. and A.I.C.	T.	N.
Gypsum Mines and Quarries ..	A.	T.	N.
Iron Ore Mining	C.B.		N.
Limestone Quarrying	J.I.C.		N.
Roadstone Quarrying	N.J.C.	T.	N.
Sand and Ballast	N.J.C.	T.	N.
Sand, Lime and Brick	J.C.	T.	N.
Silica and Moulding Sands Quarrying ..	N.J.C.	T.	N.
Slate Quarrying (N. Wales)	A.I.C.	T.	
Tin Mining	A.(L).	T.	
METAL, ENGINEERING AND SHIPBUILDING			
Agricultural Machinery Making and Repair	A.	T.	N.
Aluminium	A.	T.	N.
Blastfurnaces	J.Cte.		N.
Bobbin and Shuttle Making ..	A.		N.
Chainmaking	W.C.		N.
Cutlery	W.C.	T.	N.

Trade	*Method of Negotiation*	*T. & G.W.*	*N.U.G.M.W.*
Electrical Cable Making	J.I.C.	T.	N.
Engineering (General)	A.	T.	N.
Engineering (Agricultural Machinery) ..	A.	T.	N.
Engineering (Clerical Workers) ..	A.	T.	
Engineering (Civil Air Transport) ..	N.J.C.	T.	N.
Engineering (Government)	J.C.	T.	N.
Engineering (Heating and Ventilating)			N.
Foundries	A.	T.	N.
Galvanising	C.B.	T.	N.
Heavy Steel			N.
Hollow-ware	W.C.	T.	N.
Iron, Steel and Non-ferrous Scrap ..	C.C.	T.	N.
Light Castings	J.Cte.	T.	N.
Light Metal Trade	J.Cte.	T.	N.
Metal Finishing	J.C.	T.	N.
Motor Vehicles—Retail and Repair ..	J.I.C.	T.	N.
Needle, Fish-hook and Tackle ..			N.
Pin, Hook and Eye	W.C.	T.	N.
Railway Shops	Rail Shopmen's Cte.	T.	N.
Shipbuilding	A.	T.	N.
Shipbuilding (Government)	J.C.	T.	N.
Ship Repairing	A.	T.	N.
Stamped and Pressed Metal Ware ..	W.C.	T.	N.
Tin Box	W.C.	T.	N.
Tinplate	J.I.C.	T.	N.
Tubes (Scotland)	W.B.	T.	N.
Wire and Wire Rope	J.I.C.	T.	N.
Woven Wire (Scotland)	N.J.C.	T.	
CHEMICALS, OIL, ETC.			
Drugs and Fine Chemicals	J.T.C.	T.	N.
Fat Melting and Bone Degreasing ..	C.C.	T.	N.
Fertilisers	J.I.C.	T.	N.
Glue and Gelatine	J.I.C.	T.	N.
Heavy Chemicals	J.I.C.	T.	N.
Imperial Chemicals	J.Cte.	T.	N.
Oil Refining	A.(L).	T.	
Oxygen	A.	T.	N.
Paint, Varnish and Lacquer	J.I.C.	T.	N.
Plastics	J.I.C.	T.	N.
Salt	N.N.C.	T.	N.
Soap, Candle and Edible Fats ..	J.I.C.	T.	N.
RUBBER			
Rubber (Clerical Workers)	J.I.C.	T.	N.
Rubber Manufacture	J.I.C. and W.C.	T.	N.
Rubber Floor Laying	J.I.C.	T.	N.
Rubber Reclamation	J.I.C. and W.C.	T.	N.

Trade	Method of Negotiation	T. & G.W.	N.U.G.M.W.
BUILDING AND CIVIL ENGINEERING			
Asbestos Cement	J.I.C.	T.	N.
Ball Clay	J.I.C.	T.	N.
Boiler Construction	A.	T.	N.
Brick and Tile	J.I.C.	T.	N.
Building	N.J.C.	T.	N.
Building and Civil Engineering (Local Authorities)	J.I.C.	T.	N.
Building Brick	J.I.C.	T.	N.
Cast Stone and Cast Concrete Products	J.I.C.	T.	N.
Cement	J.I.C.	T.	N.
Civil Engineering	C.B.	T.	N.
Constructional Engineering	A.	T.	N.
Clay Industries	J.I.C.	T.	N.
Demolition	J.W.B.	T.	N.
Fence Erection	J.C.	T.	N.
Fence Manufacturing	J.C.	T.	N.
Fletton Bricks	J.C.B.	T.	N.
Monumental Masonry	N.J.C.	T.	N.
Plaster Board	A.	T.	N.
Refractories	J.W.B.	T.	N.
Refractory Users	A.	T.	N.
Salt Glazed Ware	J.I.C.	T.	N.
Sanitary Fireclay	W.Cte.	T.	N.
Silica Bricks	J.W.B.	T.	N.
Steelwork Erection	A.		N.
Stock Bricks	J.C.	T.	N.
Stoneware	J.W.B.	T.	N.
TIMBER AND WOODWORKING			
Coffin Furniture	W.C.	T.	N.
Educational and Allied Woodworking ..	J.I.C.	T.	
Furniture	J.I.C.	T.	N.
Home-grown Timber	J.I.C.	T.	N.
Imported Timber			N.
Keg and Drum	W.C.	T.	N.
Match Manufacture	J.I.C.	?	N.
Perambulators and Invalid Carriages ..	W.C.	T.	N.
Sawmilling	N.J.Cte.	T.	N.
Vehicle Building		T.	N.
Veneer and Plywood	J.I.C.	T.	N.
Wood Box and Packing Case ..	J.I.C.	T.	N.
PAPER			
Paper Bag	W.C.	T	N.
Paper Box	W.C.	T.	N.
Paper Making	N.J.S.C.	T.	N.
HIDES AND LEATHER			
Fellmongering	A.	T.	N.
Hides and Skins	J.I.C.	T.	N.
Leather and Tanning	J.Cte.	T.	N.

Trade	*Method of Negotiation*	*T. & G.W.*	*N.U.G.M.W.*
TEXTILES AND CLOTHING			
Boot and Shoe Manufacture ..	A.		N.
Boot and Shoe Repairing	W.C.	T.	N.
Button Making	W.C.	T.	N.
Carpet Manufacture	J.C.		N.
Corsets	W.C.		N.
Cotton	J.C.C.		N.
Cotton Waste Reclamation	W.C.		N.
Dressmaking	W.C.	T. (N. Ireland)	N.
Drift Net Mending			N.
Dyeing and Cleaning	W.C.		N
Flax and Hemp	W.C.	T.	N.
Flax Processing	A.	T.	N.
Fur Trade	W.C.	T.	N.
Fustian Cutting	W.C.		N.
Glove Making	N.J.S.C.	T.	N.
Hair, Bass and Fibre	W.C.	T.	N.
Harris Tweed	A.	T.	
Hat, Cap and Millinery	W.C.	T.	N.
Hosiery (Scotland)	J.N.C.	T.	N.
Jute	W.C.	T.	N.
Lace (Plain Net Branch)	T.B.C.R.	T.	N.
Linen and Cotton Handkerchief ..	W.C.	T. (N. Ireland)	N.
Made-up Textiles	W.C.	T.	N.
Narrow Fabrics	J.I.C.	T.	N.
Nylon Spinning	A.	T.	N.
Ostrich and Fancy Feather	W.C.		N.
Pressed Felt			N.
Rayon Production	J.L.C.	T.	N.
Rayon (Artificial Silk)	A.	T.	
Roofing Felt	J.I.C.	T.	N.
Rope, Twine and Net	W.C.	T.	N.
Sack and Bag	W.C.	T.	N.
Shirt Making	W.C.	T. (N. Ireland)	N.
Silk	J.I.C.	T.	N.
Surgical Dressings	J.I.C.	T.	N.
Tailoring, Ready-made and Wholesale Bespoke	W.C.	T. (N. Ireland)	N.
Tailoring, Retail Bespoke	W.C.		N.
Welsh Textiles	N.Cte.	T.	
Woolcombing	A.		N.
Woollen Textiles (Scotland) ..	J.C.	T.	N.
GLASS			
Glass Containers	J.I.C.	T.	N.
Glass Processing	J.I.C.		N.
Glass, Sheet and Plate	A.(L).		N.

Trade	Method of Negotiation	T. & G.W.	N.U.G.M.W.
FOOD, DRINK, TOBACCO, ETC.			
Aerated Waters	W.C.	T.	N.
Bacon Curing	J.I.C.	T.	N.
Baking	W.C.	T. (N. Ireland)	N.
Biscuits	N.J.W.C.	T.	N.
Brewing	A.(L).	T.	N.
Buffer Food Depots	A.	T.	N.
Cocoa, Chocolate and Confectionery	J.I.C.	T.	N.
Cold Storage	J.Cte.	T.	N.
Corn Trade	J.I.C.	T.	N.
Distilling	A.(L).	T.	N.
Fish and Fish Processing	A.(L).	T.	N.
Flour-milling	J.I.C.	T.	N.
Food Manufacturing	J.I.C.	T.	N.
Ice Cream	A.(L).	T.	
Seed Crushing	J.I.C.	T.	N.
Slaughtering	J.I.C.	T.	
Sugar Refining	J.Cte.		N.
Sugar-beet Processing	J.N.C.	T.	N.
Sugar Confectionery and Food Processing	J.I.C. and W.C.	T.	N.
Tobacco	J.N.C.	T.	N.
Yeast	J.Cte.	T.	
OTHER MANUFACTURES			
Boot and Floor Polish	W.C.	T.	N.
Brush and Broom	W.C.	T.	N.
Coir Mat and Matting	J.I.C.	T.	N.
Cellophane	A.(L).	T.	N.
Emery	A.(L).	T.	N.
Linoleum	A.		N.
Ophthalmic Optical	J.I.C.	T.	N.
Remploy	N.N.C.	T.	N.
Thermal Insulation	J.Cte.		N.
Toys	W.C.	T.	N.
Waste Reclamation	W.C.	T.	N.
CATERING			
Carlisle State Scheme	A.		N.
Catering (Civil Air Transport)	N.J.C.	T.	N.
Catering (Licensed Non-residential)	W.B.	T.	N.
Catering (Licensed Residential)	W.B.	T.	N.
Catering (Unlicensed Refreshment)	W.B.		N.
Catering (Unlicensed Residential)	W.B.	T.	N.
Industrial and Staff Canteens	W.B.	T.	N.
National Service Hostels	N.C.	T.	N.
DISTRIBUTION			
Bookselling and Stationery	W.C.	T.	N.
Milk Distribution	W.C.	T.	N.
Milk Marketing Board	A.	T.	N.

Trade	*Method of Negotiation*	*T. & G.W.*	*N.U.G.M.W.*
Retail Coal Distribution	J.I.C.(L).	T.	
Retail Co-operative Societies ..	A.	T.	N.
Retail Co-operative Societies (Clerical)	A.	T.	
Retail Co-operative Societies (Milk Distribution)	A.	T.	N.
Retail Drapery, Outfitting and Footwear	W.C.	T.	N.
Retail Food	W.C.	T.	N.
Retail Furnishing	W.C.	T.	N.
Retail Meat Trade	J.I.C.	T.	N.
Retail Newsagency, etc.	W.C.	T.	N.
Wholesale Co-operative Societies ..	A.	T.	N.
Wholesale Co-operative Societies (Clerical)	A.	T.	
Wholesale (Warehousing)	A.	T.	
Wholesale Grocery and Provision ..	J.I.C.	T.	N.
Wholesale Mantle and Costume Trade	W.C.		N.
Wholesale Meat Trade	J.I.C.(L).	T.	
TRANSPORT			
Civil Air Transport	N.J.C.	T.	N.
Civil Air Transport (Clerical and Administrative)	N.J.C.	T.	
Civil Air Transport (Surface Workers)	N.J.C.	T.	N.
Coal Tipping	J.N.C.	T.	N.
Coal Trimming		T.	
Co-operative Retail Societies (Transport)	A.	T.	
Docks	J.C.	T.	N.
Docks and Waterways (Clerical) ..	A.	T.	
Furniture Removal and Warehousing ..	J.I.C.	T.	
Harbour Employees	A.(L).	T.	N.
Inland Waterways	J.C.	T.	N.
Lightermen	A.(L).	T.	
Lighthouse Keepers	J.I.C.	T.	N.
Meat Transport (London)	J.I.C.	T.	
Omnibus (Private Companies) ..	N.C.	T.	
Omnibus (Clerical Workers) ..	A.(L).	T.	
Petroleum Transport	C.C.	T.	
Railways			N
Road Haulage	N.J.I.C. and W.C.	T.	N.
Road Haulage (Executive)	N.J.C.	T.	
Road Passenger Transport (Municipal)	J.I.C.	T.	N.
Road Passenger Transport (Clerical) ..	N.J.C.	T.	
Road Passenger Transport (London) ..	A.	T.	
Taxicabs	A.(L).	T.	
Trinity House	J.I.C.	T.	
Tugboatmen	A.(L).	T.	
Waterways	N.J.C.	T.	
PUBLIC UTILITIES			
Broadcast Relay Service .. .	J.Cte.		N.
Dredging	A.	T.	

Trade	*Method of Negotiation*	*T. & G.W.*	*N.U.G.M.W.*
Electricity Supply	J.I.C.	T.	N.
Electricity Supply (Administrative and Clerical)	N.J.C.	T.	N.
Gas	J.I.C.	T.	N.
Gas (Administrative and Clerical) ..	N.J.C.	T.	N.
Road Roller Hire Service	C.C.	T.	N.
Waterworks	J.I.C.	T.	N.
PUBLIC SERVICES			
Admiralty	I.C.	T.	N.
Air Ministry	Wh.Cte.	T.	N.
County Council Roadmen	J.I.C.	T.	N.
Government Workers	Wh.C.	T.	N.
Health Service	Wh.C.	T.	N.
Hospitals and Institutions	Wh.C.	T.	N.
Hospitals and Institutions (Administrative and Clerical)	Wh.C.	T.	N.
Land Drainage			N.
Local Authorities (Manual Workers) ..	J.I.C.	T.	N.
Local Authorities (Clerical)	J.C.	T.	N.
Ministry of Supply	J.I.C.	T.	N.
Ministry of Works	J.I.C.	T.	N.
Nurses and Midwives			N.
River Authorities	J.I.C.	T.	N.
War Department	J.I.C.	T.	N.
AGRICULTURE AND FORESTRY			
Agriculture	W.B.	T.	
Forestry	I.T.C.	T.	N.
FISHING			
Herring Trade	J.C.	T.	
Trawler Fishing	J.I.C.	T.	
MISCELLANEOUS			
Cranemen	A.(L).		N.
Hairdressing	W.C.	T. (N. Ireland)	N.
Insurance Workers (Co-operative) ..	A.	T.	
Laundries	W.C.	T.	N.
Laundries (Co-operative)	A.	T.	N.
Slag	J.I.C.	T.	N.
Stablemen (Newmarket)	A.(L).	T.	
Typewriter Servicing	A.		N.

SELECTED BENEFIT SCALES OF CERTAIN TRADE UNIONS, 1952–3

(Weekly Rates)	*Dispute*	*Unemployment*	*Permanent Disablement*	*Accident*	*Sickness*	*Superannuation*	*Funeral*	*Tool*	*Legal Aid*
Amalgamated Engineering Union*									
Section I									
Contribution 2/- ..	20/-	10/- (14-18 weeks†)	Up to £100	as Sickness	10/- (for 20-26 weeks), *plus* 26 weeks at 5/- after 25 years' membership	8/-—10/-†	£12 (£5 for wife)	Up to £10	At E.C.'s discretion
Section V									
Contribution 1/- ..	15/-	5/- (15 weeks)	—	—	—	—	—	—	In case of accident
Women's Section									
Contribution 6d. ..	10/-	5/- (6 weeks)	—	10/- (6 weeks)	—	—	Up to £5†	—	In case of accident
Transport and General Workers' Union*									
Men. Scale A									
‡Contribution 8d. ..	20/- (*plus* 6/- for wife and 2/6 for each child under 15)	— —	—	8/- (8 weeks) *plus* 5/- (further 8 weeks)	—	—	£5—£10†	—	Provided
Scale B									
‡Contribution 11d. ..	As above	—	—	As above	8/- (8 weeks) 5/- (8 weeks) 2/6d. (4 weeks)	—	As above	—	Provided
Scale C									
‡Contribution 1/2 ..	As above	—	—	As above	10/- (8 weeks) 7/6d. (8 weeks) 5/- (4 weeks)	— —	£7—£10* (wife £3—£5)	—	Provided
Women									
§Contribution 5d. ..	12/-	—	—	4/- (8 weeks) 2/6 (8 weeks)	—	—	£3—£5†	—	Provided

*There are other Sections not shown here. †According to length of membership. ‡Plus quarterly payment of 6d.
§Plus quarterly payment of 3d.

£ thousands

	Total Income	Total Expenditure	Working Expenses	Benefits: Super-annuation	Benefits: Unem-ployment	Benefits: Dispute	Benefits: Sick and Accident	Benefits: Funeral	Benefits: Others	Other Expenses	Political Fund
1946 ..	14,627	10,672	5,996	1,532	273	75	975	444	593	583	201
1947 ..	16,663	12,707	6,803	1,695	437	57	972	465	615	1,350	313
1948 ..	17,155	12,915	7,535	1,681	180	250	983	442	659	810	375
1949 ..	17,681	14,097	7,945	1,725	159	74	1,151	492	931	1,103	517
1950 ..	17,624	14,026	8,226	1,791	163	244	1,166	486	687	812	451
1951 ..	18,246	15,855	9,098	1,931	133	190	1,213	553	783	1,399	555
	101,996	80,272	45,603	10,355	1,345	890	6,460	2,882	4,268	6,057	2,412
Per cent		100	56.8	12.9	1.7	1.1	8.1	3.6	5.3	7.5	3.0
Comparative Figures for certain pre-war years:											
1926 ..	9,278	13,387	2,956	905	1,835*	5,617	803	316	225	621	108
Per cent		100	22.1	6.8	13.7	42.0	6.0	2.4	1.7	4.6	0.8
1933 ..	6,988	6,426	2,526	1,062	1,016*	190	621	344	302	271	94
Per cent		100	39.4	16.5	15.8	2.9	9.7	5.3	4.7	4.2	1.5
1935 ..	7,699	6,321	2,633	1,071	669*	232	571	341	325	311	168
Per cent		100	41.7	16.9	10.6	3.7	9.0	5.4	5.1	4.9	2.7
1938 ..	9,581	7,537	3,303	1,166	866*	148	627	378	397	535	117
Per cent		100	43.8	15.5	11.5	2.0	8.3	5.0	5.3	7.1	1.5

*Gross Trade Union expenditure *minus* repayments from Ministry of Labour in respect of benefits under the Unemployment Insurance Acts.

BROAD COMPARISON OF EXPENDITURE OF AMALGAMATED ENGINEERING UNION AND NATIONAL UNION OF GENERAL AND MUNICIPAL WORKERS IN 1951

(£'s sterling)

	A.E.U.	*N.U.G.M.W.*
Total Income	2,462,789	942,764
Total Outgoings (except Political Fund)	2,251,291	798,000
Benefits :		
Dispute and Victimisation	44,685	1,923
Unemployment, Travelling, etc.	21,585	—
Sickness and Disablement	225,316	12,263*
Funeral	41,459	68,374*
Superannuation	832,293	—
Accident, Tool, etc.	1,438	—
Benevolent Grants	31,910	1,608
Total Benefits and Benevolent Grants	1,199,186	84,168
Working Expenses :		
General Office Salaries, Wages and Allowances	206,743	195,967
Insurance Stamps	—	9,637
Council and Executive Meetings	—	2,967
Delegations and Conferences	93,566	31,540
Branch and District Committees	63,067	4,572
Payments to Branch Officers, etc.	173,618	258,765
Legal and Professional Costs	57,212	15,070
Propaganda	13,398	8,736
Rent, Rates, Taxes, Cleaning, Light	65,127	16,319
Repairs, Furniture, etc.	19,783	4,658
Postages, Parcels, etc.	52,415	11,612
Printing and Stationery	116,336	42,016
Officers' Pensions, etc.	11,920	40,000
Depreciation	—	10,000
Total Working Expenses	873,185	651,859
Affiliation Fees, Local Affairs and Grants	137,654	66,178
Other Expenses	41,266	6,470
Political Fund	48,512	51,863

MEMBERSHIP OF CERTAIN TRADE UNIONS AS RETURNED TO THE TRADES UNION CONGRESS AND TO THE LABOUR PARTY IN 1952, WITH COMPARISON FOR 1946

	Membership in thousands		*Percentage of L.P. to T.U.C. Figure*	
	T.U.C.	*L.P.*	1952	1946
Transport and General Workers' Union	1,285	835	65	37
General and Municipal Workers' Union	808	400	49	30
Amalgamated Engineering Union ..	756	586	77	32
National Union of Mineworkers ..	613	660	108	77
National Union of Railwaymen ..	396	317	80	53
Shop, Distributive and Allied Workers..	348	317	91	67
Electrical Trades Union	198	120	61	15
Amalgamated Society of Woodworkers..	196	129	66	22
United Textile Factory Workers ..	118*	144	79	?
National Union of Public Employees ..	175	45	26	17
Union of Post Office Workers ..	156	147	93	†
Civil Service Clerical Association ..	147	†	†	†
National Union of Printing, Bookbinding and Paper Workers	134	25	19	†
National Union of Tailors and Garment Workers	132	97	73	39
Iron and Steel Trades Confederation ..	102	84	82	43
Amalgamated Union of Building Trade Workers	90	60	67	17
Transport Salaried Staffs' Association ..	89	76	85	83
National Union of Boot and Shoe Operatives	84	60	71	62
United Society of Boilermakers ..	83	46	55	31
National Union of Dyers, Bleachers and Textile Workers	80	59	74	39
Amalgamated Union of Foundry Workers	76	50	66	41
Amalgamated Union of Furniture Trade Operatives	75	16	21	4
National Society of Painters	73	50	68	4
Associated Society of Locomotive Engineers and Firemen	69	38	62	36
National Union of Seamen	60	25	42	13
National Union of Vehicle Builders ..	55	36	65	44
Plumbing Trades Union	54	33	61	†
Typographical Association	49	29	59	33
Association of Engineering and Shipbuilding Draughtsmen	47	30	64	39

*The unions composing this federation are affiliated separately to the T.U.C.
†Not affiliated to the Labour Party.

STRIKES. *Number, Numbers Directly Involved. Working Days Lost*

(*a*) Number of Strikes beginning in year. (*b*) Workers directly involved. (*c*) Workers indirectly involved. (*d*) Total Working Days lost.

	(*a*)	(*b*) *thousands*	(*c*) *thousands*	(*d*) *thousands*
1900	633	132	53	3,088
1901	631	111	68	4,130
1902	432	115	140	3,438
1903	380	93	116	2,320
1904	346	56	87	1,464
1905	349	67	92	2,368
1906	479	158	218	3,019
1907	585	100	146	2,148
1908	389	221	293	10,785
1909	422	168	297	2,687
1910	521	384	514	9,867
1911	872	824	952	10,155
1912	834	1,232	1,462	40,890
1913	1,459	497	167	9,804
1914	972	326	121	9,878
1915	672	401	47	2,953
1916	532	235	41	2,446
1917	730	575	297	5,647
1918	1,165	923	193	5,875
1919	1,352	2,401	190	34,969
1920	1,607	1,779	153	26,568
1921	763	1,770	31	85,872
1922	576	512	40	19,850
1923	628	343	62	10,672
1924	710	558	55	8,424
1925	603	401	40	7,952
1926	323	2,724	10	162,233
1927	308	90	18	1,174
1928	302	80	44	1,388
1929	431	493	40	8,287
1930	422	286	21	4,399
1931	420	424	66	6,983
1932	389	337	42	6,488
1933	357	114	22	1,019
1934	471	109	25	955
1935	553	230	41	1,849
1936	818	241	75	1,726
1937	1,129	388	209	3,132
1938	875	211	63	1,329
1939	940	246	91	1,352
1940	922	225	74	938
1941	1,251	297	63	1,076
1942	1,303	349	107	1,527
1943	1,785	454	103	1,805
1944	2,194	716	105	3,687

	(*a*)	(*b*) *thousands*	(*c*) *thousands*	(*d*) *thousands*
1945	2,293	447	84	2,827
1946	2,205	405	121	2,138
1947	1,721	489	131	2,389
1948	1,759	325	100	1,935
1949	1,426	313	120	1,805
1950	1,339	269	33	1,375
1951	1,719	336	43	1,687
1952	1,718	303	112	1,770

Affiliated Organisations and Membership as stated in Report of 1951 Congress

Europe		*America*		*Asia*		*Africa*		*Oceania*	
Austria	1,279,520	*Argentina	40,000	Ceylon	43,000	Gambia	2,000	[Australia	o]
*Basque	5,000	Barbados	14,000	China	107,605	[Libya	o]	New Zealand	200,000
Belgium	631,075	Bolivia	12,500	Cyprus	4,000	Mauritius	10,000		
Denmark	630,748	Brazil	1,775,000	Hong Kong	121,000	Sierra Leone	14,000		
[Finland	o]	British Guiana	2,000	India	2,371,310	Tunisia	58,000		
France	1,000,000	British Honduras	2,500	Japan	(3,050,000)				
Germany, West	5,500,000	Canada	750,000	Korea	800,000				
Great Britain	7,883,355	Chile	1,500	Lebanon	14,000				
Greece	277,000	Columbia	400,000	Malaya	75,000				
Iceland	24,000	Costa Rica	20,000	Pakistan	276,000				
Italy	1,200,000	Cuba	1,100,000	Persia	(120,000)				
Luxemburg	20,000	Dominica	5,400	Thailand	59,000				
Malta	10,653	Dutch Guiana	23,150						
Netherlands	402,000	Falkland Islands	600						
Norway	487,000	Grenada	3,000						
Saar	80,000	[Haiti	o]						
*Spain	20,000	Mexico	1,385,000						
Sweden	1,537,692	Panama	10,000						
Switzerland	380,904	Peru	350,000						
Trieste	55,203	Philippines	10,000						
[Turkey	o]	Puerto Rico	125,000						
		St. Kitts	7,056						
		St. Lucia	1,500						
		Trinidad	3,766						
		United States A.F. of L.	7,742,603						
		United States C.I.O.	6,300,000						
		Uruguay	(20,000)						
		*Venezuela	(200,000)						

Figures in parenthesis are for December, 1949. Others for the end of 1950. "o" means that the country in question was not affiliated to the I.C.F.T.U. but sent 'observers' to the Congress. Some of the figures for non-European countries are highly speculative. The movements marked * were in exile.

SOME COMMON ABBREVIATIONS

A.A.M. .. Association of Assistant Mistresses
A.C.T. .. Association of Cine Technicians
A.E.S.D. .. Association of Engineering and Shipbuilding Draughtsmen
A.E.U. .. Amalgamated Engineering Union
A.F. of L. .. American Federation of Labor
A.M.A. .. Association of Assistant Masters
A.S.E. .. .. Amalgamated Society of Engineers (now A.E.U.)
A.S.L.E.F. .. Associated Society of Locomotive Engineers and Firemen
A.S.R.S. .. Amalgamated Society of Railway Servants (now N.U.R.)
A.S.S.E.T. .. Association of Supervisory Staffs, Executives and Technicians
A.S.W. .. Amalgamated Society of Woodworkers
A.Sc.W. .. Association of Scientific Workers
A.S.W.C.M. .. Amalgamated Society of Woodcutting Machinists
A.T.T.I. .. Association of Teachers in Technical Institutions
A.U.B.T.W. .. Amalgamated Union of Building Trade Workers
A.U.F.W. .. Amalgamated Union of Foundry Workers
A.U.T. .. Association of University Teachers

B.E.A. .. .. British Electricity Authority
B.E.A. .. .. British European Airways
B.I.M. .. .. British Institute of Management
B.M.A. .. British Medical Association
B.O.A.C. .. British Overseas Airways Corporation

C.A.W.U. .. Clerical and Administrative Workers' Union
C.E.U. .. Constructional Engineering Union
C.G.T. .. Confédération Générale du Travail
C.I.O. .. .. Congress of Industrial Organisations
C.P. .. .. Co-operative Party
C.P.F. .. .. Co-operative Productive Federation
C.P.G.B. .. Communist Party of Great Britain
C.S.A.T. .. Civil Service Arbitration Tribunal
C.S.C.A. .. Civil Service Clerical Association
C.S.U. .. Civil Service Union
C.U. .. .. Co-operative Union
C.W.S. .. Co-operative Wholesale Society
C.W.U. .. Chemical Workers' Union

E.P.E.A. .. Electrical Power Engineers' Association
E.T.U. .. Electrical Trades Union

F.B.I. ..	.. Federation of British Industries
F.B.U...	.. Fire Brigades' Union
F.O. ..	.. Force Ouvrière (France)
G.F.T.U.	.. General Federation of Trade Unions
G.I.O.	.. Guild of Insurance Officials
G.N.C.T.U.	.. Grand National Consolidated Trades Union
I.C. ..	.. Industrial Court
I.C.A. ..	.. International Co-operative Alliance
I.C.F.T.U.	.. International Confederation of Free Trade Unions
I.D.T.	.. Industrial Disputes Tribunal
I.F.C.T.U.	.. International Federation of Christian Trade Unions
I.F.T.U.	.. International Federation of Trade Unions (pre-1945)
I.L.O. ..	.. International Labour Organisation
I.L.P. ..	.. Independent Labour Party
I.S.T.C.	.. Iron and Steel Trades Confederation
I.T.F. ..	.. International Transport Workers' Federation
I.W.M.A.	.. International Working Men's Association
I.W.W.	.. Industrial Workers of the World
J.C.C. ..	.. Joint Consultative Committee
J.I.C. ..	.. Joint Industrial Council
L.C.S...	.. London Co-operative Society
L.R.C...	.. Labour Representation Committee (now Labour Party)
L.R.D.	.. Labour Research Department
L.S.C.	.. London Society of Compositors
L.T.C.	.. London Trades Council
M.F.G.B.	.. Miners' Federation of Great Britain (now N.U.M.)
M.P.U.	.. Medical Practitioners' Union
M.U. ..	.. Musicians' Union
N.A.L.G.O.	.. National Association of Local Government Officers
N.A.O.P.	.. National Association of Operative Plasterers
N.A.T.K.E.	.. National Association of Theatrical and Kine Employees
N.A.T.S.O.P.A.	National Amalgamated Trade Society of Operative Printers and Assistants
N.C.B.	.. National Coal Board
N.C.E.O.	.. National Confederation of Employers' Organisations
N.C.L.	.. National Council of Labour
N.C.L.C.	., National Council of Labour Colleges
N.F.B.T.O.	.. National Federation of Building Trades Operatives
N.I.I.P.	.. National Institute of Industrial Psychology
N.S.P.	.. National Society of Painters

N.S.P.W. .. National Society of Pottery Workers
N.U.A.W. .. National Union of Agricultural Workers
N.U.B. .. National Union of Blastfurnacemen
N.U.B.E. .. National Union of Bank Employees
N.U.B.S.O. .. National Union of Boot and Shoe Operatives
N.U.E. .. National Union of Enginemen
N.U.F.T.O. .. National Union of Furniture Trade Operatives
N.U.G.M.W. National Union of General and Municipal Workers
N.U.H.W. .. National Union of Hosiery Workers
N.U.J. .. National Union of Journalists
N.U.M. .. National Union of Mineworkers
N.U.P.E. .. National Union of Public Employees
N.U.R. .. National Union of Railwaymen
N.U.S. .. National Union of Seamen
N.U.S.M.W. .. National Union of Sheet Metal Workers
N.U.T. .. National Union of Teachers
N.U.T.G.W. .. National Union of Tailors and Garment Workers
N.U.V.B. .. National Union of Vehicle Builders

O.B.U. .. One Big Union

P.E.P. .. .. Political and Economic Planning
P.K.T.F. .. Printing and Kindred Trades Federation
P.O.E.U. .. Post Office Engineering Union
P.T.U. .. Plumbing Trades Union

R.A.C.S. .. Royal Arsenal Co-operative Society

S.C.W.S. .. Scottish Co-operative Wholesale Society
S.D.F. .. Social Democratic Federation
S.T.U.C. .. Scottish Trade Union Congress

T.A. .. .. Typographical Association
T. and G.W.U. Transport and General Workers' Union
T.S.S.A. .. Transport Salaried Staffs' Association
T.U.C. .. Trades Union Congress
T.U.C.G.C. .. Trades Union Congress General Council

U.B.M.S. .. United Boilermakers' Society
U.P.M.A. .. United Patternmakers' Association
U.P.W. .. Union of Post Office Workers
U.S.D.A.W. .. Union of Shop, Distributive and Allied Workers
U.T.F.W.A. .. United Textile Factory Workers' Association

V.A.F. .. Variety Artistes' Federation

W.E.A. .. Workers' Educational Association
W.F.T.U. .. World Federation of Trade Unions

SELECT BIBLIOGRAPHY

Second Impression 1955

A.—HISTORY

1. *General*

S. and B. Webb .. .. History of Trade Unionism (1893). (Revised edition, 1920)

G. D. H. Cole .. .. A Short History of the British Working-class Movement, 1789–1947. (First edition, in three volumes, 1925–7. Revised edition, 1947)

G. D. H. Cole .. .. Attempts at General Union, 1819–34. (First edition, 1939. Revised edition, 1953)

G. D. H. Cole and A. W. Filson .. .. British Working-class Movements : Select Documents, 1789–1875 (1951)

G. Howell .. .. Labour Legislation, Labour Movements, Labour Leaders (1902)

G. Howell .. .. The Conflicts of Capital and Labour, Historically Considered. (1877. Revised edition, 1890)

A. Aspinall .. .. The Early English Trade Unions : Documents from the Home Office Papers (1949)

Social Science Association .. Report on Trade Societies (1860)

W. H. Crook .. .. The General Strike (1931)

K. G. J. C. Knowles .. Strikes : A Study in Industrial Conflict (1952)

B. Drake .. .. Women in Trade Unions (1920)

2. *Histories of Particular Unions, etc.*

J. B. Jefferys .. .. The Story of the Engineers, 1800–1945 (1945)

R. P. Arnot .. .. The Miners (two volumes, 1949 and 1953. A third volume is to come)

R. Fynes .. .. Miners of Northumberland and Durham (1873)

E. Welbourne .. .. The Miners' Unions of Northumberland and Durham (1923)

S. Webb .. .. The Story of the Durham Miners (1921)

J. Wilson .. .. A History of the Durham Miners' Association (1907)

N. Edwards .. .. History of the South Wales Miners (1926)

N. Edwards .. .. History of the South Wales Miners' Federation (1938)

G. D. H. Cole .. .. Labour in the Coal-mining Industry, 1914–1921 (1923)

Sir A. Pugh .. .. Men of Steel (1952), dealing with iron and steel

G. D. H. Cole and R. P. Arnot .. .. Trade Unionism on the Railways (1917)

G. W. Alcock .. . Fifty Years of Railway Trade Unionism (1923)

J. R. Raynes .. . Engines and Men (1921)—Locomotive Engineers

N. McKillop .. .. The Lighted Flame (1950)—Loco. Engineers

E. Howe and H. E. Waite .. The London Society of Compositors (1948)

E. Howe and J. Child .. The Society of London Bookbinders, 1780–1951 (1952)

S. C. Gillespie .. .. A Hundred Years of Progress (Scottish Typographical Association, 1853-1952) (1953)

H. Owen .. .. The Staffordshire Potter (1901)

W. H. Warburton .. The History of the Trade Union Organisation in the North Staffordshire Potteries (1931)
H. Bending .. .. Forty Years: National Union of Scalemakers, 1909–1949 (1949)
Anon. .. .. .. Sixty Years of the National Union of General and Municipal Workers (1949)
W. Kiddier .. .. The Old Trade Unions (1930)—Brushmakers
F. W. Chandler .. .. History of the Amalgamated Society of Carpenters and Joiners (1910)
R. W. Postgate .. .. The Builders' History (1923)
D. C. Cummings .. History of the Boilermakers' Society (1905)
W. Mosses .. .. History of the United Patternmakers' Association (1922)
Sir B. Turner .. .. Short History of the General Union of Textile Workers (1920)
F. E. Green .. .. A History of the English Agricultural Labourer, 1870–1920 (1930)
E. Selley .. .. Village Trade Unions in Two Centuries (1919)
R. Groves .. .. Sharpen the Sickle: the History of the Farm Workers' Union (1949)
H. G. Swift .. .. A History of Postal Agitation (1900)
P. C. Hoffman .. .. They Also Serve (1949)—Shop Assistants
W. J. Davis .. .. Trades Union Congress: History and Recollections (two volumes, 1910, 1916)
G. Tate and others .. London Trades Council, 1860–1950 (1950)

3. *Biographies*

G. D. H. Cole .. .. Life of Robert Owen (revised edition, 1930)
Margaret Cole .. .. Robert Owen of New Lanark (1953)
Margaret Cole .. .. Makers of the Labour Movement (1948)
A. W. Humphrey .. Robert Applegarth (1913)
Tom Mann .. .. Memoirs (1923)
W. Stewart .. .. Life of Keir Hardie (1920)
G. D. H. Cole .. .. James Keir Hardie (Fabian Society, 1941)
G. D. H. Cole .. .. John Burns (Fabian Society, 1943)
W. Kent .. .. John Burns (1950)
M. A. Hamilton .. .. Life of Arthur Henderson (1938)
F. Williams .. .. Ernest Bevin (1952)

B. DESCRIPTIVE AND ANALYTICAL

Trades Union Congress .. Annual Reports
A. Flanders .. .. Trade Unions (1952)
H. Collins .. .. Trade Unions To-day (1950)
N. Barou .. .. British Trade Unions (1947)
G. D. H. Cole (ed.) .. British Trade Unionism To-day (1939)
G. D. H. Cole .. .. Organised Labour (1924)
G. D. H. Cole .. .. The World of Labour (1913, revised 1919)
W. Milne Bailey .. Trade Union Documents (1929)
W. Milne Bailey .. Trade Unions and the State (1934)
H. J. Laski .. .. Trade Unions in the New Society (1950)
J. Goldstein .. .. The Government of British Trade Unions (1952)
S. and B. Webb .. .. Industrial Democracy (1897)

Political and Economic Planning	British Trade Unionism (1948)
Acton Society Trust	The Future of the Unions (1951)
B. England	Trade Union Problems (1950)
J. D. M. Bell	Industrial Unionism, A Critical Analysis (1949)

C. TRADE UNION LAW

R. Y. Hedges and A. Winterbottom	A Legal History of Trade Unionism (1930)
A. Macdonald	The Law relating to Masters and Workmen (1867)
G. Howell	Handy Book of the Labour Laws (1876, revised edition, 1895)
H. H. Slesser and Charles Baker	Trade Union Law (3rd edition, 1927)
A. Henderson, jun.	Trade Unions and the Law (1927)
N. A. Citrine	Trade Union Law (1950)

D. INDUSTRIAL RELATIONS

Ministry of Labour	Industrial Relations Handbook (revised edition, 1953)
Ministry of Labour	Annual Reports
J. H. Richardson	Industrial Relations in Great Britain (revised edition, 1938)
P. Sargant Florence	Labour (1948)
I. G. Sharp	Industrial Conciliation and Arbitration in Great Britain (1950)
Lord Amulree	Industrial Arbitration in Great Britain (1929)
D. Sells	British Wages Boards (revised edition, 1939)
Sir C. Renold	Joint Consultation over Thirty Years (1950)
H. Somervell	Industrial Peace in Our Time (1950)
E. J. Lever and F. Goodell	Labor-Management Co-operation (U.S.A., 1948)
F. Harbison and R. Dubin	Patterns of Union-Management Relations (U.S.A., 1947)
International Labour Office	Co-operation in Industry (1951)
International Labour Office	Labor-Management Co-operation in France (1950)

E. WAGES AND PRODUCTIVITY

Ministry of Labour	Time-rates of Wages and Hours of Labour (annual)
A. Flanders	A Policy for Wages (Fabian Society, 1950)
T. E. M. McKitterick	Wages Policy ? (Fabian Society, 1949)
Margaret Cole	The Rate for the Job (Fabian Society, 1946)
F. Zweig	Productivity and Trade Unions (1951)
International Labour Office	Payment by Results (1951)
C. A. Mace	Incentives : Some Experimental Studies (Industrial Health Research Board, 1935)
M. Heinemann	Wages Front (1947)
B. Edwards	Wages, Productivity and Training (pamphlet, Chemical Workers' Union, 1952)

A. Calder and J. L. Knipe .. The Guaranteed Annual Wage (U.S.A., 1948)
Anglo-American Council on Productivity .. .. Reports on various trades—various dates to 1952

F. INDUSTRIAL DEMOCRACY AND WORKERS' CONTROL

G. D. H. Cole .. .. Self-Government in Industry (1917, revised edition, 1919)
G. D. H. Cole .. .. Guild Socialism Re-stated (1920)
G. D. H. Cole .. .. Workshop Organisation (1923)
G. D. H. Cole and W. Mellor The Meaning of Industrial Freedom (1918)
G. D. H. Cole and W. Mellor Workers' Control and Self-Government in Industry (Fabian Tract, 1933)
H. A. Clegg .. .. Industrial Democracy and Nationalisation (1951)
H. A. Clegg .. .. Labour in Nationalised Industry (Fabian Society, 1950)
C. L. Goodrich .. .. The Frontier of Control (1920)
E. Jaques .. .. The Changing Culture of a Factory (1951)
E. White .. .. Workers' Control (Fabian Society, 1949)
Fabian Society and ASSET Management by Consent (1948)
G. D. H. Cole .. .. The National Coal Board (Fabian Society, 1948)
Margaret Cole .. .. Miners and the Board (Fabian Society, 1949)
F. Pickstock .. .. British Railways, the Human Problem (Fabian Society, 1950)
L. Gossman .. .. Industrial Management (Fabian Society, 1949)
J. M. Chalmers, I. Mikardo and G. D. H. Cole .. Consultation or Joint Management ? (Fabian Society, 1949)
E. Goodman .. .. Forms of Public Ownership and Control (1951)
M. B. Reckitt .. .. Industry and Democracy (League for Workers' Control, ? 1952)
Labour Party .. .. Industrial Democracy (Discussion pamphlet)
J. B. Jefferys .. .. Trade Unions in a Planned Economy (Fabian Society, 1947)

G. POLITICS

A. W. Humphrey .. History of Labour Representation (1912)
G. D. H. Cole .. .. British Working-class Politics, 1832–1914 (1941)
G. D. H. Cole .. .. A History of the Labour Party from 1914 (1948)
F. Williams .. .. Fifty Years' March : The Rise of the Labour Party (1950)

H. EDUCATION

M. Stocks .. .. The Story of the Workers' Educational Association (1953)
S. G. Raybould .. .. The W.E.A.—The Next Phase (1949)
S. G. Raybould .. .. The English Universities and Adult Education (1951)
Workers' Educational Association .. .. Annual Reports, etc.
J. P. M. Millar .. .. Education and Power (National Council of Labour Colleges)

National Council of Labour Colleges .. .. Pamphlets and Reports
Anon. .. .. The Story of Ruskin College, 1899–1949 (1949)
Ruskin College .. .. Annual Reports, etc.
UNESCO .. .. Workers' Education: A Report. Edited by G. D. H. Cole and A. Philip (1953)

I. INTERNATIONAL

W. Galenson (ed.) .. Comparative Labor Movements (U.S.A., 1952)
H. A. Marquand (ed.) .. Organised Labour in Four Continents (1939)
J. Price .. .. The International Labour Movement (1945)
International Confederation of Free Trade Unions .. Reports
World Federation of Trade Unions .. .. Reports

INDEX

ST. MARY'S COLLEGE OF MARYLAND LIBRARY
ST. MARY'S CITY, MARYLAND

DATE

DEC 2 1 '73	
MAY 7 1982	
DEC 6 1982	
NO 14 '83	
MR 26 '85	

GAYLORD